Thomas Gray
Contemporary Essays

LIVERPOOL ENGLISH TEXTS AND STUDIES

General Editors:

JONATHAN BATE, BERNARD BEATTY
AND KELVIN EVEREST

Titles available in this series

John Keats: A Reassessment
Edited by KENNETH MUIR

Life and Letters of Sir Thomas Wyatt
By KENNETH MUIR

Elizabethan and Jacobean Drama
Critical Essays by PETER URE. Edited by J. C. MAXWELL

Literature of the Romantic Period, 1750–1850
Edited by R. T. DAVIES and B. G. BEATTY

The Singularity of Shakespeare and Other Essays
By KENNETH MUIR

Shakespeare's Chaucer: A Study in Literary Origins
By ANN THOMPSON

Dramatic Identities and Cultural Tradition:
Studies in Shakespeare and his Contemporaries
Critical Essays by G. K. HUNTER

The Pilgrim's Progress: Critical and Historical Views
Edited by VINCENT NEWEY

Essays on Shelley
Edited by MIRIAM ALLOTT

Cowper's Poetry: A Critical Study and Reassessment
By VINCENT NEWEY

Memory and Writing from Wordsworth to Lawrence
By PHILIP DAVIS

Byron and the Limits of Fiction
Edited by BERNARD BEATTY and VINCENT NEWEY

Literature and Nationalism
Edited by VINCENT NEWEY and ANN THOMPSON

Thomas Gray: Contemporary Essays
Edited by W. B. HUTCHINGS and WILLIAM RUDDICK

Thomas Gray
Contemporary Essays

EDITED BY
W. B. HUTCHINGS
Senior Lecturer in English Literature
University of Manchester
and
WILLIAM RUDDICK

LIVERPOOL UNIVERSITY PRESS

First published 1993 by
LIVERPOOL UNIVERSITY PRESS
PO Box 147, Liverpool, L69 3BX

Copyright © 1993 by
Liverpool University Press

British Library Cataloguing-in-Publication Data
A British Library CIP Record is available
ISBN 0–85323–268–7

Text set in Linotron 202 Baskerville by
Wilmaset Limited, Birkenhead, Wirral

Printed and bound in the European Community by
Redwood Books, Trowbridge, Wiltshire

Contents

Contributors

BERNARD BEATTY: Senior Lecturer in English Literature, University of Liverpool.

T. W. CRAIK: Emeritus Professor of English, University of Durham.

ANGUS EASSON: Professor of English, University of Salford.

DAVID FAIRER: Senior Lecturer, School of English, University of Leeds.

MALCOLM HICKS: Staff Tutor in Literature, Department of Extra-Mural Studies, University of Manchester.

W. B. HUTCHINGS: Senior Lecturer in English Literature, University of Manchester.

ANNE McDERMOTT: Lecturer, School of English, University of Birmingham.

VINCENT NEWEY: Professor of English, University of Leicester.

WILLIAM RUDDICK: Formerly Lecturer in English Literature, University of Manchester.

RICHARD TERRY: Lecturer in English, University of Sunderland.

PAUL WHITELEY: Lecturer, School of English, Queen's University of Belfast.

PAUL WILLIAMSON: Lecturer in English, University of Vienna.

Acknowledgements

The editors would like to thank the many undergraduate and postgraduate students with whom they have had animated discussions of the poems of Thomas Gray, Robin Bloxsidge of Liverpool University Press for his support and help, and Shelagh Aston of the Department of English Language and Literature at the University of Manchester for her expert and tireless editorial assistance.

Note

Quotations from Gray's poetry are taken from *The Complete Poems of Thomas Gray*, ed. H. W. Starr and J. R. Hendrickson (Oxford, 1966, reprinted with corrections, 1972). This is referred to as *Complete Poems*. Quotations from Gray's letters are taken from *Correspondence of Thomas Gray*, ed. Paget Toynbee and Leonard Whibley, with Corrections and Additions by H. W. Starr, 3 vols (Oxford, 1971). This is referred to as *Correspondence*.

Thomas Gray: Past Criticism and the Present Volume

W. B. HUTCHINGS

'Gray's slide into disregard continues', comments Alan Bower in his review of scholarship for the 1989 volume of *The Year's Work in English Studies*.[1] Yet Gray's remains one of the most familiar names in the history of English literature, and some of his verses (notably the *Eton College Ode* and the *Elegy*) are—or at least were—among the most commonly quoted poems in the language. Contemporary criticism's reluctance to engage fully with his work is, perhaps, a consequence of various forms of unease. It may be that the critic who aspires to sophistication instinctively shies away from a poet whose former popularity lay, to no little extent, in his capacity for memorable statement, for the expression of, in Samuel Johnson's elegant and precise phrase, 'sentiments to which every bosom returns an echo'.[2] Popularity and memorability can, all too often, appear as vices to some types of modern criticism. It may be, too, that Gray suffers from the common neglect of poetry sandwiched in time between periods defined by those neat (and glib) generalizations, 'Augustan' and 'Romantic'. Or it may even be that, as G. S. Rousseau implies in essays collected in his 1991 volume, *Perilous Enlightenment*,[3] the task of understanding Gray has been deferred out of a reluctance to accept the truly personal nature of much of his writing.

However, a degree of critical uncertainty about Gray's status is no new phenomenon. In his own time Gray became the best-known living poet, and was offered (but, characteristically, refused) the Poet Laureateship in 1757. By that year, the *Elegy Written in a Country Churchyard*—destined to remain his most famous and widely-read poem—had appeared in ten separate editions, in the 1753 edition of six poems with illustrations by Richard Bentley, and in many pirated

editions.[4] So, when, still in 1757, Dodsley paid Gray 40 guineas
for two new odes, he was rewarded by rapid sales (1200–1300
within two weeks) and the notice of the chattering classes. Yet
the odes themselves encountered a mixed response, criticisms
of their obscurity acting as a contrast, or perhaps a comple-
ment, to praise from a coterie headed by Walpole.[5] When
Johnson, in his 'Life' of Gray, later formulated an attack on
what he saw as the ungraceful ornaments, affected images and
harsh language of these poems, while simultaneously rejoicing
to concur with the common reader in his unstinting praise of
the *Elegy*, he established the pattern of Gray's popular renown
which has ever since remained largely intact: the acceptable,
the readable, Gray has the common touch whereas the
unacceptable, the unreadable, retreats into a world of poetic
artifice.

Within the literary world, however, this pattern was before
long significantly amended in a way which has come to
dominate academic thinking and put Gray's advocates on the
defensive. Wordsworth, writing in the celebrated Preface to the
second edition of the *Lyrical Ballads* on behalf of the 'language
really used by men' as that which should belong to poetry, did
what poet-critics so often do: he made a space for his own views
by convicting his predecessors, notably Gray, of the contrary
tendency, of widening the gap between poetic diction and the
language of prose.[6] As Anne McDermott argues in the present
volume, Wordsworth's criticism is not, despite superficial
similarity, a reversion to Johnsonian (or 'Augustan') principles. Johnson and 'Augustanism' never deny the existence of
'poetic diction', but insist that obscurity be avoided and that
decorum, or fitness of language to subject-matter, be retained.
It is Wordsworth's principle (however much his practice
reveals its untenability) that has remained influential. Gray's
own, oft-cited comments in a letter to West that the language of
the age is never the language of poetry seemed to many to
provide corroboration of what became in the nineteenth
century, and has largely remained in the twentieth, the critical
orthodoxy.[7] Modern critics who have sought to defend Gray's
use of a distinct, self-conscious poetic diction have mainly
argued that this language takes its place within a 'dialogic'
structure of competing voices.[8] Indeed, the recurrent aim of

the small group of twentieth-century critics who have written on him has been to define or explain Gray's particular poetic language, thus confirming Wordsworth's challenging proposition that it is this diction that is the central problem in evaluating his work, since on it depend the validity of the emotions expressed and the effectiveness of the communication achieved. Explanations have thus tended to concentrate on specific aspects of Gray's diction, such as allusion, personification and the sublime. Yet, even among Gray's advocates, uncertainty of focus can be detected. Those who argue that the force and meaning of Gray's poetry lie in its deep and complex range of allusion to classical and English predecessors would seem to propose a hermetic, inward-looking Gray, very much Gray the scholar. Those who reveal the nature of Gray's personification are essentially unfolding what they take to be a common language of eighteenth-century writing and reading, one which has become lost to subsequent generations and thus (like all lost or partly lost languages) unfairly vulnerable to charges of obscurity and irrelevance.[9] The former have Gray as self-consciously learned, the latter as available to common sight could we but recover the right way of looking. The former approach can be tilted towards either praise or blame;[10] but its interpretation remains the same, one which is consistent with the Wordsworthian position.

It is, perhaps, instructive that, right from the time that Johnson so resoundingly confirmed the common reader's belief, the *Elegy* has been regarded as in some ways exceptional within Gray's poetry. The power of this poem has produced some of the most moving tributes from the common reader, and some of the best critical essays on Gray. This is often seen as the poem which, far from retreating into an artificial world of its own creation, is most securely based in reality, whether that of society or that of personal feeling expressed with poetic decorum.[11] Yet even here the element of poetic formality has proved hard to avoid, since the kind of emotion generated has been traced by some critics to conventional poetic types; while, for others, the key to the poem lies in its particularly elaborate, even contrived, structure or in an ambiguity of stance created by the juxtaposition of conflicting attitudes to the subject-matter of retirement and rustic life.[12] This last-mentioned approach returns us very much to the 'dialogic' structure so often discerned by linguistic criticism: the attitudes, like the language, are set in a state of tension. Thus, ultimately, the same issues emerge. Does the *Elegy* achieve direct, emotional communication, or is it really an exercise in the re-statement of poetic stereotypes? Does Gray commit himself to direct expression, or does he remain concealed behind a balanced structure of conflicting and unresolved tensions?

Understandably enough when its subject is an oeuvre full of apparent self-reference, much 'traditional' twentieth-century criticism has placed emphasis upon Gray's poetry as the outcome of personal feeling, while finding post-Romantic difficulty with the apparent lack of spontaneous overflow in its expression.[13] Indeed, there has actually been an interesting, if minor, strand of criticism which, by proposing that Gray's feelings are more directly expressed in his Latin than in his English poetry, re-states our central problem in yet another form. Should we view Gray's facility for writing Latin verse as a flagrant example of his propensity to retire from the common world into his own literary retreat—the arid scholar widening the gap between himself and a vulgar public and its habitual modes of language—or should we adjust our perspective by acknowledging that, for an eighteenth-century man educated at Eton, school-exercises rendered the writing of Latin verses a perfectly natural mode of expression? One of the most impressive recent essays on Gray addresses directly the relationship between the Latin and English poetry, ultimately confirming him as a man of his own age in his recurrent endorsement of a Lockeian epistemology.[14] This setting of Gray within his own time serves as a healthy riposte to the customary (since the nineteenth century) invocation of a retrospectively defined teleology characterized by the recurrent term 'pre-Romantic'; and to an influential twentieth-century elaboration of this taxonomy which institutes an 'age of sensibility' slung between the twin poles of 'Augustan' and 'Romantic'. The effect, however, of all these enterprises is to re-play the question about where to 'place' Gray within literary history.[15]

Not all questions, of course, can be considered, let alone answered, in one volume. However, the time seems propitious for a book-length attempt to address some of the recurrent problems in evaluating Gray's writing, particularly since they raise many pressing issues concerning the establishment of critical criteria. Apart from the biographically-based studies by Martin, Ketton-Cremer and Lytton Sells, only Morris Golden's volume in the Twayne English Authors series and *Fearful Joy*, a collection of papers from the bicentenary conference at Carleton University, stand as full-scale assessments of Gray's work. The former, in its updated 1988 version, is a respectable and solid essay, but does not break much new ground; while the latter contains a number of fine essays on a healthy variety of Gray's work and associated subjects, but is inevitably something of a patchwork. The present volume, it may be, will also prove to have this last fault, if fault it be. For the editors believed that, given the need to emphasize the range within Gray's output (notwithstanding the Victorian chorus of frustration that he produced so little) and the questionable shape of his past and present reputation, a series of essays by divers hands would prove more fruitful than a single-author book. They also felt that, since—as this introduction has argued—so many of the issues and problems in Gray's reputation are the consequence of judgements and attitudes which date from Gray's own period and the next century, an effective volume ought both to consider Gray's work in its own right and to examine how it has been mediated through the perspective of the poetry and criticism of some of his contemporaries and later writers.

Thus the reader will find here essays written from differing points of view, some of which focus on various aspects of Gray's oeuvre and some on the relationship between Gray and other writers. The essays may be conveniently divided into four groups. The first group consists of three substantial essays on the poetry and its language. Vincent Newey takes the major poems as a process of shaping the poet's identity, of what he terms 'biblio-selving'. Gray emerges from his study as a key figure in the developing of Romantic selfhood, but not as a pale precursor: the paradox that the self being appraised by this process is one marked by stasis, even inertia, is not a reflection of the Victorian notion, discussed fully in Malcolm Hicks's essay which concludes the volume, of Gray as a poet stifled by an unfavourable age, but the very discovery of the identity of the self as theme. Thus the *Eton College Ode* can be ranked as the earliest notable example of what has been defined as the greater Romantic lyric. Gray's poetry is one of a desperate subjectivity, lacking as it does a generalized language of a stable philosophy of the self, and is hence caught in a continuing process of the realization of disablement. Paul Williamson, by contrast, examines the *Elegy* as a poetics of genre, not a poetics of self. The transition, he argues, between the first version of the poem and its final, published form is that from an eighteenth-century Christian ethos characteristic of the genre of 'graveyard poetry' to the form of the classical elegy. When an external theology is invoked as the resolution of elegiac verse, poetry yields to the priority of a metaphysics of transcendence: poetic status is superseded by a prior and separate 'truth' which renders the poetic voice mute. The Virgilian pastoral elegy, however, reflected a tension between tragic themes and Arcadian idyll, so that the tone of elegiac sentiment admits of no conceptual resolution. It is to this classical mood and consequent assertion of an aesthetic, not a transcendent, value, that Gray transforms his poem. Whereas poetry which invokes an external theology thereby accepts a resolution which precedes the logic of the poem and thus renders poetic form redundant, the *Elegy* achieves its logic of expression within its own formal terms. Newey and Williamson thus bring the critical methods of the present age to bear on a recurrent question in Gray criticism, answering in equally cogent but differing ways. Newey finds a modernist means of sustaining the notion of the 'self' while rejecting naive conceptions of the personal, whereas Williamson discovers in scholarship and allusion the means to revive a living, not arid, form of classicism. For Newey the poetry points forward, for Williamson it finds its life in the past.

Richard Terry's essay represents a major attempt to place the issue of Gray's language within the context of eighteenth-century notions of poetic diction. An investigation of the tendency of 'Augustan' diction to stress the distance between verse and prose through the use of archaism, personification, periphrasis and the like leads him to an analysis of Gray's paradoxical position. Gray's observations on poetic style, as in his remarks on Lyttelton's *Monody*, show his concern to break free of linguistic stiffness, and yet this is the very fault of which he himself is so often accused. But, although Gray's diction remains a genuine issue, it can be defended by seeing his ability to turn weakness into strength, as when he avoids the language of cheap and sentimental consolation in his various epitaphic writings or when he creates unresolved dramatic contrast by means of the clash of registers in his 'dialogic' poetry. The result may be a limited kind of poetry, but one in which, at its best (as in the sonnet on the death of West), the suspension of the mind between alternatives enacts possibilities of response and thus becomes a means by which the mind can better know itself. By fully examining the tradition from which Gray's poetic diction emerges, Terry allows a more informed and so truer interpretation of one of the most common issues in writing on Gray.

The two essays of the second group answer accusations that Gray's output is too small to justify the highest praise by noting his capacity to turn his hand to two common, but usually neglected, genres within eighteenth-century writing, comic poetry and travel writing. T. W. Craik takes as his starting-point Walpole's remark that humour was Gray's 'natural and original turn'. This observation might surprise those for whom the *Elegy* represents the essential Gray as well as those well-read in nineteenth- and twentieth-century views of Gray. But, as with Johnson's similarly disconcerting comment on Shakespeare's natural tendency towards the comic, the eighteenth-century view can serve as a productive rejoinder to our too easy assumptions. Gray emerges from Craik's essay as a sharper and more varied writer than is normally dreamt of in our criticism, as evidenced by one of his very finest poems, the lines 'On Lord Holland's Seat'. William Ruddick examines the travel accounts in Gray's letters, finding in them a creative tension between direct reporting and description mediated by literary or artistic conventions. The recipient of the correspondence is here important: letters from the Alps to Gray's mother are straightforward in manner, whereas those to West are more literary in flavour. The Lakes tour, above all, reveals this quality of dual vision in Gray's accounts, making them fascinating and significant documents in the development of landscape description and travel writing.

Three essays on Gray and his contemporaries follow. David Fairer counters over-simple models of 'pre-Romanticism', finding instead different relationships with the past as the crucial aspect of mid-century poetry. His contrast is between a Thomas Warton for whom the past is a productive subject of inquiry, a realm for his genuine discovery of the new (in the course of which Fairer counters another too easily accepted modern model, Bloomian anxiety of influence) and a Gray for whom the view of the past (whether on a personal level, as in the sonnet on West, or on the level of public tradition, as in 'The Bard') is of disconnection, the inability to establish such a creative relationship. Like Terry, Fairer asserts the need to situate Gray within the movements of his own age if he is to be properly understood. Like Williamson, he sees the past as a potentially fruitful area of discovery for the eighteenth-century poet. But the Gray who emerges from his study is actually closer to that of Newey, despite their very different emphases and attitudes: it is Gray who is the 'more modern figure, a poet of anxieties and disconnections'. A similar conclusion is reached in Paul Whiteley's comparison between Gray's 'Ode on the Spring' and 'The Progress of Poesy' and two odes by another contemporary, Mark Akenside. Where Akenside's view of poetry finds connection and consolation, Gray uses poetry to reveal the insecurity of the individual; and where Akenside possesses a strong sense of the possibilities of lyric expression, Gray questions the capacity of the present to recapture the lyric power of the past. Whiteley points to Akenside's popularity in his own time and subsequent neglect, and sees the unique voice of Gray as the one which emerges as the more significant for the present day. An essential lesson lies at the heart of both these essays: literary history is always more complicated and self-contradictory than critical system-builders would have us believe. The Enlightenment, we should perhaps recall, distrusted any system: empiricism discovers diversity rather than unity, and generalizations (even such a one as is implied in the term 'Enlightenment') should be distrusted.

Anne McDermott returns to the issue of language and Johnson's objections to Gray's Pindaric odes. As noted earlier, she sets out the often-missed distinction between Johnson's and Wordsworth's criticisms of Gray, before defining the central question as being about the very nature of poetic language: 'does the language of poetry have to mean in the same way as the language of prose?' If Gray's odes represent a mid-century movement towards a view of language as relative to emotional states, Johnson's criticism emphasizes the importance of sustaining a relation between language and nature. So Johnson's concern for distinctness of image and exactness of language contrasts with the synthetic, blurring and aggregating characteristics of the 'sublime'. Johnson, as ever, emerges as a key critical figure, articulating a clear point of view which has the merit of defining differences of perspective and sharply noting the limitations of poetic fashions.

A final group of three essays examines Gray in the light of subsequent writers, two of the major 'Romantic' poets, Wordsworth and Byron, and the influential critics of the Victorian age. As we have noted, Wordsworth is the Romantic poet most directly associated with a theory of poetic diction contrary to that of Gray. But in terms of theme and attitude, Angus Easson argues, his response to Gray's poetry was more complex than that of mere rejection. Although the later writer needed to distance himself from a major predecessor, Gray served Wordsworth as a recurrent point of reference and as a source of sympathetic feeling. Easson's analysis of the Robespierre passage in book X of the 1805 *Prelude* reveals how Gray could act as a focal point for ideas of loss and memory; while his comparison between Gray's West sonnet and Wordsworth's 'Surprised by Joy' indicates how, ultimately, Wordsworth had to transcend the earlier poet. Wordsworth's poetic relationship with Gray emerges as one marked by both acknowledgement and a need to supersede.

Byron, by contrast, might, at first sight, strike one as an unlikely candidate for comparison with Gray, the two poets appearing to be worlds apart temperamentally and poetically. Yet Bernard Beatty's imaginative intertextual study of aspects of their work alerts us to how a shared point of difference can indicate similarity. Distinguishing himself from Wordsworth's campaign for simple diction, Byron actually manifests some of that self-conscious variation of language which Wordsworth was unable—or unwilling—to acknowledge in Gray's poetry. Byron is equally drawn to elements of Gray's sensibility, and the result is a texture of language which demonstrates a particular energy of feeling characteristic of Gray, rather than of poets of the 'Romantic' generations. Beatty's essay thus performs its own variation on one of the motifs of this volume, the rejection of simplified categories of literary history. An earlier poet does not have to be either a representative of a dead tradition or a threatening 'precursor': such a poet as Byron can shape his individual freedom and explore his capacity for expression by means of his own creative engagement with an earlier, equally individual, writer.

Malcolm Hicks's essays on Gray's reputation among the Victorians is a fitting conclusion to the volume, since it not only examines thoroughly attitudes to Gray within a crucial period for the establishment of critical criteria, but also raises questions about the very nature of the critical endeavour. An age perhaps sees its own face in the mirror of criticism, and Hicks argues that Victorian perceptions of Gray actually reflect the age's own anxieties. Arnold—for good and ill—is the dominating figure, memorably and influentially establishing the notion of a Gray who never spoke out, a poet trapped in an age of prose. But Hicks makes it clear how concerted the chorus was: from John Mitford's concern that Gray wrote so little to Edmund Gosse's Gray as an innovatory lyricist, the 'Romantic' quality is the true touchstone for the age which so dubbed the 'Romantics' themselves. The teleology countered by Fairer is itself the product of retrospective. Perhaps this, too, no criticism can entirely escape. Such a failing will be as true of the present volume as it is of any other, and the frailties of its patterns will, no doubt, be drawn in time from their abode. The editors will be content if the book is taken as a frail memorial to the work of one of our finest and most memorable poets.

NOTES

1. *The Year's Work in English Studies*, 70 (1989), 370.
2. 'Life of Gray', in *Lives of the English Poets*, ed. G. Birkbeck Hill, 3 vols (Oxford, 1905), III, 441.
3. 'The pursuit of homosexuality' and 'Love and Antiquities: Walpole and Gray on the Grand Tour', in *Perilous Enlightenment: Pre- and Post-Modern Discourses, Sexual, Historical* (Manchester, 1991), pp. 2–43, 172–99. See also

Jean H. Hagstrum, 'Gray's Sensibility', in *Fearful Joy* (Papers from the Thomas Gray Bicentenary Conference at Carleton University), ed. James Downey and Ben Jones (Montreal, 1974), pp. 6–19.

4. C. S. Northup, *A Bibliography of Thomas Gray* (New Haven, 1917), pp. 74–76.

5. See W. Powell Jones 'The Contemporary Reception of Gray's *Odes*', *Modern Philology*, 28 (1930–31), 61–82.

6. *The Poetical Works of William Wordsworth*, ed. E. de Selincourt, 5 vols (Oxford, 1940–49), II, 384–404. For the link between Johnson's and Wordsworth's views, see Donald Greene, 'The Proper Language of Poetry: Gray, Johnson, and Others', in *Fearful Joy*, pp. 85–102. See also Roger Lonsdale, 'Gray and Johnson: The Biographical Problem', in *Fearful Joy*, pp. 66–84.

7. Gray to West, 8 April 1742. *Correspondence*, I, 192.

8. The influential essay is F. Doherty, 'The Two Voices of Gray', *Essays in Criticism*, 13 (1963), 222–30. See also Patricia Meyer Spacks, 'Statement and Artifice in Thomas Gray', *Studies in English Literature*, 5 (1965), 519–32, revised in *The Poetry of Vision* (Cambridge, Mass., 1967), chapter 5; *Selected Poems of Thomas Gray and William Collins*, ed. Arthur Johnston (London, 1967); Judith K. Moore, 'Thomas Gray's "Sonnet on the Death of Richard West": the Circumstances and the Diction', *Tennessee Studies in Literature*, 19 (1974), 107–13; Donald C. Mell, *A Poetics of Augustan Elegy* (Amsterdam, 1974), chapter 6. Typical comments on West are Spacks's assertion that the chief tension is 'between artifice and personal statement' (*Poetry of Vision*, p. 95) and Johnston's view that the 'use of the two languages helps to emphasize the poet's sense of isolation from the world of beauty outside him, which he nevertheless recognizes as beautiful' (p. 19).

9. Critics emphasizing allusion include Joseph Foladare, 'Gray's "Frail Memorial" to West', *Publications of the Modern Language Association of America*, 75 (1960), 61–65; Geoffrey Tillotson, *Augustan Studies* (London, 1961), pp. 204–15; Arthur Johnston, '"The Purple Year" in Pope and Gray', *Review of English Studies*, n.s. 14 (1963), 389–93; Thomas B. Gilmore, 'Allusion and Melancholy in Gray's *Ode on a Distant Prospect of Eton College*', *Papers on Language and Literature*, 15 (1979), 52–58; R. S. Edgecombe, 'Diction and Allusion in two early Odes by Gray', *Durham University Journal*, 48 (1986), 31–36. See also Howard D. Weinbrot, 'Gray's "Progress of Poesy" and "The Bard": An Essay in Literary Transmission', in *Johnson and His Age*, ed. James Engell (Cambridge, Mass., 1984), pp. 311–32 for a characteristically salutary warning against too simple views of the Pindaric odes as imitations of classical models. The key text for the visually imaginative nature of Gray's personification is Jean H. Hagstrum, *The Sister Arts* (Chicago, 1958), pp. 287–314. See also Eric Rothstein, *Restoration and Eighteenth-Century Poetry 1660–1780* (London, 1981), pp. 53–55; Margaret Anne Doody, *The Daring Muse: Augustan Poetry Reconsidered* (Cambridge, 1985), pp. 164–66. On the sublime, see Marshall Brown, 'The Urbane Sublime', *ELH*, 45 (1978), 236–54.

10. E.g. John Butt, *The Mid-Eighteenth Century*, ed. and completed Geoffrey Carnall (Oxford, 1979), who writes of 'a sophisticated pleasure derived from observing a great master in emulation of his predecessors, profoundly aware

of a treasury of word and phrase that they have bequeathed him, using it with distinction in a new context, or giving final expression to what oft was thought' (p. 75); A. L. Lytton Sells, *Thomas Gray: His Life and Works* (London, 1980), who curtly remarks that the 'final comment on the "Ode to Adversity" is that it suffers from an excess of erudition' (p. 169).

11. Critics emphasizing social reality include William Empson, *Some Versions of Pastoral* (London,1935), p. 4; F. R. Leavis, *Revaluation* (London, 1936), pp. 106–07; Thomas R. Edwards, *Imagination and Power: A Study of Poetry on Public Themes* (London, 1971), pp. 118–29. Critics emphasizing the truth and/or decorum of personal feeling include Bertrand H. Bronson, 'On a Special Decorum in Gray's *Elegy*', in *From Sensibility to Romanticism*, ed. F. W. Hilles and H. Bloom (New York, 1965), pp. 171–76; Thomas R. Carper, 'Gray's Personal Elegy', *Studies in English Literature*, 17 (1977), 451–62; Howard D. Weinbrot, 'Gray's *Elegy*: A Poem of Moral Choice and Resolution', *Studies in English Literature*, 18 (1978), 537–51.

12. On conventional types, see Myrddin Jones, 'Gray, Jaques, and the Man of Feeling', *Review of English Studies*, n.s. 25 (1974), 39–48; Ian Jack,'Gray's *Elegy* Reconsidered', in *From Sensibility to Romanticism*, pp. 139–69, on the *Elegy* as a poem of sensibility. Those emphasizing structure include Cleanth Brooks, 'Gray's Storied Urn', in *The Well Wrought Urn* (London, 1949), pp. 96–113; F. H. Ellis, 'Gray's *Elegy*: The Biographical Problem in Literary Criticism', *Publications of the Modern Language Association of America*, 66 (1951), 971–1008; Frank Brady, 'Structure and Meaning in Gray's *Elegy*', in *From Sensibility to Romanticism*, pp. 177–89. The influential essay on ambiguity of stance is A. E. Dyson, 'The Ambivalence of Gray's *Elegy*', *Essays in Criticism*, 7 (1957), 257–61. See also, George Watson, 'The Voices of Gray', *Critical Quarterly*, 19 (1977), 51–57.

13. Critics taking the poetry as directly personal include Roger Martin, *Essai sur Thomas Gray* (Paris, 1934); R. W. Ketton-Cremer, *Thomas Gray* (Cambridge, 1955); Morris Golden, *Thomas Gray, Updated Edition* (Boston, 1988). Even in such an essay as Wallace Jackson, 'Thomas Gray and the Dedicatory Muse', *ELH*, 54 (1987), 277–98, where the stress is on rhetoric, the author still accepts that biographical parallels can be traced.

14. W. Powell Jones, *Thomas Gray, Scholar* (Cambridge, Mass., 1937) comments that 'Gray wrote in English a stilted sonnet on West's death and put his genuine feelings into the Latin verses that he appended to his philosophical fragment, *De principiis cogitandi*' (p. 8). Roger Martin and Morris Golden also read the Latin poetry as expressive of direct feeling. The recent essay is S. H. Clark, ' "Pendet Homo Incertus": Gray's Response to Locke', *Eighteenth-Century Studies*, 24 (1991), 273–91, 484–503.

15. The influential essay on the age of sensibility is Northrop Frye, 'Towards Defining an age of Sensibility', *ELH*, 23 (1956), 144–52. For a rebuttal of 'labelling', see W. B. Carnochan, 'The Continuity of Eighteenth-Century Poetry: Gray, Cowper, Crabbe, and the Augustans', *Eighteenth Century Life*, 12 (1988), 119–27.

The Selving of Thomas Gray

VINCENT NEWEY

Memorability is one fair measure of poetic success, and Gray's *Elegy* is, as Dr Johnson famously realized, a very memorable piece, 'abound[ing] with images which find a mirror in every mind, and with sentiments to which every bosom returns an echo':[1]

> The boast of heraldry, the pomp of pow'r,
> And all that beauty, all that wealth e'er gave,
> Awaits alike th'inevitable hour.
> The paths of glory lead but to the grave.
>
> (ll. 33–36)

This is what Johnson elsewhere termed 'the grandeur of generality':[2] a frugal sublimity in keeping with the rehearsal of life's great commonplaces, eschewing elaborate ornament for the sober qualities of a strong and lucid syntax, weighty verbs, the compressed figurative eloquence of 'inevitable hour' and 'paths of glory'. Gray is here a pre-eminent practitioner of that 'artistic *kenosis*', or awesome renunciation of false riches, which has been seen as the characteristic signature of eighteenth-century classicism as it is inscribed in religious and moralistic verse, including the hymn.[3] If hymnody supplied the model for Gray's quatrains, the themes of the *Elegy* were derived from the 'graveyard school', especially the Revd James Hervey's widely influential *Meditations and Contemplations*, which offer, for example, reflections on Death the Leveller corresponding to Gray's stanzas (ll. 29–44) on 'disdainful' Grandeur that ends in futile 'Trophies' and 'silent dust':

> The poor indigent lay as softly, and sleep as soundly, as the most opulent possessor. All the distinction that subsisted, was ... a sepulchral stone ornamented with imagery ... Why should we exalt ourselves, or debase others, since we must all, one day, be upon a common

level, and blended together in the same undistinguished dust?[4]

Gray transformed a popular preacherly rhetoric into an abiding corporate wisdom.

As we shall see, however, Gray's relation to Hervey was not only that of a poet in search of a public voice: the *Meditations* were also a book he fell upon for ways of shaping his identity and writing his life into a destiny—that is, for materials of his 'biblio-selving'. Commenting upon the poetry of the second half of the eighteenth century, Northrop Frye distinguished between two views of literature, the Aristotelian (or neo-classical) and the Longinian (or Romantic), 'the aesthetic and the psychological, the view of literature as product and the view of literature as process'.[5] My own concern is primarily with 'the psychological' in Gray, with Gray's poetry as 'process'—though that does not mean forgetting the common-sense and social art of the *Elegy*, since this represents, whatever else, an escape from silence and the fear of waste.

Roger Lonsdale, one of the critics most committed to reading the *Elegy* as personal statement, takes as his focus the fact that it exists in 'two distinct versions': the version which originally ended with the four rejected stanzas of the Eton manuscript, and the revised and expanded version which reached print in 1751.[6] Lonsdale remarks that in its first form[7] the *Elegy* makes a 'well-constructed poem', more balanced in structure and meaning than the final version. The opening three stanzas 'brilliantly [set] the poem and the poet in the churchyard'; or, more precisely, they create a mood of heightened meditative tranquillity, a trance or half-conscious state in which the sights and sounds of the external world are interiorized as vivid slow-motion dream-impressions and sensations—the miniature herd that 'wind slowly o'er the Lea', the shadowy ploughman that 'homeward plods his weary way', the gradual withdrawal of material bearings as 'fades the glimm'ring Landscape on the Sight' and the strange answering plenitude as magically 'all the Air a solemn Stillness holds'. There then follow four complementary units each of four stanzas, dealing in turn with the lives of the humble villagers, highlighting their happiness and honourable toil; with the lives of the great, steeped in power and splendour but equally subject to death; with the way in which the poor are deprived of opportunity in the spheres of art, knowledge and political action; and, by contrast, with the fact that this same obscurity ensures their innocence of crimes involved in worldly success. The last three stanzas, matching the opening three, return us to the poet, making plain that the whole piece has been a *psychomachia*, or mind-debate, in which, having reflected upon the relative drawbacks and privileges of the sequestered life and the life of ambition, he makes choice of the former model of existence:

> Hark how the sacred Calm, that broods around
> Bids ev'ry fierce tumultuous Passion cease
> In still small Accents whisp'ring from the Ground
> A grateful Earnest of eternal Peace
>
> No more with Reason & thyself at Strife;
> Give anxious Cares & endless Wishes room
> But thro' the cool sequester'd Vale of Life
> Pursue the silent Tenour of thy Doom.[8]

This we may describe as an attitude of Christian stoicism, in which the consoling sense of an afterlife blends with resigned dedication to the private places of retirement. But in what sense, exactly, are the stanzas 'personal'? F. W. Bateson, among others, takes a frankly biographical approach, reading in Gray's rejection of the 'thoughtless World' references to his quarrel with Horace Walpole and consequent estrangement from aristocratic circles, and in the stance of acceptance his response to 'anxious Cares' and 'endless Wishes' arising from the death of his father and that of his friend, Richard West.[9] There may be something in this even though the *Elegy* was probably not begun until some four years after 1742 when all these events took place:[10] poetry can be written out of a long arc of feeling. Yet there is another kind of autobiography in Gray's writing, where recurrent tropes express general preoccupations and not least a persistent apprehension of aimlessness, futility and confinement:

> I am got into a room; ... when I get up in the morning, I
> begin to travel [tow]ards the middle of it with might &

main, & with much ado about noon bate at a great Table,
which stands half-way it: so then, by that time, (after
having pursued my journey full speed); that I arrive at the
door, it is so dark & late, & I am so tired, that I am obliged
to turn back again: so about Midnight I get to the
bedside.[11]

[my days] go round and round like the blind horse in the
mill, only he has the satisfaction of fancying he makes a
progress, . . . my eyes are open enough to see the same dull
prospect, and to know that having made four-and-twenty
steps more, I shall be just where I was.[12]

To these examples might be added the well-known observations on 'low spirits', his 'true and faithful companions', or
brief asides complaining of a shut-in state—'no Wonder then
. . . if my Spirits, when I return'd back to my Cell, should sink
for a time'.[13] Claude Lévi-Strauss points out that reduction to
small-scale makes reality less threatening—'diminishes or
eliminates the resistance that [it] poses to the ordering instincts
of the human mind'.[14] In his statements here, however, Gray
enacts an almost parodic version of this strategy for psychic
control: nervously balanced between playfulness and horror,
his imagination transforms his surroundings into a prison,
movement into non-progression, aloneness into haunted
isolation. But what we then have in the ending of the first *Elegy*
is the upside of this characteristic negative vision, and embodi-
ment, of self: no lament but rather a confident embrace of the
'Doom' of solitude; no oppressive limits, or endless circling, or
an expense of energy in getting nowhere, but, as the word
'Pursue' in particular suggests, a resolute journeying along the
benign track of the 'cool sequester'd Vale of Life'. The source of
Gray's sentiments may well be in Hervey's twin themes of *de
contemptu mundi* and self-mastery—exhortations to 'get above
the delusive amusements of honour', to seek the scene where all
concurs to 'hush our Passions, and sooth our Cares' and 'where
I may, with advantage, apply myself to subdue the *rebel within*,
and be master, not of a sceptre, but of myself'.[15] But they are
sentiments driven radically inwards: like Cowper the recluse of
Olney in his great coda to Book VI of *The Task* ('He is the
happy man, whose life ev'n now / Shows somewhat of that

happier life to come...'),[16] Gray the Cambridge introvert found in the *topos* of contemplative retreat a positive pattern on which to base his own being-in-the-world—or being out of it. Poetry becomes the context for stabilizing the individual present.

Yet the Eton MS *Elegy* is not so rounded-off as this account might suggest. Its conclusion is a holding operation rather than a resolution, and there are in the text layers of signification that the ending does not encompass, or that remain to unsettle it. One of the most intriguing of these is the imagery— as in 'Forbad to wade thro' Slaughter to a Throne' (*PW*, p. 183)—which implies a puzzling interest in violence on Gray's part. We must return to this in another context. Of more immediate relevance is the undertow of denial that pulls at the poem despite the closing affirmative poise. Some motifs are turned, others are not; and among the latter are configurations above all of obscurity as waste:

> Full many a Gem of purest Ray serene
> The dark unfathom'd Caves of Ocean bear.
> Full many a Flower is born to blush unseen
> And wast its Sweetness on the desert Air.

> (*PW*, p. 183)

The miracle is that worth and beauty are bred in the darkest and most arid of places, at the bottom of the sea and in the desert; but this celebration is compromised by the implication that 'Gem' and 'Flower' have no point because they are not seen: their existence is, paradoxically, a form of non-being. The philosophy at the end of the poem does nothing to erase either this sense of unfruitfulness or the accompanying images of cruel restriction where the literal 'narrow Cell' in which the dead villager lies (*PW*, p. 181) seems but an extension of the limitations that before 'froze the genial Current of the Soul' (*PW*, p. 183).

Of the figures on the dark side of Gray's imagination, however, it is that of silence which finally disturbs the poem most. The 'mute inglorious' condition of the countryman has its counterpart in the 'silent Tenour' of the poet's 'Doom'; but Gray's ease with that 'Tenour' proves more apparent than real, for he actually pursues it only to renounce it by crossing out the original ending in favour of a continuation of his poetic voice. The decision to accept silence and a hidden life becomes the point at which both are refused and the poem undone. In rewriting the *Elegy* Gray declared its first conclusion a context—a counterfeit or deception. He was driven to a different 'selving', in which both his uncertainty about the value of sequestration and the concomitant claims of worldly status were emphatically acknowledged.

The most important changes to the *Elegy* are the addition of the speech of the 'hoary-headed Swain', which describes the poet roaming the landscape, and of the epitaph on the grave of that same poet. In Bateson's view the purpose of these new segments was to 'depersonalize' the poem for an age which recoiled from the publication of private griefs: 'the central figure is no longer Thomas Gray' but 'a conventional figure, the Melancholy Man, who could not possibly be identified with anybody'.[17] This is to stay too much on the surface. The whole of the *Elegy* is what Christine Gallant usefully calls 'concentrical'[18]—that is, the outcrop of a single mind. The swain's account of the poet-outsider is Gray's view of himself and how others might see him—a projection of his concern with his place and standing. The picture is profoundly ambiguous:

'Oft have we seen him at the peep of dawn
'Brushing with hasty steps the dews away
'To meet the sun upon the upland lawn.

'There at the foot of yonder nodding beech
'That wreathes its old fantastic roots so high,
'His listless length at noontide wou'd he stretch,
'And pore upon the brook that babbles by.

'Hard by yon wood, now smiling as in scorn,
'Mutt'ring his wayward fancies he wou'd rove,
'Now drooping, woeful wan, like one forlorn,
'Or craz'd with care, or cross'd in hopeless love.

(ll. 98–108)

There is, on the one hand, a manifest assertive aspect to this (self-)portrait: the Poet is, as Lonsdale puts it, a man of 'unique and somehow valuable sensibility';[19] he dwells apart, deep in feeling and in a special relationship with nature. Yet, on the other hand, the imagery is packed with suggestions of stasis and enervation: the energy of 'Brushing' and 'hasty' seems frantic, and leads only to an end-stopped encounter with the rising sun; the idea of contemplative ease is lost in impressions of 'listless' vacuity, and if this Poet repeatedly ponders the language of nature it is but to experience an incomprehensible 'babble'; imagination and emotion are no channels of inspiration but threads that bind him, 'drooping', 'craz'd' and 'cross'd'. These stanzas echo Spenser, Shakespeare and early Milton,[20] and Gray is clearly making trial of an alternative conception of creative life to that of neo-classical tradition. Is there something beyond the swain's ken, a mystery he cannot penetrate? Perhaps so: what *he* hears as 'babble' might be, to the seer, meaningful sounds; in the solitary Poet we discern the possible contours of the Wordsworthian *vates*, who, communing with nature, sees into 'the life of things'.[21] But Gray does not fill out those contours: for that we must go to Cowper's *The Task* and its influential arguments in favour of a wise passiveness where 'Meditation ... / May think down hours to moments' and 'the heart / May give an useful lesson to the head'.[22] In Gray the Poet's *via obscura* remains a condition of impasse—a state where inner process, like the wreathing and fantastic roots of the 'nodding beech', is wayward and involuted. The poetry conforms to the motifs of circling, confinement and 'low spirits' that are his customary autograph. If the Romantic idea of the Poet *is* apparent, it is rather in its unhappy reverse—the self-absorbed melancholic of Wordsworth's 'Lines, left upon a Seat in a Yew-tree', the maniac of Shelley's 'Julian and Maddalo', Keats's 'dreaming thing, / A fever of thyself'.[23]

The Epitaph, however, then comes at the problem of self-appraisal and self-worth from another angle. One of the themes of the *Elegy* is humankind's desire to be remembered after death ('On some fond breast the parting soul relies...' [l. 89]), and Gray, queerly, conjures up his own memorial, inscribing his future small corner of the earth with his 'merits'. Both apologia and personal consolation, the verses show Gray's interest at last in laying claim to *social* virtues; solitari-

ness and the life of imagination are finally no more acceptable
to him than silence:

> *Large was his bounty, and his soul sincere,*
> *Heav'n did a recompence as largely send:*
> *He gave to Mis'ry all he had, a tear,*
> *He gain'd from Heav'n ('twas all he wish'd) a friend.*
>
> (ll. 121–24)

The word 'bounty' is often interpreted as 'blessings' granted to
the poet,[24] but the whole drift of the Epitaph makes clear that
it refers to the benevolence—if only 'a tear'—that he shows to
others. Similarly, in the previous lines, 'Melancholy', which is
placed on an equal footing with 'Science', is to be taken as an
active and superior quality, rather than an affliction: it
appears in 'Ode to Adversity' (ll. 25–32) alongside Wisdom,
Justice, Charity and Pity, and seems to indicate, as it does in
Milton's 'Il Penseroso', a receptivity to philosophic truth.[25] If
Milton's early poem helped Gray to upvalue the life of
academic seclusion, however, it was James Hervey who
supplied the more solid model of usefulness: 'Let surviving
friends bear witness, that I have not lived to myself alone, nor
been altogether unserviceable to my generation ... Let the
poor, as they pass by my grave, point at the little spot, and
thankfully acknowledge—"There lies the man whose unwear-
ied kindness was the constant relief of my distress ... Here are
the last remains of that sincere friend, who watched for my
soul"'.[26] As is further suggested by the cancellation of the
'Red-breast' stanza that precedes the Epitaph in the Eton MS,
which is an alternative 'plate' depicting the secret tribute of
nature as 'little Footsteps lightly print the ground' (*PW*,
p. 187), Gray cannot rest content with any surmise that
consigns him to invisibility, but wishes to be seen as an
exemplary and 'serviceable' figure. It is true that at the end he
follows Hervey's reminder that what really matters is God's
judgement, for, however 'disregarded or forgotten' our
'characters' might be on earth, they will 'be had in everlasting
remembrance before the Lord':[27]

> *No farther seek his merits to disclose,*
> *Or draw his frailties from their dread abode,*

(There they alike in trembling hope repose)
The bosom of his Father and his God.

(ll. 125–28)

Yet the entire added section of the poem actually works against the grain of any notion of being 'disregarded' or 'forgotten'. In the Eton MS Gray had left the Churchyard *Elegy* to speak for itself—to be his memorial; in the revised version his urge to make his mark and establish his image extends even to writing the text of his own demise and immortality.

For Matthew Arnold, the whole history of Thomas Gray was that '*He never spoke out*'; and Graham Hough in *The Romantic Poets*, a book now much undervalued, takes up this approach by noting the recurrence in Gray's texts of 'despairs and frustrations' and ascribing them to the difficulty of being a poet 'in a climate . . . that did not suit what ought to have been [his] kind of poetry': 'When Shelley feels as Gray must often have felt, the result is "Stanzas written in Dejection". But the strong social sense of eighteenth-century poetry . . . made this kind of self-expression quite impossible.'[28] I would like, of course, to reverse the emphasis. Gray not so much lacked a convention for 'self-expression' as inaugurated one in a climate of change. His interest in his own identity is clearly interwoven with concern over the role of poetry itself: what the *Elegy* dramatizes is, as Lonsdale begins to suggest,[29] an uneasy suspension between dispensations—the poet as anxious outsider, no longer 'the urban, urbane, worldly, rational Augustan' but at the same time unable to embrace a Romantic faith in solitude, in intercourse between self and nature, or in the imagination as the most productive of human capacities. Like Collins, who talked of 'this laggard age', and Cowper, who lamented that 'Whate'er we write, we bring forth nothing new', Gray belonged to a generation uncertain of its direction: and in the fragment entitled 'Stanzas to Mr. Bentley' the text actually peters out as he reflects upon the absence in 'this benighted age' (l. 17) of both the 'diviner inspiration' of the Renaissance and the 'energy' and 'harmony' of Dryden and Pope.[30] In the void, however, emerges psychodrama—the self on the periphery, bidding for the centre.

We must come back later to these broader issues. First, the

psychodrama itself is worth distinguishing further. Gray could
certainly speak out in his way but could find no way to break
out, either from 'despairs and frustrations' or from the constant
cycle of making and unmaking the self. 'Ode on the Spring' is
an early case in point.

The original title of this poem, 'Noontide, an Ode',[31] would
have been appropriate for Gray, implying as it does an in-
between position. The designation 'Ode on the Spring' raises
ideas of growth and development, but these expectations are
not borne out. This is a two-part text with a definite down-
wards curve. The first part proclaims retirement as a site of
superior wisdom from which the unthinking life of 'the Busy
and the Gay' may be nonchalantly denounced:

> Beside some water's rushy brink
> With me the Muse shall sit, and think
> (At ease reclin'd in rustic state)
> How vain the ardour of the Crowd,
> How low, how little are the Proud,
> How indigent the Great!
> (ll. 15–20)

The insects that surround the poet become emblematic of 'the
race of Man', where all 'Shall end where they began', brushed
away by 'rough Mischance' or 'chill'd by age' (ll. 31–40).
Already, however, the parenthesis—'(At ease reclin'd in rustic
state)'—allows us a glimpse of ambiguity in the poet's situation, the impression of magisterial authority in 'rustic state'
being queried by that of mere otiose retreat in the preceding
image of stretched-out ease; and in the second half of the poem
denial is well and truly snatched from the jaws of affirmation as
the 'sportive kind' are given the right of reply:

> Methinks I hear in accents low
> The sportive kind reply:
> Poor moralist! and what are thou?
> A solitary fly! ...
> Thy sun is set, thy spring is gone—
> We frolick, while 'tis May.
> (ll. 41–44, 49–50)

The overplayed ventriloquism and clever twisting of the theme of *carpe diem* create humour, but this cannot mask the serious edge of Gray's gesture of self-derision. In turning the irony upon himself he enacts a pattern of non-progressive being—a kind of ontological paralysis—that dominates his writing and interior life. This pattern exists, moreover, not only in the thought structure of individual poems but in the chain of repetition that forms between them: the figure here 'At ease reclin'd' beside the stream is reproduced in the poet of the swain's speech in the *Elegy*, where, as we have seen, the signs of privilege are similarly, if less explicitly, undermined by suggestions of worthlessness and lack.

Self-realization in Gray, then, is closely bound up with self-limitation and incompleteness. Another example comes immediately into view. Gray sent 'Ode on the Spring' to Richard West in June 1742 without knowing that West was already dead:[32]

> In vain to me the smileing Mornings shine,
>   And redning Phoebus lifts his golden Fire:
> The Birds in vain their amorous Descant joyn;
>   Or chearful Fields resume their green Attire:
> These Ears, alas! for other Notes repine,
>   A different Object do these Eyes require.
> My lonely Anguish melts no Heart, but mine;
>   And in my Breast the imperfect Joys expire.
> Yet Morning smiles the busy Race to chear,
>   And new-born Pleasure brings to happier Men:
> The Fields to all their wonted Tribute bear:
>   To warm their little Loves the Birds complain:
> I fruitless mourn to him, that cannot hear,
>   And weep the more, because I weep in vain.

Few readers can be ignorant of Wordsworth's contempt in the Preface to *Lyrical Ballads* (1800) for the 'curiously elaborate ... poetic diction' of lines 1–5 and 9–12 of 'Sonnet on the Death of Richard West'.[33] Yet it is clear that this diction functions as part of an overall mental topography, not least in contrast with the remaining lines, which Wordsworth found more 'interesting' because more natural, 'the language of prose ... when prose is well written'.[34] The phrases of the opening section are taken from Virgil, Ovid, Pope's *Odyssey* and Milton's *Paradise Lost*;[35] and the effect of this artifice is to stress the pressure of the poet's aloneness by signifying that he can find contact with the external world only at second-hand, through borrowed language. The collective voice of epic formulae has been appropriated to the expression of isolate subjectivity, and tells of disability—the natural man struck blind and deaf by loss (the emphasis is all on 'Eyes' and 'Ears'). The metaphor then switches to that of dumbness, as the 'Sonnet' voices a condition of voicelessness; that is, the lack of communication, or of conversation: 'I fruitless mourn to him, that cannot hear'. The irony is that the only source of relief for Gray is he whose death causes his grief. Wordsworth complained of ' "fruitless" for fruitlessly' as a single 'defect' in two otherwise successfully plain lines; but this misses the point that 'fruitless' is both adverb *and* adjective, telling not only of the sterility of the present utterance but also (the more forcibly if we carry over echoes of the previous reference to 'little loves') to the equally issue-less relationship of Gray and West in life (and we realize that this elegy is a species of 'amorous Descant', too). And so desire—*want* in both its meanings—becomes an added factor in the poem's experiential content: a thread in the pattern of helplessness which is projected on other levels by the repetition of 'In vain', which mirrors the poet's shut-in state, or by the anthropomorphic and prosopopeial effects which locate the speaker in a field of uncontrollable forces, including his own senses and emotions ('these Eyes require', 'My lonely Anguish' ...).

There is, however, a further point, which has firm bearing on the standing of Gray's texts. Part of the deprivation expressed in this lament is the absence of an audience, whether the public readership evoked by the 'heroic' idiom of the opening lines or the private addressee who is Richard West. But another audience emerges in the form of our own trespass and overhearing. We again catch the marginal subject in process of moving, if inadvertently, to the fore: the repeated phrase, 'in vain', that draws a circle round the text signalizes not only that subject's confinement—the impossibility of escaping impotent self-consciousness—but also the satisfying completeness of the inner drama we have tumbled upon. The

emptiness of Thomas Gray, so perfectly framed, is our plenitude.

If the 'Sonnet' is Gray's most concentrated poem of personal
reflection, *Ode on a Distant Prospect of Eton College* is his most
extended, and has some claim to being the earliest notable
example of that dominant site of post-Enlightenment subjectivity which M. H. Abrams identified as 'the greater Romantic
lyric', a genre taking in Coleridge's 'Frost at Midnight' and
'Dejection', Wordsworth's 'Tintern Abbey', Shelley's 'Stanzas
written in Dejection', all of which are 'a varied but integral
process of memory, thought, anticipation, and feeling which
remains closely intervolved with the outer scene ... [while] in
the course of this meditation the lyric speaker achieves an
insight, faces up to a tragic loss, comes to a moral decision, or
resolves an emotional problem'.[36] It is worth noting, however,
that in the first stanza the 'prospect' is, rather, an unsolicited
occasion for reaffirming a continuity in history and a social
hierarchy endorsed by nature and by myth: spatial and
temporal references—'Ye distant spires, ye antique towers, /
That crown the watry glade'—situate Eton on a venerable
eminence, in whose precincts Science worships the originary
spirit of the place (the 'holy Shade' of Henry VI, founder of the
College); alongside, the royal castle of Windsor dominates a
harmonious and fertile landscape through which the tutelary
figure of 'hoary Thames' takes his 'silver-winding way'. School
and State, bastions of established rule, are legitimized as
features of a numinous and unified topography in which past
and present commune and the gods abide. There are no people
here, only the attractive and unquestionable hegemony of
impersonal forces—History, Knowledge, Nature.

There are in this text, then, buried ideological assumptions—how far buried being apparent by comparison with
Pope's manifest proclamation of the Stuart peace and Britain's
imperial destiny in *Windsor-Forest*, with 'Old father Thames'
prophesying the kingdom's future as both universal emporium,
where 'nations enter with each swelling tide', and its political
hub, where 'Kings shall sue, and suppliant States be seen'.[37]
Reinforcement, however, can be all the more effective for being
concealed or undeclared, and it seems that a case could be
made for seeing the poem as an instance of that 'Romantic

ideology' whereby conservative power structures are endorsed
and awkward questions are elided by diverting attention on to
the interior life of the 'free' individual.[38]

But such an approach would have the drawback of ignoring
just how decisively the focus shifts and how deep the attention
goes—that is, of cancelling the *dynamis* of the rest of the text. In
the second stanza history becomes recollection and the
inscribed values of the scene are no longer covertly socio-
political but patently subjective:

> Ah happy hills, ah pleasing shade,
> Ah fields belov'd in vain,
> Where once my careless childhood stray'd,
> A stranger yet to pain!
> I feel the gales, that from ye blow,
> A momentary bliss bestow,
> As waving fresh their gladsome wing,
> My weary soul they seem to sooth[e],
> And, redolent of joy and youth,
> To breath a second spring.
>
> (ll. 11–20)

The words 'happy', 'pleasing', 'belov'd' bring in a note of
simple emotional bonding and gain, which is, with equal
speed, unsettled by thoughts of the inevitable passing of
unselfconscious childhood ('in vain' again working to evoke the
individual's ultimate impotence in the face of experience). The
interesting thing about this stanza, however, is that Gray does
take a forwards ontological step, by making trial of the
redemptive possibilities of contemplation, memory and a sense
of place: the winds ('gales') that blow across the landscape are
also the regenerative in-fluences that come to the poet from the
past, or rather from the field of idealized retrospection. 'There
are in our existence spots of time, / That with distinct pre-
eminence retain / A renovating virtue', says Wordsworth in a
maturer intellectual context; Gray's passage predicts the
Romantic theme of grace through recall, and recall to grace, so
forcibly embodied in Cowper's 'On the Receipt of My Mother's
Picture', Wordsworth's 'Tintern Abbey', or Coleridge's 'This
Lime-tree Bower'.[39]

Yet no sooner does the way to a philosophy of renewal open

than it closes down. The 'bliss' is but 'momentary' (l. 16), and 'seem' (l. 18) then casts doubt on its very authenticity. More significantly, the next stanza declares, not connectedness with the past, but separation from it, as the poet asks Father Thames about the 'race' whose sports He has witnessed generation after generation:

> Who foremost now delight to cleave
> With pliant arm thy glassy wave?
> The captive linnet which enthrall?
> What idle progeny succeed
> To chase the rolling circle's speed,
> Or urge the flying ball?
>
> (ll. 25–30)

For Lonsdale, these lines, 'self-conscious and ponderous', merely betray Gray's 'dislike of boyish games'.[40] More to the point is the effect of the circumlocutory, semi-scientific diction in signifying the poet's psychological distance from childhood's 'paths of pleasure': as with the formulaic idiom of the opening section of 'Sonnet on the Death of Richard West', the periphrasis indicates a mind cut off from all but mechanical contact with potential sources of consolation. There is, after all, neither imaginative interiority nor therapeutic yield.

What this detachment does allow, however, is the construction, in the following two stanzas, of a myth of Innocence. Not only is childhood powerfully defamiliarized, it is envisioned as a prelapsarian realm—or, more exactly, is created backwards from the present as a paradise where the constrictions of Experience exist only for their sting to be drawn. Thus, 'labours' and 'constraint' but 'sweeten liberty' (as the boys learn lessons for recitation); ambition drives the bold beyond 'The limits of their little reign' but does no harm, bringing at worst a 'fearful joy'; 'hope' is a constant nourishment 'by fancy fed', no source of grim dissatisfaction; sorrow departs in a moment:

> The thoughtless day, the easy night,
> The spirits pure, the slumbers light,
> That fly th'approach of morn.
>
> (ll. 48–50)

There are echoes here of Milton's account of Adam's life in Eden before the Fall, and of Thomson's Golden Age in *The Seasons*.[41]

Yet, typically, the pendulum swings once more—never to return. In the event childhood is for Gray no myth to rest upon or live by; on the contrary, his paradise is there to throw the bleak future into relief:

> Alas, regardless of their doom,
>   The little victims play!
>   (ll. 51–52)

'Victims' is a harsh, arresting word. 'Victims' of what? Gray's answer is the 'Ministers of human fate', a 'griesly troop' which he enumerates with remorseless vigour and comprehensiveness. The 'fields' of regenerative imagination become now the nightmare 'vale of years' (l. 81) inhabited by every ill, mental or physical, which humankind may suffer, ranging from such 'vultur[e]s of the mind' as 'pineing Love', through 'hard Unkindness' and 'moody Madness laughing wild', to the 'painful family of Death' and

> Poverty, to fill the band,
> That numbs the soul with icy hand,
> And slow-consuming Age.
>   (ll. 88–90)

The impulses that seemingly enhance childhood—the courage of the 'bold adventurers' who seek out 'unknown regions', 'Gay hope', the 'tear forgot'—are in truth but a training for subsequent devastating vulnerability, where, for example, to aspire is to be a sacrifice to 'grinning infamy' (ll. 71–74), unfulfilled desire 'inly gnaws the secret heart' (ll. 61–70), and 'Unkindness ... mocks the tear it forc'd to flow' (ll. 76–77). In the long run, delight and liberty are a delusion: the boys may 'disdain / The limits of their little reign' (ll. 35–36), but the truth is that humankind has reign over nothing, and is subject ever to malign forces ruled by that 'hideous ... Queen', Death (ll. 83–84).

'Ah, tell them, they are men!' (l. 60). No poet has put more graphically on parade the evils of living, and it is hard not to wonder why. One reason no doubt is the painful nature of

Gray's own experience in the months preceding the composition of the 'Ode' in August 1742, which, as we know, had
seen not only the death of West and (in the previous year) the
bitter quarrel with Horace Walpole, but also the loss of his
father in November 1741 and the onset of severe financial
insecurity. If this last circumstance lies behind the lines on
Poverty, those on the precariousness of fame might have been
suggested by the fall of his former friend's father, Sir Robert
Walpole, the Prime Minister, early in 1742. Yet there may
also be another, curious motivation at work in the poem—
revenge. As schoolboys, Gray, West and Walpole, with
Thomas Ashton, had formed the 'Quadruple Alliance' in
defence against those who, as an Etonian contemporary put it,
'treated them as feminine characters, on account of their too
great delicacy, and sometimes too fastidious behaviour'.[42]
Gray never did rough it on the playing fields of Eton, and
would not have been among those on whom his poem casts a
lingering glance. It is true that in his troubled frame of mind
he 'could easily idealize his schooldays'.[43] West had done that
very thing in verses he had sent to Walpole; but these tell of
straying 'with those, / Whom first my boyish heart had
chose',[44] while Gray's focuses on those from whom he and
West had been apart and felt themselves different. Does
Gray's chilling catalogue of horrors reflect a subterranean
delight in the hurt of those who had given hurt? If there *is* a
driven politics in the *Eton Ode*, is it not a politics of cultural
dissidence—the 'Good' against the 'Great',[45] Gray the
effeminate intellectual loosing his fantastical demons upon the
'sprightly race'?

Be that as it may, Gray moves at last to studied generalization:

> To each his suff'rings: all are men,
> Condemn'd alike to groan,
> The tender for another's pain;
> Th'unfeeling for his own.
> Yet ah! why should they know their fate?
> Since sorrow never comes too late,
> And happiness too swiftly flies.
> Thought would destroy their paradise.

> No more; where ignorance is bliss,
> 'Tis folly to be wise.
>   (ll. 91–100)

This takes the prize for memorability. In context, however, Gray's words have a precise and discomforting edge. They lock humankind in a tragic condemnation: the second half of the stanza, turning on 'Yet ah!', promises to alleviate the stress on inescapable suffering, but it does not, for the 'thought' that ruins paradises is itself unavoidable; 'innocence', though much to be desired, cannot last. To recall Abrams's positivist terminology in his definition of 'the greater Romantic lyric', Gray does not so much resolve an emotional problem or achieve a stabilizing philosophic perspective as repeat his familiar fall into mental paralysis: 'men' are put in a no-win situation, unable to remain blissfully ignorant or to enjoy wisdom, and in that formulation we read the mind of the 'man' Thomas Gray who, like the sadly knowing 'I' of the 'blind horse' letter or 'Ode on the Spring', thinks himself into traps.

What is also disturbing about the *Eton Ode* is that it has no place for the values of development or maturation; change is a process only of incremental torment. This becomes all the clearer if we compare it with a poem for which it supplied several cues—Wordsworth's 'Immortality Ode'.[46] Where Gray sees a break between past and present, Wordsworth, for all that has been lost of 'glory', finds continuity: 'The Child is Father of the Man'. Both poets keep faith with childhood, but Wordsworth looks beyond its scene of 'joy and youth' (*Eton Ode*, l. 19) to those profounder feelings that bear witness to an other-worldly 'home'—'High instincts before which our mortal Nature / Did tremble like a guilty Thing surprised' (ll. 146–47)—and proclaims that these are 'truths' which nothing can 'abolish or destroy' (ll. 155–60). The 'Immortality Ode' reads here as a deliberate transcending of Gray's *Ode*: the 'unknown regions' explored by the boys of Eton become 'worlds not realized', the snatching of a 'fearful joy' becomes a trembling that betokens more than mortal origins; and in all of this Wordsworth insists that he holds allegiance to more than 'Delight and liberty, the simple creed / Of childhood, whether busy or at rest, / With new-fledged hope still fluttering in his breast' (ll. 136–38). Above all, even while acknowledging the ravages of mortality, 'all the Persons, down to palsied Age, / That Life brings with her in her equipage' (ll. 104–05), he is able to embrace Experience and its challenges—'the soothing thoughts that spring / Out of human suffering', 'the faith that looks through death, / In years that bring the philosophic mind' (ll. 183–86).

We think of the 'Immortality Ode' as connected with Wordsworth's reading of Plato. In part it emerged from an encounter with Thomas Gray, the limits of whose vision Wordsworth made manifest and outran. But this engagement is of course a compliment to Gray's originality as well as a rebuttal, and suggests the paradox, so eloquently proposed by Donald Davie, that those who set new bearings for poetry in the later-eighteenth century were not figures of radical zeal but anxious introspective writers—'One comes to think ... that it was enervation, not energy, that fretted most under the Augustan dispensation. The Augustan chains were chafed away; they were not broken'.[47] Davie oversimplifies, but has a point.

As we noted earlier, the new bearings signalled in Gray include concern over the very function of poetry. The most direct instance of this, perhaps, is 'The Bard', whose eponymous hero defiantly declaims a belief in the interdependence of poetry, liberty and the well-being of the nation. Yet the Bard's victory over the forces hostile to art and to freedom—here, beyond all, those of political tyranny—is a truly pyrrhic one, for, like the poet-figure at the end of the *Elegy*, he is isolated and, if more spectacularly, doomed: 'Deep in the roaring tide he plung'd to endless night' (l. 144); and the poem is in any case set back in an improbable bygone age, implying that neither the role of seer nor the grand gesture—'To triumph, and to die, are mine' (l. 142)—are available as self-justification to the modern poet. These ironies link 'The Bard' to a whole contemporary tradition of attempts and failures to make fruitful connections with the public world. Cowper's programme in *The Task* constitutes the most significant of these, but we may settle for the more circumscribed example of the split between art and the practical realm, and between value and that realm, in Goldsmith's *The Deserted Village*. This is an apt text, since, like Gray, Goldsmith makes of the past a prelapsarian landscape—'Sweet Auburn' with its 'lovely bowers of innocence and ease' (ll. 1–5)—though this paradise is destroyed not by 'thought' but by the advent of materialist culture, led by commerce and profit-oriented agrarian reform, 'trade's unfeeling train', 'the tyrant's power' (ll. 63, 76).[48] So complete is the 'fall' that the Muse itself is exiled along with the refugees from Enclosure in 'these degenerate times of shame' (l. 409).

Out of alienation, however, comes selfhood, and even as 'sweet Poetry' is bidden farewell at the end of *The Deserted Village* it is endowed with a coming purpose, which is to teach that 'trade's proud empire hastes to swift decay, / ... While self-dependent power can time defy' (ll. 427, 429).[49] The triumphs, and trials, of 'self-dependent power', set against the near or far-distant background of corruptness in the social and political spheres, is one of the main stories told by Romanticism: as by Cowper, who, fascinated yet repelled by a world reforming itself on newly acquisitive principles of economic expansion guided by 'the Midas finger of the state', establishes the credentials, both as moral exemplar and the source of *true* creativity, of the 'self-sequestered man' in whom 'contemplation is his bliss';[50] or by Wordsworth, for the 'Immortality Ode' brings definitively to the fore, in the face of a deep sense of being as a condition of psychic dislocation, the individual of modern humanist tradition, whole, at the centre, spreading meaning upon the world.

But this is not quite Gray's story. Certainly, his poetry expresses a historic shift from mythopoeic to psychopoeic ends, and we might remind ourselves how tellingly this is figured in the *Eton Ode* in the subsuming of the socio-political map of Pope's *Windsor-Forest* into the happenstance of personal reverie and the scene of childhood. And it is true, as we have seen, that in setting the virtues and gains of the sequestered life against the dangers and hollow rewards of greatness, the *Elegy* itself is both ethical statement and a quest for identity. Yet Gray differs from Goldsmith, Cowper and Wordsworth in salient ways. It is obvious but very striking that he has no metacomment, no generalizing language, which would turn the expression or valorization of self into a philosophy to exist by; and it should always be remembered that in one substantial

dimension of his work he retreated to the arcane recesses of
Norse and Celtic mythology, as far as possible from any project
in writing either social *or* psychological truth. His is an
altogether more raw and more desperate subjectivity than that
of the others—unsettled, wavering, never reaching beyond
itself to be resolved in stable self-appraisal or turned outwards
into shareable wisdom—always 'process', never 'product',
except where the product is, as so fully in 'Sonnet on the Death
of West', a realization of the nature, the very quality, of
disablement, impotence, and loss.

None of this, however, makes the subjectivity of Gray
insignificant or less real. Not only does it lay out the bare
grounds on which progressive Romantic individualism was
predicated (whether or not, as in the crucial case of Wordsworth's intervention, this was by reaction as much as
extension), it also looks forward to a more distant species of
modernity which may be brought back into focus by reference
to his customary tropes.

Gray sometimes had his happy dreams of rest, like that
which came to him when visiting Grasmere in the Lake
District:

> ... not a single red tile, no flaring Gentleman's house, or
> garden-walls, break in upon the repose of this little
> unsuspected paradise, but all is peace, rusticity, & happy
> poverty in its neatest most becoming attire.[51]

As we well know, the run of his thoughts and psychic currents
is more often in a darker vein, telling of silence and solitariness,
marginality, being hedged in or caught out, trembling even in
repose. 'Put your ear to the cage! / You will hear the bustle of
little caged poets', says Paolo Buzzi in 'La Gabbia'.[52] In falling
short by the measure of one tradition—that of Romantic
humanism—Gray pointedly foreshadowed another: in him,
not only does the enigmatic figure of the poet get firmly in the
picture but the curious consciousness of the captive artist, or
artist *manqué*, becomes the subject of art; the 'happy man' of the
classical and neo-classical world, all 'peace', 'rusticity' and
contented penury, yields to the happy-unhappy shut-in of our
own.[53] At the same time, moreover, if we slightly adjust our
perspective, the comparative crudeness, limitations and

incompleteness of Gray's 'selving' take us back behind the Romantic ideal of free, stable and creative selfhood and remind us subversively of the fracture and faintness, the *vita negativa*, to which that selfhood might regress, or which it barely covers up. Seen in this deconstructive light, Thomas Gray appears a 'subject' well in tune with the bent of one major branch of recent critical theory—that carried forward, of course, primarily by Foucault and Lacan, whose desire has been to unmake 'the notion of a constituting ego which offers itself as a phenomenological centre from which *free will* radiates into the world', in favour of the idea of 'man' as 'the great absence' or prisoner in a network of exterior or psychic determinants, or as one irreducibly 'split', fragmented, unable truly to become.[54] But to elaborate that approach to Gray would be yet another story.

NOTES

1. Samuel Johnson, 'Life of Gray', *Lives of the Poets*, ed. G. Birkbeck Hill, 3 vols (Oxford, 1905), III, 441.

2. 'Life of Cowley', *Lives*, I, 45.

3. See Donald Davie, *A Gathered Church: The Literature of the English Dissenting Interest, 1700–1930* (London, 1978), pp. 106–07 especially.

4. Hervey's popular *Meditations among the Tombs* appeared in 1746, and was gathered with subsequent works in the collected edition, *Meditations and Contemplations*, 2 vols (London, 1748). I quote from the one-volume edition of 1812, p. 9 (hereafter, *Meditations*). Several, but by no means all, of the close parallels between Hervey and Gray are noted by Roger Lonsdale in his edition of *The Poems of Gray, Collins and Goldsmith* (London, 1969), pp. 140–41.

5. Northrop Frye, 'Towards Defining an Age of Sensibility', in *Eighteenth-Century English Literature: Modern Essays in Criticism*, ed. James L. Clifford (New York, 1959), p. 312.

6. *The Poems of Gray, Collins and Goldsmith*, pp. 114–16 (hereafter, Lonsdale). Lonsdale's commentary and annotations on the *Elegy* (pp. 103–41) are invaluable. There are some measured insights into the relationship between the two versions of the poem in Ian Jack, 'Gray's *Elegy* Reconsidered', in *From Sensibility to Romanticism*, ed. F. W. Hilles and H. Bloom (New York, 1965), pp. 139–69. Other noteworthy treatments of the 'personal' element in Gray include: F. Doherty, 'The Two Voices of Gray', *Essays in Criticism*, 13 (1963), 222–30; P. M. Spacks, *The Poetry of Vision: Five Eighteenth-Century Poets* (Cambridge, Mass., 1967), pp. 90–118; Clarence Tracy, 'Melancholy Marked Him For Her Own', in *Fearful Joy: Papers from the Thomas Gray Bicentenary Conference at Carleton University*, ed. J. Downey and Ben Jones

(Montreal, 1974), pp. 37–49. Kenneth MacLean, 'The Distant Way: Imagination and Image in Gray's Poetry', in *Fearful Joy*, pp. 136–45, advances recognition that 'it is of the mind that Gray is chiefly poet' (p. 138) in a stimulating account of some of his recurrent tropes.

7. For the Eton Ms *Elegy* (not all the variants of which are recorded in the apparatus of *Complete Poems*) I have used Appendix I of *The Poetical Works of Gray and Collins*, ed. Austin Lane Poole, Oxford Standard Authors, third edition (London, 1961), which conveniently prints the full text (pp. 181–87).

8. *Poetical Works*, ed. Austin Lane Poole, p. 184 (hereafter, *PW*: with references bracketed in the main text).

9. F. W. Bateson, *English Poetry: A Critical Introduction*, second edition (London, 1968), pp. 130–31. See also, for example, Tracy, 'Melancholy Marked Him' (n. 6 above), p. 41.

10. Lonsdale, pp. 106–10, sets out the highly persuasive case for the later dating.

11. *Correspondence*, I, 5.

12. *Correspondence*, I, 34.

13. *Correspondence*, I, 66, 255.

14. Bruce Redford, *The Converse of the Pen: Acts of Intimacy in the Eighteenth-Century Familiar Letter* (Chicago, 1986), p. 55; paraphrasing Claude Lévi-Strauss, *La Pensée Sauvage* (Paris,1962), pp. 34–35.

15. *Meditations*, pp. 55, 218.

16. Cowper, *The Task*, VI. 906 ff.: *The Poetical Works of William Cowper*, ed. Sir Humphrey Milford, fourth edition, revised by Norma Russell (London, 1971), p. 239. All references to Cowper's poems are to this edition. For a detailed discussion of Cowper's appropriation of the *topos* of 'the happy man', see my *Cowper's Poetry: A Critical Study and Reassessment* (Liverpool, 1982), pp. 196–207.

17. Bateson, *English Poetry*, p. 131.

18. Christine Gallant, *Shelley's Ambivalence* (London, 1989), p. 21.

19. Lonsdale, p. 116.

20. See Lonsdale, pp. 135–37.

21. Wordsworth, 'Tintern Abbey', l. 49: *The Poetical Works of William Wordsworth*, ed. E. de Selincourt and H. Darbishire, 5 vols (Oxford, 1940–49), II, 260. All references to Wordsworth's poetry are to this edition.

22. Cowper, *The Task*, VI. 84–117.

23. Keats, 'The Fall of Hyperion', ll. 168–69. For relevant analysis of this underside of Romantic identity, see my 'The Shelleyan Psycho-Drama', in *Essays on Shelley*, ed. Miriam Allott (Liverpool, 1982), pp. 84–91.

24. See, for instance, Tracy, 'Melancholy Marked Him', p. 42.

25. Milton writes of the getting of mystical illumination:

Where I may sit and rightly spell
Of every Star that Heav'n doth shew,
And every Herb that sips the dew;
Till old experience do attain
To something like Prophetic strain.
('Il Penseroso', ll. 170–74)

26. *Meditations*, pp. 49–50.

27. *Meditations*, p. 50.

28. Arnold, 'Thomas Gray', *Matthew Arnold's Essays in Criticism*, Everyman Library (London, 1964), p. 267; Graham Hough, *The Romantic Poets* (London, 1953), pp. 11–12.

29. Lonsdale, pp. 115–16.

30. In 'The Passions' Collins prays for the revival of an ancient lyricism whose

> humblest reed could more prevail,
> Had more of strength, diviner rage,
> Than all which charms this laggard age.
> (ll. 110–12)

See Cowper, 'Table Talk', l. 733 and passim; and, for another expression of Gray's own sense of the inferiority of his generation, 'The Progress of Poesy', ll. 107–23.

31. See Lonsdale, p. 49.

32. Ibid.

33. *The Prose Works of William Wordsworth*, ed. W. J. B. Owen and Jane Worthington Smyser, 3 vols (Oxford, 1974), I, 133.

34. Ibid.

35. See Lonsdale, p. 67.

36. M. H. Abrams, 'Structure and Style in the Greater Romantic Lyric', in *From Sensibility to Romanticism*, ed. Hilles and Bloom, pp. 527–28.

37. See Pope, *Windsor-Forest*, ll. 355–422: *Pope: Poetical Works*, ed. Herbert Davis (London, 1966), pp. 48–49.

38. I refer in particular, of course, to the argument advanced in Jerome J. McGann, *The Romantic Ideology* (Chicago, 1983). Gray wrote the occasional piece on contemporary political issues, such as the satire 'On Lord Holland's Seat'; and it has been claimed, with some brilliance, that the *Elegy* itself was written out of a response to historic events witnessed by Gray in August 1746, especially the momentous trial in Westminster Hall of the Jacobite peers involved in the '45 rebellion, for several of whom the 'paths of glory' certainly did lead to 'the grave' (see W. M. Newman, 'When Curfew Tolled the Knell', *National Review*, 127 [1946], 244–48). The *Elegy* may well record Gray's preoccupation with the 'pomp of pow'r' which he saw at Westminster and during the Duke of Cumberland's triumphal metropolitan appearances as victor of Culloden—or with, say, the readiness to 'wade through slaughter to a throne', as Frederick the Great had just done, Bonny Prince Charlie had tried to do, and the Bourbons were currently doing. If the poem has a message about politics, however, it is to keep out of them—including any committing of poetry itself to the service of 'heap[ing] the shrine of Luxury and Pride / With incense kindled at the Muse's flame'. Gray's ideology is in a sense an ideology of rejection—the artist's moral vision, and in the context of the *Elegy* as a whole his inner drama, being elevated above the demands of the public world. Gray's reaction to that world leads, for better or for worse, to the erasure of its 'pull' and precise lineaments, and to self-consciousness.

An interesting contrast to Gray's moral-aesthetic occlusion of the political scene is provided by the opening pages of Hervey's 'Contemplations on the Night', which give overt thanksgiving for the preservation of 'liberty' and 'property, that best of charters' by the defeat of 'the malignant spirit of Popery' and 'an abjured pretender' who would 'cut his way to our throne'. Far from placing meditative sequestration in opposition to active allegiance, Hervey makes the one dependent on the other, declaring that it is owing to 'our present happy constitution, and auspicious government', gloriously upheld at Culloden, that he 'can ramble unmolested along the vale of private life, and taste all the innocent satisfactions of a contemplative retreat' (*Meditations*, pp. 209–12). But the difference between Gray and Hervey does not go deep: the former was silently loyal to the established order, or at least not one for rocking the boat, while the latter, for all his outspoken partisan nationalism on this occasion, put his energy as comprehensively as anyone into cultivating the fruits of 'contemplative retreat' and exhorting others— Romantically—to do so. Gray's solidity with 'our present constitution' is underlined in his substitution in the *Elegy* (ll. 57–60) of the classical *exempla*, Cato, Tully and Caesar, by Hampden, Milton and Cromwell, heroes of the English Revolution and forebears of the Act of Settlement of 1789 upon which the Protestant succession and future parliamentary 'system' were founded; but these sympathies do not prevent him from insisting on the moral point that Cromwell was by no means 'guiltless of his country's blood'.

39. Wordsworth, *The Prelude* (1850), XII. 208–10: ed. E. de Selincourt and H. Darbishire (Oxford, 1959), p. 445. For the importance of Cowper's poem in this regard, see Newey, *Cowper's Poetry*, pp. 245–70.

40. Lonsdale, p. 55.

41. See Lonsdale, p. 59.

42. Jacob Bryant, letter of 24 December 1798, first printed in *Gentleman's Magazine*, New Series 25 (1846), 140–43; quoted by Lonsdale, p. 55.

43. Lonsdale, p. 55.

44. West, 'Ode to Mary Magdalene'; quoted by Lonsdale, p. 55.

45. Gray, 'The Progress of Poesy', l. 123.

46. Lonsdale, p. 54, reports the information that Wordsworth owned a manuscript of Gray's *Ode*.

47. Introduction, *The Late Augustans*, ed. Donald Davie (London, 1958), p. xxii.

48. References to *The Deserted Village* are to Lonsdale, pp. 675–94.

49. These lines were added by Dr Johnson, but that of course supports rather than detracts from my point about the general bearings of poetry in the period.

50. See the relation between the passages (from which I quote here respectively) at *Task*, IV. 465–510 and VI. 924–1004: discussed in Newey, *Cowper's Poetry*, chapter 6.

51. *Correspondence*, III, 1099.

52. Paolo Buzzi, 'The Cage', trans. Dora M. Pettinella, in *Arts in Society*, 6 (1969), 113.

53. I follow here the theme of the excellent study by W. B. Carnochan,

Confinement and Flight: An Essay on English Literature of the Eighteenth Century (Berkeley, Calif., 1977), pp. 171 ff.—though, surprisingly, no texts by Gray are included in Carnochan's outline of the 'evolutionary process' in question.

54. See J-M. Benoist, *The Structural Revolution* (London, 1978), p. 14.

Gray's *Elegy* and the Logic of Expression

PAUL WILLIAMSON

I

When Gray wrote to Horace Walpole in June 1750 to inform him that he had 'put an end to a thing' whose 'beginning' Walpole had seen 'long ago', it seems beyond doubt that he was referring to the final version of the *Elegy Written in a Country Church-Yard*.[1] When the poet further insists that this version of the poem is ended, explicitly asking that Walpole should 'look upon it in the light of a *thing with an end to it*',[2] his criterion of completeness acquires a highly formal character. The poem is now satisfactorily concluded, 'structurally unified',[3] and Gray's announced completion of it implies a criterion of completeness which is as much formal as thematic or, indeed, temporal. Yet even if Walpole himself had not actually seen it, the 'beginning' to which Gray refers had an ending of its own. In this earlier version of the poem, now preserved in the Eton Manuscript, the first 18 stanzas of the poem culminate in four stanzas with which it appears the *Elegy* was originally intended to conclude.[4] Although these 18 stanzas appear 'substantially' as in their later, published form, the four deleted stanzas still provide a conclusion to them which may be regarded as 'perfectly coherent'.[5] It has even been argued that in some respects the early version of the *Elegy* is more finished, more formally complete, than the poem finally regarded as such by Gray himself.[6] Why, then, did Gray reject that earlier 'balanced' structure in favour of the conclusion as it now stands? In the analysis which follows I will try to suggest an answer to that question by placing the earlier version of the *Elegy* in its generic context, in terms of both contemporary, eighteenth-century poetry and its historical forbears. In this context it can be shown that the set of metaphysical beliefs on which this version of the poem depends, by which I mean the complex of moral, intellectual, and spiritual concerns that underpins the work, actually tends to disable poetic expression. Gray's response to this problem, embodied in the transition from the earlier to the later versions of the *Elegy*, involves a reorientation of the poetic genre away from its eighteenth-century Christian ethos towards its broadly classical origins. The implication of this is a reinterpretation of the function and purpose of elegy which bases the poem in a logic of expression, in a recognition and affirmation of the intrinsic value of poetic utterance.

II

The four stanzas which conclude the earlier version of the poem (in which form it may be referred to as 'Stanzas'[7]) make clear that Gray originally had in mind a very specific kind of poem. A highly conventional linguistic texture gives rise to certain generic expectations, which, in the poem's conclusion, are amply fulfilled. As critics have often remarked, 'Stanzas' constitutes a recognizable type of retirement poem in which the poet's meditations are concerned with death and whose setting is the graveyard.[8] The conventional elements of the concluding self-apostrophe direct the poet to take the Christian-Stoic way:

> Hark how the sacred Calm, that broods around
> Bids ev'ry fierce tumultuous Passion cease
> In still small Accents whisp'ring from the Ground
> A grateful Earnest of eternal Peace
>
> No more with Reason & thyself at Strife
> Give anxious Cares & endless Wishes room
> But thro' the cool sequester'd Vale of Life
> Pursue the silent Tenour of thy Doom.
>
> (ll. 81–88)

One may compare Robert Blair's *The Grave*:

> . . . Sure the last end
> Of the good man is peace!—How calm his exit!

Night dews fall not more gently to the ground,
Nor weary worn-out winds expire so soft.
Behold him in the evening tide of life,
A life well spent, whose early care it was
His riper years should not upbraid his green:
By unperceiv'd degrees he wears away;
Yet, like the Sun, seems larger at his setting:
(High in his faith and hopes) look how he reaches
After the prize in view! and, like a bird
That's hamper'd, struggles hard to get away:
Whilst the glad gates of sight are wide expanded
To let new glories in, the first fair fruits
Of the fast-coming harvest ...

                                    (ll. 712–26)[9]

In both poems the approach of death is seen, in a Christian
context, as the way to new life. It is in view of such a 'grateful
Earnest of eternal Peace' that the poet of the 'Stanzas' exhorts
himself to Christian-Stoicism; because his meditations result
in the recognition and acceptance of the promise of a world to
come. Poetic meditation concludes with the poet's divination of
religious truth; hence Blair's apostrophe to death and his
emblematic description of it:

    But know that thou must render up the dead,
And with high int'rest too.—They are not thine;
But only in thy keeping for a season,
Till the great promis'd day of restitution;
When loud diffusive sound from brazen trump
Of strong-lung'd cherub, shall alarm thy captives,
And rouse the long, long sleepers into life,
Day-light and liberty.—
[...]
'Tis but a night, a long and moonless night;
We make the grave our bed, and then are gone.
    Thus at the shut of ev'n, the weary bird
Leaves the wide air, and in some lonely brake
Cow'rs down, and dozes till the dawn of day,
Then claps his well-fledg'd wings, and bears away.
                              (ll. 654–61, 762–77)

In the connections made between evening and old age, night and death, new day and new life, Blair affirms an analogical truth. The blowing of the angelic trumpet and the recognition of Christ's triumph over death, occurring in the same part of the poem (ll. 667ff.), link such analogical imagery with Christian, biblical truth. The image of the bird which, after a night of rest, flies at dawn, works in the same analogical context; in so doing it identifies the natural bird with the Christian soul while maintaining a connection with the traditional symbol of the dove as spirit and, in the natural provision of the 'lonely brake', recalling *Matthew* 6:26.[10] Similar analogical elements are aso found in the closing lines of Thomas Parnell's 'A Night-Piece on Death':

> Such joy, though far transcending sense,
> Have pious souls at parting hence.
> On Earth, and in the body plac'd,
> A few, and evil years, they waste:
> But when their chains are cast aside,
> See the glad scene unfolding wide,
> Clap the glad wing, and tower away,
> And mingle with the blaze of day.
>
> (ll. 83–90)[11]

Again, if night is an emblem of death then the idea of a new day dawning acts as 'Earnest' of a new life, when the soul as bird may take to the heavens. The underlying equation, night equals day, death equals life, is directly stated in Edward Young's *Night Thoughts*:

> Ev'n silent Night proclaims my soul immortal:
> Ev'n silent Night proclaims eternal Day:
>
> ('Night I', ll.102–03)[12]

Understood as an example of the type of poem represented by Blair's *Grave*, Parnell's 'Night-Piece', and Young's *Night Thoughts*, then, the resolution of Gray's 'Stanzas' consists in the poet's acceptance of the Christian promise of new life, a life in which present inequalities—such as those with which Gray is concerned in the body of the 'Stanzas'—will also be rectified. The manner and tone of the concluding lines of the poem which was later to become the *Elegy* thus reinforce the poem's identity of form and purpose with its eighteenth-century cognates rather than with its classical forbears. For it is important to recognize that, although the graveyard poem is essentially an eighteenth-century invention, it incorporates certain formal and thematic elements of classical pastoral.[13] The classical basis of the meditation on death is systematically transformed in a fundamentally Christian manner—beginning with the removal to the graveyard of the original pastoral setting—and the poet's Christian-Stoic attitude is then maintained in the context of his special access to a realm of analogical truth.

With respect to its classical origins, and as is made clear in the latter half of Gray's *Elegy*, the graveyard poem may be understood as a variation of the pastoral funeral elegy. One source for the eighteenth-century meditation among the tombs can be found in Virgil's fifth *Eclogue*. As Erwin Panofsky remarks, the tombstone first makes its appearance in Arcadia when Mopsus and Menalcas sing of Daphnis:[14]

> Strew the turf with leaves, ye shepherds, curtain the springs with shade—such honours Daphnis charges you to pay him. And build a tomb, and on the tomb place, too, this verse: 'Daphnis was I amid the woods, known from here even to the stars. Fair was the flock I guarded, but fairer was I, the master.'[15]

Virgil's interpretation of death in Arcadia, however, is radically different from that of the graveyard poets. For Virgil the presence of the tombstone and the consequent recognition of human mortality strike a dissonant note amidst the pastoral setting. Here, as elsewhere in Virgil, the pastoral is pervaded by an insistent ambiguity which is caused by the eruption into Arcadia of potentially tragic themes: death, frustrated love, and, perhaps surprisingly, contemporary, historical reality.[16] Virgil offers no argued resolution to the tensions caused by such dualities; rather, their place in the poetic texture invests them with a value beyond any which they might have intrinsically, one which is a direct consequence of their incorporation into the artificial, aesthetic world of the *Eclogue*, and which may even be said to sustain them. The presence of death in the *Eclogues* is 'resolved in that vespertinal mixture of

sadness and tranquillity which is perhaps Virgil's most
personal contribution to poetry'.[17] But the idea of resolution
does not mean that the dissonance created in the combination
of pastoral bliss with human mortality is harmonized either in
any absolute, or, as Panofsky says, 'factual' sense; Virgilian
resolution consists rather in sustaining the juxtaposition of
such ideas, holding them in 'vespertinal' or 'elegiac' tension by
incorporating them into a highly crafted aesthetic texture, by
depriving them of their 'factuality' and then transforming
'mythical truth' into 'elegiac sentiment'.[18]

One way in which such a transformation is achieved is by an
adherence to memory. Bringing death into the world of
pastoral, classical elegy is concerned to hold the two together
in an aesthetic order—*in memoriam*, as it were—and so to
maintain the memory of the dead shepherd. Hence the
attention given by Virgil to the making of the tangible
memorial, the tombstone, which is emblematic of both the
aesthetic and the memorial functions of the elegy in which it is
described. And yet 'elegiac sentiment' may be characterized as
'vespertinal'. Evening is the time of Virgilian elegy because the
transition from daytime to evening to night is made symbolic of
that dissonance produced by the presence of human tragedy—
of dissipation—in Arcadia. For example, when evening falls at
the end of the first *Eclogue*:

> Yet this night you might have rested here with me on
> the green leafage. We have ripe apples, mealy chestnuts,
> and a wealth of pressed cheeses. Even now the house-tops
> yonder are smoking and longer shadows fall from the
> mountain-heights.[19]

Similarly, in the closing lines of the tenth:

> Let us rise; the shade oft brings peril to singers. The
> juniper's shade brings peril; hurtful to the corn, too, is the
> shade. Get ye home, my full-fed goats—the Evening-star
> comes—get ye home![20]

Here the equation of evening with elegiac meaning is radically
unchristian; for, as the evening which sustains human tragedy
in a texture of tranquillity gives way to night, so life gives way
to death, and memory to oblivion. *Eclogues* IX:

Time robs us all, even of memory; oft as a boy I recall
that with song I would lay the long summer days to rest.
Now I have forgotten all my songs.[21]

Interpreted in this way, 'elegiac sentiment' is consummately
classical. It originates in that Greek poetry upon which Virgil
was so closely dependent, and specifically in the *Lament for
Bion*, attributed to Moschus, the 'genuine archetype or model
of the funeral elegy':[22]

> ... as for me, this song shall be my weeping sad lamen-
> tation for thy decease. Could I but have gone down into
> Tartarus as Orpheus went and Odysseus of yore and
> Alcides long ago, then would I also have come mayhap
> to the house of Pluteus, that I might see thee, and if so
> be thou singest to Pluteus, hear what that thou singest
> may be. But all the same, I pray thee, chant some song
> of Sicily, some sweet melodious country-song, unto the
> Maid; for she too is of Sicily, she too once sported on
> Etna's shores; she knows the Dorian music; so thy
> melodies shall not go without reward. Even as once she
> granted Orpheus his Eurydicè's return because he
> harped so sweetly, so likewise she shall give my Bion
> back unto the hills; and had but this my pipe the power
> of that his harp, I had played for this in the house of
> Pluteus myself.[23]

The Virgilian transformation of the mythical and factual into
the specifically elegiac noted by Panofsky is here prefigured.
The poet's grief for Bion finds a mythical dimension in the grief
of Orpheus for Eurydice; the sorrow of both poets is then
subsumed into elegy because intrinsic to the presence of the
Orpheus legend in the *Lament for Bion* is the knowledge that,
just as Orpheus's quest to bring Eurydice back from the
underworld ended in failure, so Moschus's song will not restore
Bion to the hills. Bion's continued existence depends on the
memory of the poet and thereafter on the memorial efficacy of
the elegy. But the afterlife of memory is one where the dead
Bion's existence is merely a shadow, an image, of that life
which he once led. As the poet says in a trope later taken up by
Gray:

He that was lovely and pleasant unto the herds carols
now no more, sits now no more and sings 'neath the desert
oaks; but singeth in the house of Pluteus the song of Lethè,
the song of oblivion.[24]

Bion's memory is presented in terms of his activity as a living
man, but radically qualified in the repeated 'no more', a
negative which leads into the recollection of his present
oblivion. Just as Bion's song becomes a song of his own
oblivion, so the poet's lament, like even the song of Orpheus, is
inefficacious in the face of death, tending also to oblivion, and
taking with it the inevitably fading memory of Bion.

Such dissipation is utterly unchristian. In the Christian
conception of the afterlife, not only does the soul of the dead
one have a continued objective, even super-objective, existence, but also the life to come is qualitatively better than the
present, earthly one. For that reason it is practically impossible
for the Christian pastoral to sustain a truly elegiac sentiment.
Even in the conclusion of Milton's *Lycidas*, where, by introducing a second poetic voice in the highly formal coda, the poet
achieves the impossible and sustains at least a note of quasi-
Virgilian elegy, Virgilian dissonance is transposed into a song
of rejoicing:

> Weep no more, woeful shepherds weep no more,
> For Lycidas your sorrow is not dead,
> Sunk though he be beneath the water floor,
> So sinks the day-star in the ocean bed,
> And yet anon repairs his drooping head,
> And tricks his beams, and with new spangled ore,
> Flames in the forehead of the morning sky:
> (ll. 165–71)[25]

Similarly, when transposed into its eighteenth-century setting, the essential, 'vespertinal' quality of Virgilian elegy
functions not as the vehicle of 'elegiac sentiment' but rather
analogously, as a way of expressing the basically religious truth
that death is the pathway to new life as surely as night gives
way to day. In such analogy, however, the poignancy and
finality of Arcadian death are denied, as is the elegy's basis in
memory, and the significance of the elegiac form is under-

mined. In the eighteenth-century meditation among the tombs, the tragic dissonance of Arcadian death is resolved in an acceptance of death as the necessary means to a new and better life, so that the elegiac quality of Death's famous pastoral motto, *et in Arcadia ego*, is inverted.[26] When Death speaks in Parnell, for example, its message entails a radical denial of classical 'elegiac sentiment':

> 'When men my scythe and darts supply,
> How great a king of fears am I!
> They view me like the last of things;
> They make, and then they draw, my strings.
> Fools! if you less provok'd your fears,
> No more my spectre-form appears.
> Death's but a path that must be trod,
> If man would ever pass to God:
> A port of calms, a state to ease
> From the rough rage of swelling seas.'
>
> (ll. 61–70)

Similarly, in Blair's *Grave* the desire to overcome the oblivion of death through memory is made ridiculous:

> Absurd to think to over-reach the Grave,
> And from the wreck of names to rescue ours.
> The best concerted schemes men lay for fame
> Die fast away; only themselves die faster.
> The far-fam'd sculptor, and the laurell'd bard,
> Those bold insurancers of deathless fame,
> Supply their little feeble aids in vain.
>
> (ll. 183–89)

Such a radical reinterpretation of classical form and ethos begs a very significant question. By what means does the graveyard poet gain access to the analogical knowledge on which his poem depends? It is achieved in view of the further component of the graveyard poem: the poet's melancholy. In the epitaph of Gray's *Elegy* the poet is described as a melancholy man: '*And Melancholy mark'd him for her own*' (l. 120). A similar contemplative melancholy underlies the poetic musings of the 'Stanzas'. The brief reference to the poet's contemplative motivation in the second of the deleted stanzas—

later revised and incorporated into the *Elegy* proper—draws on
the terminology of melancholy:

> And thou, who mindful of the unhonour'd Dead
> Dost in these Notes their artless Tale relate
> By Night & lonely Contemplation led
> To linger in the gloomy Walks of Fate

The poet is 'mindful', pensive like the 'pensive Spirit' later
introduced to seek him out;[27] he is led by 'Night' and 'lonely
Contemplation'.[28] The 'Walks of Fate' are 'gloomy', a word
with specifically contemplative-melancholy, gothic connotations.[29] Accordingly, it is the poet's melancholy temper
which provides him with the mental attitude appropriate to his
night-time meditations, and so permits expression of the sort of
faithful resolution that occurs in the 'Stanzas' as in the equally
melancholic graveyard poetry to which it is related.[30]

    For the poets of the first half of the eighteenth century the
immediate source of melancholy is Milton's 'Il Penseroso':[31]

> But hail thou goddess, sage and holy,
> Hail divinest Melancholy,
> Whose saintly visage is too bright
> To hit the sense of human sight;
> And therefore to our weaker view,
> O'erlaid with black staid wisdom's hue.
>
> (ll. 11–16)

In 'Il Penseroso' Milton sustains and transmits the Neoplatonic notion that the poet's special access to divinely given truth,
his capacity for poetic ecstasy and indeed for prophecy, is a
result of his melancholy temperament; it is the melancholy
man who is subject to poetic 'divine frenzy':[32]

> And may at last my weary age
> Find out the peaceful hermitage,
> The hair gown and mossy cell,
> Where I may sit and rightly spell
> Of every star that heaven doth shew,
> And every herb that sips the dew;
> Till old experience do attain
> To something like prophetic strain.

These pleasures Melancholy give,
And I with thee will choose to live.

(ll. 167–76)

Although the idea of the poet as prophet is famously stated in Plato's *Ion* (534b–e), its special association with the poet's melancholy disposition derives from Pseudo-Aristotle, who argues that the poet's 'divine frenzy' arises because the heat generated by 'hot bile' is 'located near the seat of the intellect'.[33] This intimation of a natural-philosophical explanation of the poet's *furor*, based on the doctrine of the humours, was developed by the Florentine Neoplatonists, principally Ficino, into a complete 'equation' of Aristotelian melancholy with Platonic 'divine frenzy'. It was Ficino who, 'in the magic chiaroscuro of Christian Neoplatonic mysticism', 'gave shape' to the idea of the 'melancholy man of genius', and through him that it was transmitted to England.[34] Such a Neoplatonic tendency underlies the melancholy graveyard poet's access to analogical truth.[35] It is in the context of a melancholy-contemplative inclination that the poets of such poems as Gray's 'Stanzas', Parnell's 'Night-Piece', Blair's *Grave*, and Young's *Night Thoughts* may perceive the characteristically 'sacred Calm' of evening as 'Earnest of eternal Peace'.

And yet it must be observed that a strongly-held Neoplatonism is relatively rare in the mid-century. Although the sorts of truthful conclusions found in Blair's *Grave* and Parnell's 'Night-Piece' are underpinned by the Neoplatonic concept of melancholy, they are intensely formulaic. For, juxtaposed with that ultimately religious melancholy, one finds what may be referred to as a purely 'poetic melancholy',[36] in which the religious basis of Neoplatonic melancholy is redefined. The former humour is transposed into a purely subjective mood, into a mere facet of the poet's sensibility, and such visionary passages as one finds in Parnell become radically rhetorical.[37] Such a subjective and finally secular tendency is present in Milton's 'Il Penseroso', indicated even by the pensiveness of the poem's title, where it stands beside the religious, Neoplatonic notion and prefigures the later, picturesque, gothic development of the idea of melancholy in the graveyard poets of the eighteenth century:

> But let my due feet never fail,
> To walk the studious cloister's pale,
> And love the high embowed roof,
> with antique pillars' massy proof,
> And storied windows richly dight,
> Casting a dim religious light.
>
> (ll. 155–60)

The 'dim religious light' illumines the poet's way to an elaborate and sensual ecstasy in which his visionary capacity is mixed with an utterly aesthetic pleasure:

> There let the pealing organ blow,
> To the full-voiced choir below,
> In service high, and anthems clear,
> As may with sweetness, through mine ear,
> Dissolve me into ecstasies,
> And bring all heaven before mine eyes.
>
> (ll. 161–66)

Such passages, very influential in the early part of the eighteenth century, help to foster an emasculated, aesthetic concept of melancholy amongst the poets of that period. One may compare Thomas Warton's *Pleasures of Melancholy*:

> The taper'd choir, at the late hour of pray'r
> Oft let me tread, while to th' according voice
> The many-sounding organ peals on high,
> The clear slow-dittied chant, or varied hymn,
> Till all my soul is bath'd in ecstasies,
> And lapp'd in paradise. Or let me sit
> Far in sequester'd iles of the deep dome,
> There lonesome listen to the sacred sounds,
> Which, as they lengthen through the Gothic vault
> In hollow murmurs reach my ravish'd ear.
>
> (ll. 196–205)

The significant change in this close imitation of 'Il Penseroso' is that the subjective nature of melancholy, its basis in the poet's sensibility, is here still further intensified and overt. Whereas in 'Il Penseroso' the poet's perception of 'heaven' remains, in the Neoplatonic manner, essentially visionary, based in the faculty of sight (l. 166), Warton's 'paradise' is felt rather than seen; it is a purely sensual state of the poet's soul, which is 'lapp'd in paradise' (l. 201). Similarly, versions of the first-person pronoun—'me' (ll. 197, 201), 'my soul' (l. 200), 'my ear' (l. 205)—abound, each of the two possessives indicating ways in which the poet receives experiences of an order which is fundamentally sensual.[38] Alongside the older, Neoplatonic melancholy is thus developing a secularized, aesthetic—gothic and picturesque—and, above all, increasingly subjective idea of melancholy which may be referred to as 'modern', a state of 'enhanced self-awareness' in which the 'ego is the pivot round which the sphere of joy and grief revolves'.[39]

The shift from an earlier, religiously oriented melancholy to a later, purely 'poetic' melancholy is significant for the change that takes place between the first and second versions of the *Elegy*. It is part of the more general transition taking place at this period: away from a didactic, objectified, religious manner in poetry towards one which is ever more subjective, emotional, and sensual-aesthetic. In the two versions of Gray's poem these concerns are present in such a way that the whole process of transition may be illuminated.

III

The resolution of the 'Stanzas' indicates an authority over the world outside its formal confines. The poem embodies a metaphysical reality which enables it to pronounce upon that world, and when the poem proclaims its meaningful authority the poet reaffirms his faith in the metaphysical structure on which his composition finally depends. In graveyard poetry the poetic viewpoint is then made objective and the poet's statements are held to be universally truthful. In the 'Stanzas', for example, a transition is made from the apparent subjectivity of the poem's opening lines (culminating in the fourth, 'And leaves the world to darkness and to me'[40]) to the objectivity of its Christian-Stoic conclusion. At the moment of resolution, however, the poet abdicates his own creative autonomy. As a consequence of his faith, the poet's viewpoint becomes objective and on that basis the meaningful relation between the world and the work is thought to persist in a manner which is unproblematical, natural. Accordingly, when the Virgilian 'discovery'[41] of evening is Christianized and analogized, the tension between pastoral innocence and human tragedy is resolved. But such tragic dissonance is the *raison d'être* of the graveyard poem, as indeed of the pastoral elegy from which it is ultimately derived, and when generic dissonance is harmonized in an order of objective, analogical and universally truthful imagery, the poetic voice is effectively silenced. In the consolatory conclusions of Blair and Parnell the sensational, gothic effect which death has on the poet's imagination is rationalized, calmed, like the 'last end' of the 'good man' (*The Grave*, ll. 712ff.), in the image of the bird. Blair:

> Thus at the shut of ev'n, the weary bird
> Leaves the wide air, and in some lonely brake
> Cow'rs down, and dozes till the dawn of day,
> Then claps his well-fledg'd wings, and bears away.
> (ll. 764–67)

Even the extravagant verbosity of Young inclines to silence, to 'more than words', in the ultimately harmonizing relationship which the poet discerns between time and eternity and by which his poem is both governed and transcended:

> THUS, *Darkness* aiding Intellectual Light,
> And Sacred *Silence* whispering Truths divine,
> And *Truths Divine* converting Pain to Peace,
> My Song the Midnight Raven has outwing'd,
> And shot, ambitious of unbounded Scenes,
> Beyond the flaming Limits of the World,
> Her gloomy Flight. But what avails the Flight
> Of *Fancy*, when our *Hearts* remain below?
> *Virtue* abounds in Flatterers, and Foes;
> 'Tis Pride, to praise her; Penance to perform:
> To more than Words, to more than Worth of Tongue,
> LORENZO! rise, at this auspicious Hour;
> ('Night IX', ll. 2411–22)

One may compare the Christian-Stoic self-address with which Gray's 'Stanzas' concludes. When the poet perceives the 'sacred Calm' of evening analogously, as 'Earnest of eternal

Peace' (ll. 81–84), when he recognizes the Christian truth uniting his meditations with the world, he also exhorts himself to poetic silence:

> No more with Reason & thyself at Strife
> Give anxious Cares & endless Wishes room
> But thro' the cool sequester'd Vale of Life
> Pursue the silent Tenour of thy Doom.
>
>   (ll. 85–88)

And yet there is a problem here. In this final stanza the apparent subjectivity of the beginning of Gray's poem is made objective by its assumption into the order of Christian truth, when the 'isolation' of the poetic self before 'absolute blankness'[42] is absorbed into the truthful order. But the subjective quality of Gray's verse is not entirely overcome. It resists objectification even in the problematic formulation of generic silence—in an oxymoron, the idea of the silent poet—and in closing his poem with what amounts to a radically anti-poetic self-address Gray sustains a level of dissonance. The presence of such a subjective residue is further confirmed by the recognition of an alternative model for the conclusion of the 'Stanzas', Joseph Warton's 'Ode to Evening':

> Now every passion sleeps; desponding love,
> And pining envy, ever-restless pride;
> An holy calm creeps o'er my peaceful soul,
> Anger and mad ambition's storms subside.
>
>   (ll. 21–24)

The idea of a 'holy calm' does not represent a metaphysical resolution of the sort of problematical state of affairs presented in the body of the 'Stanzas'. By contrast, it is sensual, the achievement of a purely sensual calm in which only the turbulent states of the poet's sensible soul, of his sensibility, are harmonized. Religious resolution is replaced by a subjective mood. Characteristically, in the final stanza of the poem, the poet's contemplative sensibility is both 'soothed' and 'nourished' by natural music:[43]

> O modest Evening, oft let me appear
> A wandering votary in thy pensive train,

List'ning to every wildly-warbling throat
That fills with farewell notes the dark'ning plain.

(ll. 25–28)

Just as one may juxtapose the ultimately Neoplatonic theory of
melancholy with 'poetic' melancholy, so one may place beside
the analogous interpretation of evening the more aesthetic and
sensual idea of evening exemplified in Warton's lines.

The existence of such a subjective possibility leads to the
very heart of the difficulty presented by the graveyard poem.
Generically, like the classical elegy, the graveyard poem turns
on the problem of death. In this case the problem is both
universal and particular—it refers to an abstract idea of death
and its effect on all humanity as well as to the death of the
individual, of the subjective self and, ultimately, of the poet.
The inherited task of the pastoral elegy consists in an
attempted union of the general and the particular, in understanding each in the context of the other.[44] That is why, in its
classical phase, the blatant artifice of the form is not only
tolerated but valued, because by its formal expression the most
primary of all concerns may be realized in its inherent
duality—as particular and subjective but also as general. To
invest poetic form with such central importance, however,
involves a logic of expression. For, so understood, the sort of
resolution which naturally takes place in the funeral elegy is
not that of the particular into the general or *vice versa*, but rather
of both the particular and the general into an order which is
specifically aesthetic. Poetic form becomes an end in itself
because it is in the perfection of form that the idea of death may
be expressed and comprehended. That is why Virgil's *Eclogues*
are a work of 'original and immortal genius';[45] because he
sustains tragic dissonance by resolving human tragedy into the
tranquillity of his formal perfection. So stated, however, this
logic of expression is essentially humanistic and unchristian.[46]
It presupposes no metaphysics of resurrection or transcendence: its idea of salvation is the memorial efficacy of the
artefact—and in Virgil and Moschus even that fades into
oblivion with the passing of time. Indeed, in its radical form
the metaphysical basis of this logic is no more than will
facilitate expression. In Virgil's fifth *Eclogue*, for example,

Daphnis's death and apotheosis do not signify any general redemption. First and foremost they provide an occasion for the making of songs whose perfection is rewarded by the exchange of Menalcas's 'reed' (which 'taught' him to sing the second and third of the *Eclogues*) for Mopsus's 'crook' (ll. 81ff.), an emblem of his status as shepherd and so, in this context, of his status as poet. Subsequently, when the poem is viewed as part of Virgil's wider intention, in the ultimately mythical Virgilian context, serving the cause of the 'new *Romanitas*',[47] his 'portrait of death and resurrection' becomes a way of expressing 'the change by which a brutal murder—*crudele funus*—had led to new *otia* and security', a way of understanding 'historical actuality' such that the poet's 'bucolic *otium*' is sufficiently secure for him to 'sing'.[48] And even in the largest context of all—that of the story of the founding of Rome—might not Virgil's guiding myth be regarded as nothing other than a way of understanding the historical actuality of imperial civilization that makes possible its crowning achievement, an epic poem?

The problem of the graveyard poem is that it would both accept and deny this logic of expression. In some degree its poetic form implies and requires the same logic; it is on that basis that poetic form has some intrinsic worth. And yet this poetry embodies Christian truth in such a way that the importance of the poetic, formal status is transcended and the logic of expression effectively denied. Regarding the duality of the idea of death, for example, the graveyard poet does not wish to juxtapose the general and particular aspects of that conflict but rather to resolve the particular into the general. In Parnell's 'Night-Piece', when exhorted to remember his end by the 'visionary crowds' of ghostly dead(l. 50), the individual poet is transformed into a common denominator: '*Think, mortal, what it is to die*' (l. 52). This address is symptomatic of the generalizing tendency that works throughout the poem to transform the studious ego of its opening lines into the generic body and soul of its conclusion:

> By the blue taper's trembling light,
> No more I waste the wakeful night,
> Intent with endless view to pore

The schoolmen and the sages o'er:
Their books from wisdom widely stray,
Or point at best the longest way.
I'll seek a readier path, and go
Where wisdom's surely taught below.
[. . .]
   Nor can the parted body know,
Nor wants the soul these forms of woe;
As men who long in prison dwell,
With lamps that glimmer round the cell,
Whene'er their suffering years are run,
Spring forth to greet the glittering Sun:
Such joy, though far transcending sense,
Have pious souls at parting hence.

(ll. 1–8, 77–84)

The image of the prisoners in their cell who see glimmering
lamps rather than the true brilliance of the sun recalls Plato's
image of the cave (*Republic*, VII.514ff.), through which is
expressed the idea that earthbound man may perceive only
reflections, insubstantial images, of the universal and eternal
world beyond earthly reality. By drawing on this Platonic
contrast Parnell comprehends the translation of the soul from
this world to the next in terms of a contrast between particulars
and universals. The passage through death to new life is
represented as the assumption of the individual soul into a
world of universals, of eternal truths. Similarly, Blair's *Grave*
uses particular ideas and descriptions in a thoroughly sensa-
tionalist manner to reinforce and, as it were, to vivify his
extreme generalizations. The poet seems ready to contemplate
his own death:

Sure 'tis a serious thing to die! my soul!
What a strange moment must it be, when near
Thy journey's end, thou hast the gulf in view!

(ll. 369–71)

   Any idea of the fearful strangeness of the individual soul's
last living moment, however, is immediately swamped in
reflections of a wildly general sort, and when a more detailed
description finally does appear (in the image of the 'pitcher'

with which the passage concludes) its function is not to develop
the first idea of the awesome sense of seriousness and strangeness felt by the individual at the moment of death, but rather to
elaborate on the general thesis that, when death occurs, the
immortal soul is sundered from the body:

> That awful gulf, no mortal e'er repass'd
> To tell what's doing on the other side.
> Nature runs back, and shudders at the sight,
> And every life-string bleeds at thought of parting;
> For part they must; body and soul must part:
> Fond couple! link'd more close than wedded pair.
> This wings its way to its Almighty Source,
> The witness of its actions, now its judge;
> That dops into the dark and noisome Grave,
> Like a disabled pitcher of no use.
>
> (ll. 372–81)

The implications of this procedure reach still further. For the
graveyard poet does not wish to juxtapose some general idea of
death with his own particular, subjective concerns within the
confines of the artefact; rather, he would resolve the particular
into the general beyond the formal boundaries of the poem, in
the absolute truthfulness of Christian salvation. This is the
meaning of the poet's silence in Young, for example: the idea of
resurrection transcends poetic form because the very reason for
the existence of the poem—the problem of death—is resolved
in a truthful order that has an objective existence outside the
poem's formal limits. As argued by the conventional origins of
the poet's silence in the conclusion of Gray's 'Stanzas', when
generic dissonance is harmonized in an affirmation of objective, analogical, and universally truthful imagery, poetic form is
transcended, the poet's subjective authority over his poem is
absorbed in the objective order, and the poetic voice is
effectively silenced.

In graveyard poetry, moreover, such relief is always imman-
ent because the point of resolution precedes the logic of
expression. Its truth transcends poetic form even before the
poem itself has come into existence, and the poem is always
tending to irrelevance just as the poetic voice tends to fade into
a radically unpoetic silence. This is clear in the analogical

linguistic procedure of such verse. In Blair's *Grave*, for example, there occurs a description of the day of judgement. On that day all deaths—even death itself, as it were—are finally overcome in the great reawakening. In the following passage the triumph of life is characteristically realized as the new day which follows a night of sleep:

> But know that thou must render up the dead,
> And with high int'rest too.—They are not thine;
> But only in thy keeping for a season,
> Till the great promis'd day of restitution;
> When loud diffusive sound from brazen trump
> Of strong-lung'd cherub, shall alarm thy captives,
> And rouse the long, long sleepers into life,
> Day-light and liberty.—
>
> (ll. 654–61)

But the omnipresence of this truth is continually impressed on the reader by the poem's analogical imagery. Even the poem's generic, night-time setting, its apparently naturalistic starting point, expresses the same truth that as night becomes day so death becomes life. The poem's very location testifies to death's inefficacy:

> 'Tis but a night, a long and moonless night;
> We make the grave our bed, and then are gone.
>
> (ll. 762–63)

As Young puts it:

> Ev'n silent Night proclaims my soul immortal:
> Ev'n silent Night proclaims eternal Day:
>
> ('Night I', ll. 102–03)

The generic setting of the graveyard poem embodies the affirmation of Christian truth to which the poem itself is subordinate. The metaphysics of the poetry works through its most fundamental imagery to deny the generic point of tension—the problem of life and death which is the poem's starting point—and the efficacy of poetic expression is radically denied.

In this way all particular, subjective concerns are subsumed into a structure of objective truth so that the poem tends constantly to negate its own *raison d'être*. This self-refutation argues a contradiction at the heart of the genre. Truthful resolution does not depend on its appearance in the poem, but is prior to it; poetic form thus becomes redundant. The poem is predicated on a truth that transcends its formal significance and even disallows its existence by disabling the requisite basis of expression. This contradiction is felt in the oxymoron at the close of Gray's 'Stanzas' where a level of poetic, subjective expression remains recalcitrant to generic consolation. A similar contradiction may be observed in the opening of Parnell's 'Night-Piece'. Even as he begins to write, the poet declares literary activity to be useless:

> By the blue taper's trembling light,
> No more I waste the wakeful night,
> Intent with endless view to pore
> The schoolmen and the sages o'er:
> Their books from wisdom widely stray,
> Or point at best the longest way.
> I'll seek a readier path, and go
> Where wisdom's surely taught below.
>   How deep yon azure dyes the sky!
> Where orbs of gold unnumber'd lie,
> While through their ranks in silver pride
> The nether crescent seems to glide.
>   (ll. 1–12)

The truthful order simply does not require poetic expression—hence the poet's desire to abandon books in favour of the night-time excursion into nature—and the existence of the poem becomes paradoxical. The same implication underlies Young's assertion of the priority of nature over poetry:

> But why on *Time* so lavish is my Song?
> On this great Theme kind *Nature* keeps a School,
> To teach her Sons Herself. Each Night we Dye,
> Each Morn are born anew; Each Day, a Life!
>   ('Night II', ll. 284–87)

And yet the very fact of the existence of such poetry requires some level of adherence to the logic of expression, some basis

on which the poet's activity is not only possible but worthwhile. Consciously or otherwise, therefore, graveyard poetry
presupposes a dual, mutually contradictory basis: firstly, the
generic interpretation of Christian truth which disallows the
intrinsic significance of the artefact by resolving all particular,
subjective concerns into its own universal and objective
validity, transcending the import of poetic form; and,
secondly, an intransigent affirmation of the value of literary
expression, necessitated even by the existence of the poem.
This is the meaning of the subjective elements discernible in
the genre. The emergence of the poet's sensual rather than
visionary melancholy, the possibility of a subjective response
to evening, the transformation of religious themes into aspects
of the picturesque, and the radical sensationalism of the genre
are all ways of incorporating a level of subjectivity into the
poem which is required by the logic of expression, but
disallowed by the sort of objective resolution required by the
generic presupposition of Christian truth. In terms of his idea
of Christian consolation, for example, Blair's descriptive catalogues illustrating different types of death serve no purpose;
they are at best tangential and at worst mildly impious. But
their real function is not related to Blair's avowed beliefs.
Indeed, their real purpose is rather physiological than metaphysical; they are an imaginative-sensual substitute for that
generic and subjective tension which, on the level of Christian-
metaphysical resolution, is denied:

> Here is the large-limb'd peasant:—here the child
> Of a span long that never saw the Sun,
> Nor press'd the nipple, strangled in life's porch.
> Here is the mother, with her sons and daughters;
> The barren wife, and long-demurring maid,
> Whose lonely unappropriated sweets
> Smil'd like yon knot of cowslips on the cliff,
> Not to be come at by the willing hand.
> Here are the prude severe, and gay coquet,
> The sober widow, and the young green virgin,
> Cropp'd like a rose before 'tis fully blown,
> Or half its worth disclos'd. Strange medley here!
>
> (ll. 517–28)

The strangeness of such a 'medley' is not integrated with the poem's consolatory conclusion but is rather an end in itself; like the gothic elements and the elements of popular super-stition, it is simply juxtaposed with the poem's assertion of metaphysical truths to introduce an interest that may be referred to as poetic, a poetic *raison d'être*:

> The wind is up:—hark how it howls!—Methinks,
> 'Till now, I never heard a sound so dreary:
> Doors creak, and windows clap, and night's foul bird,
> Rook'd in the spire, screams loud; the gloomy aisles
> Black plaster'd, and hung round with shreds of
>   'scutcheons,
> And tatter'd coats of arms, send back the sound,
> Laden with heavier airs, from the low vaults,
> The mansions of the dead.—Rous'd from their slumbers,
> In grim array the grisly spectres rise,
> Grin horrible, and, obstinately sullen,
> Pass and repass, hush'd as the foot of night.
>   (ll. 32–42)

The Shakespearean echoes heard in such passages are part of the same tendency:[49] they represent a recalcitrant level of purely poetic expression on which their function is to make sense of poetic form in a way that is not possible in the context of Blair's Christian resolution. Similarly, the spectres which appear to Blair, though a part of the apparatus of the melancholy poet, are here utterly formulaic—they are an aspect of that same emergent, purely 'poetic' sensibility, in the context of which the melancholy mood becomes 'more of a convention' and 'the feeling itself' becomes increasingly 'emas-culated'.[50]

Graveyard poetry is constructed on a self-contradictory foundation. The requirements of the logic of expression are fulfilled apart from the poet's presupposition of Christian truth, and the poetic expression of that truth is only possible on a basis which is not comprehended in the truthful order. The principles of composition are confused. This is the problem that is manifested in the oxymoron at the end of Gray's 'Stanzas' and which governs the transition from the 'Stanzas' to the *Elegy*.

IV

The conclusion of Gray's 'Stanzas' resolves the debate that has taken place in the elegist's mind during the course of the poem: 'No more with Reason & thyself at Strife' (l. 85). The 'Strife' between 'Reason' and the elegist's 'self' is caused not only by the presence of death but also by the dual way in which the villagers, the 'rude Forefathers' (l. 16), are regarded in the poem. The conventional picture of idyllic village life, conventionally disrupted by Arcadian death, is pervaded by a second dissonance. Amidst the poem's graveyard rhetoric a further problem is raised. As A. E. Dyson remarks concerning the *Elegy*, 'Gray is seeing the "rude Forefathers" of the hamlet in two rôles simultaneously, both as the happiest of men, and as victims'.[51] As the 'happiest of men' the 'rude Forefathers' are people from a pastoral world and, in order to express the discordant presence of death amidst pastoral happiness, Gray imitates the *Lament for Bion*:[52]

> For them no more the blazing hearth shall burn,
> Or busy houswife ply her evening care:
> No children run to lisp their sire's return,
> Or climb his knees the envied kiss to share.
>
> (ll. 20–24)

In its contemporary context such 'obscurity' may be regarded as part of the poem's 'new pastoralism'[53] and so as attractive; and yet, as Dyson rightly remarks, the 'rude Forefathers' are 'simultaneously' viewed as 'victims'. In the 'Stanzas' the lines where they are so described contain classical exempla:

> Some Village Cato   with dauntless Breast
> The little Tyrant of his Fields withstood;
> Some mute inglorious Tully here may rest;
> Some Caesar, guiltless of his Country's Blood.
>
> (ll. 49–52)

Dyson:

> The words 'mute' and 'inglorious' acquire an ambiguity from their context. They are words of deprivation and

defeat, but they are here levelled up by juxtaposition with the 'guiltless' Cromwells [here Caesars] almost to the status of happiness.[54]

That 'ambiguity' is the 'Strife' which is resolved in the Christian-Stoic conclusion of the 'Stanzas'. It is caused by the emergence, alongside the problem of death, of a level of 'historical actuality'[55] in the mythical world of the 'rude Forefathers'; Gray's pastoral 'hamlet' (l. 16) is invaded by the realism of the villagers as victims. As though to confirm that incursion of 'actuality', in the revised version of this stanza the exempla are no longer classical but modern:

> Some village-Hampden, that with dauntless breast
> The little Tyrant of his fields withstood;
> Some mute inglorious Milton here may rest,
> Some Cromwell guiltless of his country's blood.
>
> (ll. 57–60)

Recalling the Virgilian pastoral, there are two sources of tension in the 'new pastoral' setting of Gray's *Elegy*, as of the 'Stanzas': death and 'contemporary reality'.[56] By contrast with the Christian-Stoicism of the 'Stanzas', however, in the *Elegy* the resolution of the 'Strife' caused by the juxtaposition of pastoral innocence, death, and an encroaching social realism is here postponed:

> Far from the madding crowd's ignoble strife,
> their sober wishes never learn'd to stray;
> Along the cool sequester'd vale of life
> They kept the noiseless tenor of their way.
>
> Yet ev'n these bones from insult to protect
> Some frail memorial still erected nigh,
> With uncouth rhimes and shapeless sculpture deck'd,
> Implores the passing tribute of a sigh.
>
> (ll. 73–80)

The elegist's internal debate is now sustained by the word 'Yet'; perhaps with a slight echo of the closing lines of *Paradise Lost*,[57] his own 'silent Tenour' now becomes the 'noiseless tenor' of the unfulfilled villagers and, as in Virgil, dissonance is

'resolved' into memory and poetic form. The locus of resolution
shifts from a point external to the poem—the interpretation of
Christian truth that entails poetic silence—to poetic form
itself. Virgilian dissonance is now resolved in a Virgilian
manner and, as in the fifth *Eclogue*, the tombstone, the 'frail
memorial', is not viewed as a necessary stepping-stone on the
'path that must be trod'[58] to the afterlife, but is rather made
emblematic of the poem in which it occurs—hence Gray's
introduction of the tombstone and epitaph in the conclusion of
the *Elegy*. Moreover, poetic form may be governed by memory
but, as in the classical elegy, memory is governed by time, by
the inevitable passing of life and mind:

> For who to dumb Forgetfulness a prey,
> This pleasing anxious being e'er resign'd,
> Left the warm precincts of the chearful day,
> Nor cast one longing ling'ring look behind?
>
> (ll. 85–88)[59]

The syntax of Gray's lines opens the possibility that the
memorial itself is subject to the ravages of 'dumb Forgetfulness'; one casts the 'longing ling'ring look behind' despite the
inevitable demise into oblivion. The introduction of the
memorial indicates the resolution of the crisis of priority
caused by the precedence of Christian truth over poetic form in
the logic of expression. Poetic form is governed not by eternal
truth but by uncertainty, dissonance, memory and time, and
its function is to 'deprive' such dissonance of its 'factuality', to
transcend it by sustaining it within an aesthetic texture,
transforming it into 'elegiac sentiment'.[60] For the same reason
it sustains within itself the dialectic of formal, aesthetic
transcendence and temporal decay; the *ricorso* to memory and
poetic form reinstates the Virgilian discovery of evening as
emblematic of the uncertain ability of the artefact to resist
temporal decay. In the transition from the 'Stanzas' to the
Elegy, the optimistic, eighteenth-century interpretation of
evening in terms of the divine analogy is abandoned. Evening
is again governed by the temporal transience which it embodies and expresses in Virgil, permeated by a radical 'ambiguity',
a Virgilian uncertainty, which, as Hutchings argues, pervades
even the *Elegy*'s syntax: 'And all the air a solemn stillness

holds'(l. 6). Does the 'air' hold the 'stillness' or 'stillness' the 'air'?

> ... the obscurity Gray is creating is also infiltrating his language, loosing his hold on stable syntax. As night falls, as the world fades on the sight, reality can no longer be firmly and clearly perceived. It is a time when distinctions become blurred, when objects cannot be surely grasped, but only held as nebulously as stillness the air, or air the stillness.[61]

But Gray's procedure is not simply mimetic of the time of day. Evening is as emblematic of the pre-eminence of temporal transience as of its transcendence in the artefact: does the poem 'hold' the evening or evening the poem? Further, to acknowledge the dialectic obtaining between transience, memory, and the artefact entails an acceptance of the broader temporal basis of poetic composition. Gray, as Panofsky says of Virgil, is here 'opening up the dimension of the past'.[62] Hence the *ricorso* to classical elegy that occurs in the shift from the 'Stanzas' to the *Elegy*; it also governs the introduction of the 'kindred Spirit' (l. 96) and the 'hoary-headed Swain' (l. 97) with which the latter is continued. For by the conventional, rhetorical nature of the portrait that is painted of the elegist, Gray's poet-figure is made, in part, to occupy a past, ideal world, a poetic Arcadia. The description is 'riddled with phrases and diction borrowed from Spenser, Shakespeare and Milton', 'fanciful, consciously "poetic", archaic in tone'.[63] By connecting with the equally 'archaic' shepherd-poets of classical pastoral, Gray's mythically distant poet-figure further opens up the 'dimension of the past'. The historical continuity of the 'new pastoralism' of Gray's *Elegy* with the pastoral elegies of Virgil's *Eclogues* and thence Theocritus is confirmed. As a contemporary, 'currently fashionable' 'man of sensibility',[64] moreover, the poet-figure of the *Elegy* is a particular type in a particular historical situation—hence the critical willingness to identify him with Gray himself.[65] And yet, as 'archaic', as 'distant' in the same Arcadian sense as the 'rude Forefathers' who 'broke' the 'stubborn glebe' and 'jocund' drove 'afield' (ll. 16–28), as also the classical Arcadian shepherds, he is mythical and general. In accordance with the logic of expression, that is, Gray resolves particular and general into the artefact, thereby sustaining the dissonance of pastoral elegy and so achieving elegiac sentiment. In the *Elegy*, therefore, the introduction of the tombstone and the reading of the epitaph do not express the certainty of Christian resurrection; rather, as Hutchings argues, the 'conventionally Christian context' of the epitaph merely allows Gray to 'sustain the uncertainty'.[66] The first stanza continues the ambiguous themes of fame, obscurity, and circumscribed opportunity expressed earlier in the poem:

> *HERE rests his head upon the lap of Earth*
> *A Youth to Fortune and to Fame unknown,*
> *Fair Science frown'd not on his humble birth,*
> *And Melancholy mark'd him for her own.*

(ll. 117–20)

The dubious blessing of knowledge is summed up in the phrase '*Fair Science frown'd not*', where Science is not simply 'fair' but also (where present at all) 'frowning'. Also, like the ambivalently blessed yet 'victimized' villagers, the '*Youth*' of the epigraph is '*to Fortune and to Fame unknown*'. Similarly, the apparently conventional *hic jacet* of line 117 seems to invert the sense of unwilling submission to death expressed in the lines concerning 'dumb Forgetfulness' (ll. 85–88). As B. H. Bronson has argued, in the context of the first two lines of the poem the verb 'rests' has a transitive force: 'It is not a mere *Hic jacet*. A more willing submission is implied: not simply *lies* but *lays to rest*.'[67] And yet, such 'active', 'willing submission' now takes place in death. Earlier, one asked whether the air held the stillness or stillness the air, and so whether evening holds the poem or *vice versa*; similarly, the question here is not simply whether the youth is active or passive in death but how the uncertainty of the passage from life to death may be contained in the poem, in Gray's own 'willingness to drive literary expression "beyond common apprehension"'.[68] The same uncertainty pervades even the final stanza of the poem. Here, as elsewhere, Gray does not allow death unequivocally to signify the passage to new life. Grammatically, the '*bosom*' of his '*Father and his God*' (l. 128) does not follow on from the youth's '*dread abode*' (l. 126), the grave, but rather stands in apposition to it. It also recalls the '*lap of Earth*' of the epitaph's opening line. As Hutchings observes, the poem's final stanza 'hovers in suspension of certainty':[69]

> *No farther seek his merits to disclose,*
> *Or draw his frailties from their dread abode,*
> *(There they alike in trembling hope repose)*
> *The bosom of his Father and his God.*
>
> (ll. 125–28)

That is not to say that the epitaph contains no conventional Christian sentiments; it is replete with conventional Christianity, but presented in a way that is 'still making us think, still disturbing us'.[70] For the issues raised by the poem are not resolved in a world of universal truth extrinsic to poetic expression, but sustained within the boundaries of poetic form. Gray does not rest with the metaphysical certainties of the genre in which he is working but—in the transition from the 'Stanzas' to the *Elegy*—turns instead towards a radical uncertainty through whose expression the poem maintains its *raison d'être* and so admits the logic of expression.

It is in this way that Gray acknowledges the formal and thematic continuity between his own version of the 'new pastoral' and the classical pastoral upon which it ultimately depends. This occurs in the stanzas which Dr Johnson praised as original:

> The four stanzas beginning 'Yet even these bones' are to me original: I have never seen the notions in any other place; yet he that reads them here persuades himself that he has always felt them.[71]

These are the lines where the elegist takes up the internal debate which, in the 'Stanzas', was resolved in Christian-Stoicism. In the *Elegy* the word 'Yet' signifies an anastrophe, a 'turning back' to a point in the argument which seems already past—here to the inherent frailty of the 'memorial'. But this is the anastrophe of pastoral elegy. It serves a function in Gray's poem comparable with that served by the lines beginning 'Weep no more, woeful shepherds...' (ll. 165ff.) in Milton's *Lycidas*. Gray's anastrophe, however, does not signify a turning back to life—the 'he is not dead, he lives' of *Lycidas*—but to the dubious existence conferred by the artefact, by the tombstone, the epitaph, and so by elegy itself. It is that which makes these lines at once original and familiar. The ideas of transience and memory are familiar because they are classical; the 'turning back' to them is original. For the *Elegy* turns not to the generic affirmation of Christian faith—to eternal, extemporal' truth—but away from such truth to the aesthetic and the temporal. In this acceptance of the intrinsic significance of the artefact, moreover, in the rapprochement of artfice and time, and the tenuous reincorporation of a level of 'historical actuality' into elegy, the ultimate implication of Gray's 'turning back' in these lines is the tentative emergence of a poetics of history.

NOTES

1. *Correspondence*, I, 326. On the poem to which Gray refers see *The Poems of Gray, Collins and Goldsmith*, ed. R. H. Lonsdale (London, 1969, repr. 1980), p. 103.

2. *Correspondence*, I, 327.

3. F. Brady, 'Structure and Meaning in Gray's *Elegy*', in *From Sensibility to Romanticism*, ed. F. W. Hilles and H. Bloom (New York, 1965), p. 178. Brady refers to the same passage from Gray's letter to Walpole.

4. There has been some critical disagreement about the date of the earlier version, some scholars arguing for William Mason's suggestion of 1742 (notably F. W. Bateson in his *English Poetry*, 2nd ed. [London, 1966]); others, perhaps the majority, accepting a date of about 1745–46, on the basis of Walpole's recollection of having seen the first twelve lines of the poem sometime before 1750 (see I. Jack, 'Gray's *Elegy* Reconsidered', in Hilles & Bloom, op. cit., pp. 139ff.). A dating of Gray's handwriting in the Eton MS testifies to a fairly substantial gap between the two versions: on this evidence the first version (in any event a fair copy of it) appears to have been set down some time in 1748; its continuation, as Gray seems to imply in the letter to Walpole, in 1750. See A. Macdonald's facsimile edition of the *Elegy* and the Eton MS (Ilkley & London, 1976), pp. 12–17. All references to the Eton MS are to the reprint in *Thomas Gray and William Collins: Poetical Works*, ed. Roger Lonsdale (Oxford, 1977), pp. 101ff.

5. *Gray, Collins and Goldsmith*, ed. Lonsdale, p. 104.

6. E.g., ibid., pp. 114–16 and Bateson, op. cit., pp. 128ff. In his edition of *The Complete English Poems of Thomas Gray* (London, 1973) J. Reeves regards the first version of the poem as a 'simple but exquisite exercise in Christian stoicism' (p. 15). See also Jack, op. cit., Brady, op. cit., and F. H. Ellis, 'Gray's *Elegy*: The Biographical Problem in Literary Criticism', *Publications of the Modern Language Association*, 66 (1951), 971–1008.

7. After Gray's 'Stanzas Wrote In A Country Church-Yard', the poem's

title in the Eton MS. By his own account it was Mason who suggested the later title, 'elegy'. See *The Poems of Mr. Gray* (York, 1775): *Poems*, p. 108.

8. Cp. Jack, op. cit., p. 145, and Reeves, op. cit., pp. 13ff.

9. Published 1743. Quoted from *The Works of the English Poets from Chaucer to Cowper*, ed. A. Chalmers, 21 vols (London, 1810), vol. 15. Regarding the apparent similarity of the *Elegy* and Blair's *Grave*, it is noteworthy that from 1751 to 1830 the two poems were printed together a total of 17 times. See E. M. Sickels, *The Gloomy Egoist* (New York, 1932), pp. 92–93.

10. See R. Poggioli, *The Oaten Flute* (Cambridge, Mass., 1975), pp. 174ff.

11. 1721; quoted from Chalmers, op. cit., vol. 9.

12. Quoted from *Edward Young: Night Thoughts*, ed. Stephen Cornford (Cambridge, 1989). Also noteworthy is James Hervey's very popular *Meditations among the Tombs* (1746).

13. In this regard the graveyard poets followed Fontenelle's definition of pastoral, in his *Discours sur la nature de l'églogue* (1688), as a celebration of the 'quiet Life' illuminated by the 'Natural Light of Reason', rather than Rapin's more academic recommendation to follow the objective authority of the ancients and so to imitate ancient pastoral models with some exactitude (*Dissertatio de Carmine Pastorali*, 1659). See J. E. Congleton, *Theories of Pastoral Poetry in England 1684–1798* (Florida, 1952) and R. Trickett, *The Honest Muse* (Oxford, 1967).

14. See *'Et in Arcadia Ego*: "On the Concept of Transience in Poussin and Watteau"', in *Philosophy and History*, ed. R. Klibansky and H. J. Paton (Oxford, 1936) and, a variant of the same essay, '*Et in Arcadia Ego*: Poussin and the Elegiac Tradition', in *Meaning in the Visual Arts* (Harmondsworth, 1970). All references are to the latter.

15. *Eclogues* V: 'spargite humum foliis, inducite fontibus umbras, / pastores (mandat fieri sibi talia Daphnis), / et tumulum facite et tumulo superaddite carmen: / "Daphnis ego in silvis, hinc usque ad sidera notus, / formosi pecoris custos, formosior ipse."' All references are to *Virgil*, ed. & trans. H. R. Fairclough, vol. i, rev. ed. (Cambridge, Mass. & London, 1935, repr. 1978).

16. For Virgil's concern to relate the 'mythical world directly and explicitly to contemporary reality' see R. Coleman's edition of the *Eclogues* (Cambridge, 1977), pp. 28–36; J. Griffin, *Virgil* (Oxord & New York, 1986), pp. 21ff. Also the last chapter of B. Snell, *The Discovery of the Mind*, trans. T. G. Rosenmeyer (Oxford, 1953) and P. V. Marinelli, *Pastoral* (London, 1971).

17. Panofsky, op. cit., p. 346.

18. Ibid., p. 346.

19. 'Hic tamen hanc mecum poteras requiescere noctem / fronde super viridi: sunt nobis mitia poma, / castaneae molles et pressi copia lactis; / et iam summa procul villarum culmina fumant / maioresque cadunt altis de montibus umbrae.'

20. 'surgamus: solet esse gravis cantantibus umbra, / iuniperi gravis umbra, nocent et frugibus umbrae. / ite domum saturae, venit Hesperus, ite capellae.'

21. 'Omnia fert aetas, animum quoque; saepe ego longos / cantando puerum memini me condere soles: / nunc oblita mihi tot carmina . . .'

22. Poggioli, op. cit., p. 68.

23. *Lament for Bion*, ll. 114–26. Quoted from *The Greek Bucolic Poets*, ed. & trans. J. M. Edmonds (London & New York, 1919). The 'Maid' is Persephone.

24. *Bion*, ll. 20–22; cp. Gray's *Elegy*, 19–24. For a discussion of *Bion* see Poggioli, op. cit., p. 72. Poggioli's translation of *Bion* further emphasizes the repeated 'no more' (ibid.): 'Alas, the man who dear was to the herds sings no more in their midst; he sits no more, he sings no more under the lonely oaks'.

25. Quoted from *The Poems of John Milton*, ed. John Carey and Alastair Fowler (London, 1968). Also important in this Christian transformation is Spenser's 'Nouember Æglogue' in the *Shepheardes Calender*.

26. For *et in arcadia ego*, interpreted by King George III in the words 'Ay, ay, death is even in Arcadia', see Panofsky, op. cit., p. 340.

27. Eton MS, l. 110. In the *Elegy* proper this becomes 'kindred Spirit', l. 96.

28. By the mid-century Melancholy and Contemplation were largely interchangeable (cp. the 'sober Contemplation' of Gray's 'Ode on the Spring); see, e.g., Thomas Warton's *Pleasures of Melancholy* (1747).

29. Cp. 'glooms' in the opening of Warton's *Melancholy*: 'O lead me, queen sublime, to solemn glooms / Congenial with my soul; to cheerless shades, / To ruin'd seats, to twilight cells and bow'rs, / Where thoughtful Melancholy loves to muse, / Her fav'rite midnight haunts...', ll. 17–21. Quoted from Chalmers, op. cit., vol. 18.

30. Sickels, op. cit., p. 38. Also A. L. Reed, *The Background of Gray's 'Elegy'* (New York, 1962; 1st pub. 1924), p. 246. Cp. the 'melancholy state' of Parnell's 'Night-Piece' (23) and the 'dark pencil', in 'melancholy dipt', 'darker still' than natural darkness, of Young's *Night Thoughts* ('Night V').

31. See Reed, op. cit., p. 20.

32. See R. Klibansky, E. Panofsky and F. Saxl, *Saturn and Melancholy* (London, 1964), pp. 250ff.

33. See *Problem* 30.I, here quoted from Klibansky *et al.*, op. cit., p. 18, where the complete text is given. See also E. Panofsky, *Albrecht Dürer*, 2 vols (Princeton, 1945), I, 156ff.

34. Klibansky *et al.*, op. cit., pp. 250, 255. The principal text is Ficino's *Libri de vita triplici* (*c.* 1482–89), for which see ibid., pp. 259–60.

35. See Sickels, op. cit., p. 38. For further examples of the combination of melancholy with poetic inspiration in the mid-eighteenth century, see the description of Melancholy in William Collins's 'The Passions' (pub. 1746) and the passage concerning Philosophic Melancholy in James Thomson's *The Seasons* (1746 ed.; 'Autumn', ll. 1004ff.).

36. Klibansky *et al.*, op. cit., pp. 217ff.

37. Sickels (op. cit., p. 182) notices a 'shift of emphasis from philosophical or religious doctrine to emotional realization'. For the secularization of melancholy cp. Reed, op. cit., p. 187.

38. Also important for a sensually experienced contemplative melancholy is Joseph Warton's 'Ode to Fancy', which, like Thomas Warton's *Melancholy*, contains a number of imitations of Milton's 'Il Penseroso'. E.g.: '... suddenly awak'd, I hear / Strange whisper'd music in my ear, / And my glad soul in bliss is drown'd / By the sweetly-soothing sound!' (ll. 45–48; quoted from Chalmers, op. cit., vol. 18).

39. Klibansky *et al.*, op. cit., p. 231.

40. In the context of its later appearance in the *Elegy*, this line has been described as 'zeugma', the yoking together of 'darkness and the self'. See W. Hutchings, 'Syntax of Death: Instability in Gray's *Elegy Written in a Country Churchyard*', *Studies in Philology*, 81 (1984), 496–514.

41. Panofsky, *Visual Arts*, p. 346.

42. Hutchings, op. cit., p. 501.

43. For the growing association of melancholy with music, observed in Milton's 'Il Penseroso', see Klibansky *et al.*, op. cit., p. 231.

44. Cp. Poggioli, op. cit., pp. 20, 85–86.

45. Panofsky, *Visual Arts*, p. 347.

46. Which may perhaps lie behind Dr Johnson's famous dislike of Milton's use of the 'disgusting' pastoral convention in *Lycidas* and his view of the poem as 'indecent'. *Lives of the English Poets*, ed. G. Birkbeck Hill, 3 vols (Oxford, 1905), I, 165.

47. B. Otis, *Virgil* (Oxford, 1963), p. 142.

48. Ibid., pp. 135–36.

49. Cp. especially the ghost scenes in *Hamlet*, Act I; also the various moments in *Macbeth* when the hero is wrestling with the consequences of his past actions (e.g. Act 3, scene 4) and when he is contemplating the world in terms of his own intentions and desires (e.g. 1.7, 2.1, 2.2, 4.1).

50. Klibansky *et al.*, op. cit., p. 237.

51. 'The Ambivalence of Gray's *Elegy*', *Essays in Criticism*, 7 (1957), 257.

52. *Bion*, ll. 20–22, quoted above.

53. Cp. Trickett (op. cit., pp. 259–66) on the 'new pastoralism' of the period which underlies Gray's *Elegy*.

54. Op. cit., p. 257.

55. Otis, op. cit., p. 135.

56. Coleman, op. cit., p. 28. Cp. W. Empson's interpretation of ll. 53–56: this means that 'eighteenth-century England had no scholarship system or *carrière ouverte aux talents*'. *Some Versions of Pastoral* (London, 1935, repr. 1979), p. 4.

57. Cp. *Paradise Lost*, XII, 648–49: 'They hand in hand with wandering steps and slow, / Through Eden took their solitary way'. The notion of the villagers as 'never' having 'learn'd' to 'stray' may imply a view of their existence as almost unnaturally prelapsarian in a post-lapsarian world and so perhaps sustain the oxymoron present in the idea of the silent poet.

58. From Parnell's 'Night-Piece', l. 67.

59. Cp. Virgil's *Eclogues* IX: 'Time robs us all, even of memory...' ('Omnia fert aetas, animum quoque...').

60. Panofsky, *Visual Arts*, p. 346.

61. Op. cit., p. 501.

62. *Visual Arts*, pp. 346–47.

63. *Gray, Collins and Goldsmith*, ed. Lonsdale, p. 116.

64. Hutchings, op. cit., p. 509.

65. E.g., *Gray, Collins and Goldsmith*, ed. Lonsdale, p. 115; Jack, op. cit., p. 145; and B. H. Bronson, 'On a Special Decorum in Gray's *Elegy*', in Hilles & Bloom, op. cit., p. 174.

66. Op cit., p. 512.

67. Op. cit., p. 173.

68. Ibid. See also Hutchings, op. cit., p. 511, who argues that uncertainty about 'the extent of active or passive being implied ... continues the whole poem's concern with the possibility of action; but now the action is within the realm of death. Is the youth actively resting his head, or is his head passively resting?'

69. Op. cit., p. 512.

70. Ibid., p. 513.

71. *Lives of the English Poets*, III, 441–42.

Gray and Poetic Diction

RICHARD TERRY

I

Long before Wordsworth branded him 'more than any other man curiously elaborate in the structure of his own poetic diction',[1] the stock of Gray's reputation had come to rest upon parallel consideration of the studied and formulaic phraseology used within much Augustan poetry. This essay explores the morphology of poetic diction, examines what can be gleaned of Gray's attitude towards it, and interprets afresh some of his early poems on the basis of diction's being a constitutive part of them. Gray's poetic career is of signal interest for having straddled a watershed of taste. Despite dying at fifty-five, in 1771, he still outlived the point at which the tide of literary opinion began to turn against the stylistic principles his own works upheld. Signs of Gray's embattlement against the emerging climate are increasingly manifest. His own poetic diction, as has been zealously documented, was more strongly tied to the actual wordings of earlier writers than that of any other eighteenth-century poet; and he became nervous that the growing cult of literary 'originality' could see these borrowings being put down as evidence of unoriginality or sleight of pen. In 1756, for instance, he listed for a friend some conscious allusions inserted in 'The Bard', adding with cynical resignation: 'do not wonder therefore, if some Magazine or Review call me Plagiary'.[2] Similarly, Roger Lonsdale has suggested that what might ultimately have stilled Gray's creative hand (he wrote no major poetry in the last ten years of his life) was the appearance of Richard Hurd's *Discourse on Poetical Imitation* (1753), which freed from reproach poets whose subject-matter or sentiments were repetitious while tarring as plagiarists those whose phraseology was derivative from other writers.[3]

Hurd was an appreciated friend, so the severity of his stance must have provided Gray with persuasive evidence of the way the critical wind was blowing. After Gray's death, his poetry suffered the ignominy of Johnson's belittling 'Life' (1781) and Wordsworth's adduction, in the 'Preface' to the second edition of the *Lyrical Ballads* (1800), of the 'Sonnet on the Death of Richard West' as an example of the futility of stock diction.[4] While Wordsworth's cavils about the West sonnet have never seemed wholly cogent, the general rebuke that he fleshed out against diction, that it strove to emulate the language of earlier poets without being privy to the experience which first engendered it, has an application to Gray which is not easily dismissed. The terms of Wordsworth's critique were revived much later in T. S. Eliot's influential essay on eighteenth-century poetry, which argued that, after Pope's death, a peculiar badness sets in amongst poets who hang on to the Popean idiom, not realizing that by this time the expressive technique has become an anachronism.[5] The subject-matter of Gray's poem has little in common with Pope's, yet it was just because Gray's poetry (unlike that of his contemporary, Johnson) progressively yields quarter to the new aesthetic tendencies, towards a poetry of introspection, sublimity and prophecy, that his adherence to traditional phraseology made his style all the more acutely vulnerable to the charge of being a relic.

It is as well that I should say something of what constitutes diction and from where it takes its origin. All writing is stylized, and no form of expression possesses any 'natural' relation to the subject it details, so the idea that stock diction comprised a peculiarly artificial stylistic discipline should be discredited. However, diction, in its customary sense of a poetic lexis, is conceptually artificial in one sense, in predicating that words, particularly seen as inhering within registers of poetic expression, can be clearly extrapolated from the larger schemata, figurative, rhythmical and acoustic, to which poets consign them: that words possess properties independent of poetic context. Discussions of diction have habitually assumed that they do, while conceding at the same time that responses to diction are governed by larger linguistic and social contexts. Even Johnson's notorious sniffiness at low words in *Macbeth* ('dun', 'knife') brought out a guarded denial that such words as these were *absolutely* mean: 'No word is naturally or intrinsically meaner than another; our opinion therefore of words as of other things arbitrarily and capriciously established, depends wholly upon accident and custom'.[6] Shakespeare's dictional tactlessness becomes not so much a stutter of aesthetic technique as a misguided collusion with the language of the vulgar. Wordsworth's repudiation of diction, in the *Lyrical Ballads*, though expressing an opinion almost diametrically opposite to Johnson's, is set down in terms which are markedly similar. Not the dictional terms themselves are deplored but their insipid reverberations through the mouths of generations of bad poets, until 'such feelings of disgust are connected with them as it is scarcely possible by any art of association to overpower'.[7]

The *O.E.D.* defines diction (4a) as 'The manner in which anything is expressed in words; choice or selection of words and phrases; wording; verbal style'. The word seems to have entered literary parlance in the late seventeenth century: Dryden, in his *Sylvae* (1685), glossed it as still a neologism when he spoke of Horace's 'diction, or (to speak English) ... his expressions'.[8] In the first instance, diction was used uncertainly to include metre, poetic lexis and rhetorical figures: a hold-all term for traits which constituted poetry's singularity. Dryden gave a later definition (1700) as consisting of both 'the choice of words, and harmony of numbers'; while John Dennis stated (1701) that 'Numbers distinguish the Parts of Poetick Diction, from the Periods of Prose', some years later(1717) adding the further condition that where 'there is no Use of Figures, there we may justly conclude, that the Diction is Prosaick'.[9] It was not to be long, though, before diction started disassociating itself from metrics. One early example of their being clearly differentiated comes in the 'Preface' to Pope's *Homer* (1715), where Pope observes that Homer's compound-epithets had the effect of throwing his language out of prose 'not only as it heighten'd the *Diction*, but as it assisted and fill'd the *Numbers* with greater Sound and Pomp'.[10]

Virtually from the term's inception, 'diction' became an accessory to the view that poetry and prose were wholly distinct media, commitment to diction being almost inevitably

an expression of that belief. There has always been a tendency
to think that the Augustan poetry of plain statement had more
truck with prose than poetry of most other periods, yet poetry
was widely eulogized in the period as distinct and especial.
Dennis noted bullishly that 'Poetry ... is Poetry, because it is
more Passionate and Sensual than Prose'.[11] Dennis, being one
of the first to take on board the ramifications of Longinus's *On
the Sublime*, was admittedly slightly out on a limb in the first
decade of the century, but by 1728, Joseph Trapp was throwing his appreciable authority behind the general idea, claiming
that 'as Poetry requires a peculiar Way of Thinking, it
affects, likewise, a peculiar Manner of Writing and Speaking,
that so it may be set off at as great a Distance from Prose as
possible'.[12] Belief in the abrupt separation of poetry from prose
took strongest hold during the period of Gray's poetic career.
James Beattie, with whom Gray corresponded, argued that
poetry was improved by the introduction of words and phrases
'which, because they rarely occur in prose, and frequently in
verse, are by the grammarian and lexicographer termed
Poetical'; and he coined an ingenious explanation for why prose
writers did not employ such a fixed phraseology, arguing that
as prose lacks the mnemonic properties of poetry, writers
would have been less likely to have remembered and revived
the wordings of their prose forbears.[13] The singularity of poetry
was addressed also in a contribution to the *British Magazine*,
'On Poetry, As Distinguished from Other Writing', which
ventured that it was set apart not merely by its versification
but by 'a species of painting with words'; and Johnson chided
Collins, as well as 'some later candidates for fame' (amongst
whom he may have intended Gray), for succumbing to the
delusion 'that not to write prose is certainly to write poetry'.[14]

Poets' adoption of diction was charged with both a positive
and a negative purpose. The negative aspect consisted of the
perpetuation of a poetic lexicon purged of the corruptions and
vulgarisms of common speech; the concept of diction, as in
Johnson's caveats about indelicate words in *Macbeth*, provided
a sanction for certain usages being expelled from the literary
domain. The obviously élitist nature of the programme was
candidly brought out by Johnson's glossing of poetical diction,
in the 'Life of Dryden', as a 'system of words at once refined

from the grossness of domestick use and free from the harshness of terms appropriated to particular arts'.[15] On the more
positive side, diction contributed to the larger category of
'ornamentation', consisting of images, figures of speech,
digressions, as well as dictional felicities, which was thought
integral to poetry's fulfilling its twofold purpose—to represent
known truths and to please.[16] The idea of poetic ornament was
fundamental to neo-classical aesthetics, and was built upon
two principles which, during the span of Gray's own poetic
career, became progressively outdated. First of these was the
notion that the stock of expressible truths was finite, which
caused poetry to be seen as mainly the business of better
expressing ideas that were already known and familiar; second
was that the content of utterances could be separated from
their means of expression, which allowed that any one speech-
content could in theory be couched in a number of different
ways.

   Although these ideas belonged with an early-century out-
look, it should not be imagined that the decorative view of
poetry, within which poetic diction bulked large, was only to
come under fire with proto-Romantic scepticism about the
rigid separation of poetry from prose and from common
speech; for poetic ornament had been under intermittent
threat from the beginning of the eighteenth century, primarily
from a view of poetic practice that valued 'simplicity'. Simplicity could paradoxically be assimilated as a quality of diction
itself, as was sometimes noted about Spenser, but this only
intermittently confused an essentially antithetical relation.[17]
Addison's criticism, in particular, tended to swing between
allegiance to either concept: his early 'Essay on Virgil's
Georgics' (1697), a definitive construction of Virgilian georgic,
praised the poet's deployment of '*Metaphors, Grecisms*, and
Circumlocutions, to give his verse the greater pomp and preserve
it from sinking into a *Plebeian* stile'; yet, in *Spectator* 70, he
applauded the old English ballad *Chevy Chase* for a sublimity
seen as arising from its achievement of simplicity.[18] The vogue
enjoyed by the Longinian sublime, pioneered by Boileau's
translation of 1674 and assisted by Dennis's enthusiastic
whistle-blowing, helped institute the idea that the most arresting literary utterances could be characterized by starkness and

clarity: Longinus had selected as a paradigm of the sublime effect God's majestically plain fiat 'Let there be light'.[19] One representative attack on the artifice of poetic adornment occurs in *Guardian* 15, where Steele advises that 'gentle Subjects' profit from simplicity of conception on account that the 'Figures of Stile added to them serve only to hide a Beauty, however gracefully they are put on, and are thrown away like Paint upon a fine Complexion'; while, perhaps surprisingly, Gray himself expressed one of the cases against ornament, that it detracted from a poem's ostensible 'sincerity', when he tempered his general regard for Lord Lyttelton's controversial *Monody* on his dead wife by saying that 'poetical ornaments are foreign to the purpose; for they only show a man is not sorry'.[20]

Probably the most important single element within diction was archaism. Linguistic pessimism amounted to an orthodoxy in the early decades of the century, with many writers picking up from Thomas Sprat's influential proposal that the language be placed under the stewardship of an instituted Academy by themselves contending that the English tongue had become beleaguered and corrupted. In the face of linguistic discontent, poets found solace, as creative writers always have, in the recuperation of words made sterling through usage by their predecessors. Dryden, for example, believed that the language unassisted could no longer furnish the ornamental beauties so necessary for poetry, and professed willingness to 'trade both with the living and the dead, for the enrichment of our native language'.[21] Pessimism took one form in a certain jaundice about the luck of earlier poets in being able to call upon a language which remained much closer to mint condition, and therefore afforded much more expressive potential. Richard West raised this matter with Gray in trying to legislate for how far a writer should be free to revive outdated phraseology, confessing that Shakespeare's 'old expressions have more energy in them than ours'.[22] The facilities of one language, as against those of others, inevitably become more poignantly apparent during the process of translation, and much worthwhile deliberation over the efficacy of diction grew out of the special problems posed by translating classical authors. Pope, in the 'Postscript' to the *Odyssey*, remarked wistfully on the advantage accruing to the Homeric original as a result of its inherent felicities having become further gilded by remoteness. Whether a translation should want to reproduce that slight estrangement which we invariably feel from the artefacts of remote cultures is a dubious point, but Pope's *Odyssey* deliberately sought to recover Homer's supposed exoticism by introducing Miltonic phraseology, on the grounds that 'A just and moderate mixture of old words may have an effect like the working old Abbey stones into a building, which I have sometimes seen to give a kind of venerable air'.[23]

The practice of a 'judiciously antiquated' style, as Pope tagged it, was not the preserve solely of translators. When West wrote to Gray on 4 April 1742, chivying him over the length of speech given by Agrippina, the eponymous heroine of Gray's attempted tragic drama, he also counselled against the 'antiquated' style adopted throughout the piece. The letter contrasted this with the more contemporary style of Racine, a tragedian whom Gray much admired, and urged Gray to look to Addison's *Cato* as a celebrated tragedy which managed to remain fully in tune with its linguistic times. West's heterodoxy emerges most starkly in the phlegmatic suggestion (something that a few decades later would have become unthinkable) that 'were Shakespear alive now, he would write in a different style from what he did'.[24] This amicable debunking drew from Gray a famous letter setting out grounds for the proper composition of poetic language:

> As to matter of stile, I have this to say: The language of the age is never the language of poetry; except among the French, whose verse, where the thought or image does not support it, differs in nothing from prose. Our poetry, on the contrary, has a language peculiar to itself; to which almost every one, that has written, has added something by enriching it with foreign idioms and derivatives: Nay sometimes words of their own composition and invention. Shakespear and Milton have been great creators this way; and no one more licentious than Pope or Dryden, who perpetually borrow expressions from the former.[25]

Gray's manifesto endorses not just the separating of poetry from prose but the idea of a poetic dialect, consisting of phraseology invented by poets and passed down from one

generation to another. Gray, in fact, took the autonomy of
poetic language one stage further in a passage in his *Common-
Place Book* which formed part of his sketched literary history of
Britain. Here he contended that poets should shoulder the
principal onus of reinvigorating the language of general usage,
for 'to Poetry Languages owe their first formation, elegance &
purity'.[26]

That archaism provided the readiest means of distancing
poetic language from that of prose (a desirable end) continued
to be upheld as late as Beattie's systematic exploration of
English 'Poetical words'(1783): Beattie even went so far as to
venture that Homer's language would probably, for poetic
reasons, not have been contemporary with that of his own
culture, but would instead have harked back to 'some ancient
dialect'.[27] The concept of archaism, and its facilitation of what
was effectively a poetical argot, runs as a thread through
Beattie's taxonomies of diction; yet the sub-categories are of
sufficient independent interest to warrant being set down.
They are seven: (1) the interpolation of Greek and Latin
idioms, as reversed word-order in Gray's 'destiny obscure' or
'the air a solemn stillness holds';(2) the tacking on to words of
solemnizing suffixes, as 'distain' or 'disport';(3) archaism narrowly conceived as the preservation within poetry of words
extinct in common usage, as (according to Beattie) 'anon', 'aye'
(ever), 'brand' (sword), 'host' (army); (4) poetical coinages, as
'darkling', 'pinion' (wing), 'madding'; (5) words subject to
elision or syllabic retrenchment, as ' 'Tis', ' 'twas', 'eve', 'morn';
(6) compound-epithets, as Gray's 'rosy-bosom'd', 'long-expecting' and 'moss-grown' from 'Ode on the Spring'; and (7) the
improvisation of words from one part of speech to another, as
noun to verb (to 'crown') or noun to participial adjective
('curtained').[28] Yet even Beattie's diligence makes for a less
than definitive list. One could also add, from Gray's poetry
alone, invocational formulae ('Ye distant spires, ye antique
towers'), personification ('grateful Science'), transferred
epithets ('smileing Mornings', 'chearful Fields'), revival of
Latin root meanings ('pliant'), periphrases ('Attic warbler',
'rolling circle's speed'), plus some incidence of nouns of
category ('grisly troop') and -y epithets formed from nouns
('watery glade', 'glassy wave').

Diction owed much to the regular consorting together of words which had long and fixed associations; indeed, towards the end of the century, John Aikin complained of the phrasal degeneracy compelled by routine combinations of words 'which have so long been coupled together, that, like the hero and his epithet in Homer, they are become inseparable companions'.[29] During the Augustan period, more than in any other, predictability could give a sound gauge of where writing was merely routine or even feckless. As an evil it was not restricted merely to hackneyed turns of phrase but could also be detected in the repetitiveness of rhyme words. Diction skirted with the predictable mainly in its richness of adjectives, a phenomenon best measured by counting the number of a poem's nouns not subject to modification. Take the opening lines of Gray's 'Sonnet on the Death of Richard West':

> In vain to me the smileing Mornings shine,
> And redning Phoebus lifts his golden Fire:
> The Birds in vain their amorous Descant joyn;
> Or chearful Fields resume their green Attire.

Only 'birds' here stands in the raw; each other noun (six in all) is coupled with a more or less formulaic epithet. Getting the right concentration of adjectives was something that critics such as Trapp expressly urged on poets. While epithets are thick on the ground in eighteenth-century poems, they are not generally clustered, though the Miltonic device of adjectivally encircling a substantive ('sad task and hard') had some influence. For the most part, though, adjectives functioned within fairly static binary compounds. Poetry, conceived as enunciating general truths in an arresting manner, was itself a binary phenomenon; and the idea that poetry should simultaneously render the things of the world and diversify them was instrumental within diction.

During the first half of the eighteenth century, epithets were fast going up in the world, as 'engines of mighty use, and conveniency among ... poets'.[30] Both the seventeenth and eighteenth centuries saw a rapid increase in the adjectival stock with the improvising of numerous new adjectives from nouns. Additionally, the Augustan period witnessed the growing availability of poetical dictionaries which guided budding poets in the selection of appropriate modifiers: Joshua Poole's *The English Parnassus* (1657) instigated a vogue for handbooks which listed epithets suitable for use with literally hundreds of different nouns. Handbooks of this sort exploited what the best poets, too, understood—that the ability judiciously to dispose adjectives was the most crucial of poetry's technical hurdles, barely separable, indeed, from the poetic art itself. Pope proclaimed that 'the right use of [epithets] is often the only expedient to render ... narration poetical'; while, typically of the Augustans' alertness to the corruptibility of even the best principles, critics regularly berated the maladroit deployment of adjectives.[31] Trapp claimed nothing to be 'of greater Difficulty, or Moment, in the Poetic Style, than the true Use of Epithets', but also identified as the greatest fault of which a work could be guilty the insertion of epithets 'only to fill up a Verse, when they are entirely idle and useless'.[32] This folly was commonly reprehended, one example being Swift's line in 'On Poetry: A Rapsody' (1733) exposing how the worst poets inserted epithets only 'In gaping Lines to fill a Chink' (l. 168). The duress of regular metrical lines, as well as the fact that epithets could be fished out of poetical dictionaries, means that much that is locally dislikeable in Augustan poems stems from their stale application of adjectives. Gray's friendship with Mason seems to have been placidly untroubled by the obvious disregard he felt for his friend's poetry, yet he might still have done better by Mason's future reputation had he not confided in Norton Nicholls that, when composing, Mason 'never waited for epithets if they did not occur readily but left spaces for them & put them in afterwards'. Gray thought not just the effects to be dispiriting, but the compositional method to be flawed, 'for nothing is done so well as at the first concoction'.[33]

Probably the quintessential dictional device was periphrasis, examples of which abound in the period. Some evidence of its favouritism can be gleaned from examples plucked from just one poem, John Gay's *Rural Sports* (1713): 'feather'd choir' (l. 95), 'verdant mantle' (l. 124), 'finny brood' (l. 127), 'reptile race' (l. 168), 'scaly breed' (l. 173), 'scaly prey' (l. 258), 'thorny brake' (l. 371), 'fleecy care' (l. 399).[34] Such instances reveal the

extent to which eighteenth-century periphrases fixed themselves upon noun-derived -y adjectives, a convergence much
less apparent earlier. Selection of an isolated one or two
dictional traits helps to clarify diction's lengthy genealogy,
something prone to be overlooked, partly as a result of
Johnson's statement that 'there was before the time of Dryden
no poetical diction'.[35] John Arthos's compendious study of the
lexicon of Augustan nature poetry brings to light myriad noun-
formation periphrases in poetry of the previous century, the
principal exponents being Milton, Joshua Sylvester in his
influential translation of Du Bartas's *Divine Weeks*, and
Dryden.[36] Yet epithets constructed with the suffix -y, which
Arthos finds endemic in scientific writing of the period, also
crop up in earlier writing: Shakespeare, for instance, crams
four ('starry', 'testy', 'batty', 'wormy') into a short exchange
between Oberon and Puck in *A Midsummer Night's Dream* (III.
ii. 356–84). That diction was not, in the eighteenth century, a
newly-instigated technique should hardly surprise, granted
that by this time datedness was part and parcel of its appeal.

Critical debate about the efficacy of diction has rested
heavily on appraisal of periphrases as paradigmatic of the
broader dictional agenda. Diction, as something manifestly
constitutive of much Augustan poetry—and debatably irk-
some in some of it—certainly invites some overall appraisal.
Arthur Sherbo, author of the most reliable study of the topic,
grimly cannot get beyond concluding that any poem exhibiting
diction needs strong compensatory features to offset such an
intrinsic set-back; and even Donald Davie's defence of
'chastity', as diffusely a virtue of poetical language, offers such
praise of diction as scarcely avoids prejudicing its larger case.[37]
Defence of diction has made much of the thesis, weightily
corroborated by Arthos, that Augustan poetic language looked
for a quasi-scientific calibre of denotation. Before Arthos's
clinching research, F. W. Bateson had contended that 'the
special vocabulary of poetic diction can be paralleled in the
numerous technical terms of science, philosophy, and politics
that were coined in the eighteenth century'; and he had likened
the periphrastic impulse to call fishes a 'finny tribe' to the
scientific one to coin such a world as 'phlogiston' (1733).[38]

A marked sub-species of Augustan periphrasis involved

nouns of category as 'race', 'breed', 'tribe' etc., and this fact has given some substance to the claim mounted by Arthos that dictional periphrases, with their habitual coupling of one noun with one adjective, operated like the Linnaean system of classification in biology. Looked at under a favourable light, Gay's 'scaly prey', say, has a smaller sub-category fish ('scaly') embedded within the larger one of creatures preyed on by man—all the animals which figure in the poem being shown belonging to this larger category. The efficacy of such periphrases turns on whether in a given circumstance there is some referential and implicative gain from not saying baldly what is being denoted: as 'fish'. Dryden's 'finny Flocks' (*Georgics* IV. 621) or Thomson's 'finny Swarms' ('Autumn', 922), for example, can be viewed as bearing some incremental yield by introducing a sense both of the dense shoals within which fish move and of how, when seen from the angler's vantage, their activity loses itself in a swirl and shimmer of fin movements. Ralph Cohen has adopted an argument of this type in defence of James Thomson, one of the most zealous exponents of periphrases; and his remarks amount to one of the more spirited explications of the quasi-scientific exactness of periphrastic figures:

> 'Lucid moisture' is not an image but a factual description, and in the language of growing nature there was a distinction between 'falling verdure', 'treasures of the clouds', and 'milky nutriment'. The first was an example of the falling shower seen in terms of its natural product— the second was part of a formal contrasting with an informal image and 'milky nutriment' was scientific terminology. Each of these functioned as a special way to achieve poetic meaning, and it [would be] an unfortunate reduction to attribute one function to all these images.[39]

In spite of its local cogency, this does not, in my own opinion, add up to a persuasive case; indeed, its closure with regard to 'function', always a depressingly reductive note, shows the fairly limited stakes for which Cohen is emboldened to play. Notably, the excerpt gives no indication of whether 'falling verdure', 'treasures of the clouds' and the like actually make for good poetry.

The routine collocation of particular epithets and nouns may have owed something to the fact that their grammatical separation was not fully respected until the late eighteenth century.[40] Ephraim Chambers, in his magisterial *Cyclopaedia* (1743), defined 'epithet' as 'a noun adjective, expressing some quality of a substantive to which it is joined'; and, under the head of 'substantive', advised that 'when the object is considered, as clothed with certain qualities, the noun is said to be adjective'. As late as 1762, Robert Lowth felt obliged to set the record straight:

> Adjectives are very improperly called Nouns; for they are not the *Names* of things. The Adjectives *good, white*, are applied to the Nouns *man, snow*, to express the Qualities belonging to those Subjects; but the Names of those Qualities in the Abstract, (that is, considered in themselves, and without being attributed to any Subject) are *goodness, whiteness*; and these are Nouns, or Substantives.[41]

Chambers's gloss has an oddly matrimonial ring: epithet and noun join to make one flesh (the 'noun adjective'); and it should be noted how poetry of our own day, with its much more chancy and irregular combinations of modifier and substantive, could hardly support such a formulation. Seeping through the words of both Chambers and Lowth is also a larger philosophical issue, to do with the relation of attributes to the entities in which they inhere. For example, Lowth's contention that 'blackness' is a noun formed from the adjectival 'black' is not narrowly grammatical, but is an ontological assertion that predicates can be conceived to exist separately from their inherence within substantives.

Amongst early criticis, Joseph Trapp was the one most tenacious in teasing out differing forms of possible relatedness between adjectives and nouns. These are broadly three: first, where an epithet brings out some accidental feature of a substantive, as in the 'black cat'; second, where the attribute is one inherent in the object, as in 'scaly fish'; third, where the duplication between epithet and noun becomes a straight compounding of a single idea, as saying 'hot heat' or 'audible noise'. Trapp summed up the distinction between (2) and (3) on the grounds that although the second group 'border upon the general Nature of their Substantives, expressing . . . some of their inherent Qualities; yet . . . they don't perfectly coincide with them, but express an Idea somewhat different, and yet not totally so': the intended sense probably being that even an inherent feature (as scaliness in fish) will vary in its intrinsic importance to contexts in which its substantive might be invoked.[42] There could, however, be no context in which the audibility of noise would not be integrally understood.

It is a marked feature of dictional usage (and arguably the predominant stylistic trait of Augustan poetry) that poets habitually favour epithets which, in Trapp's words, 'are of near Affinity with the Substantives': that is, have an inherent rather than accidental relation to the nouns they govern.[43] One test-case might be Gray's 'Sonnet on . . . West', which packs six epithet-noun combinations into the first four lines: 'smileing Mornings', 'redning Phoebus', 'golden Fire', 'amorous Descant', 'chearful Fields', 'green Attire'. Amongst these, two epithets ('smileing', 'chearful') are transformed, educing as attributes of the perceived world qualities which reflect the poet's own emotions. The three colour epithets ('redning', 'golden', 'green') are formulaic tags more than modifiers, indicative of a low level of specification; only 'amorous' stays the reader by imparting an accidental: that the birds' song is bent towards mating aspirations rather than perhaps simply being a dawn chorus. Another feature of epithet-noun combinations worth mention, as what may have helped fuel the grammatical confusion surrounding the two parts of speech, is that in such periphrases as 'finny prey' or 'fleecy substitutes', the epithet and noun effectively transpose roles. It is the noun which supplies the narrowing term, for that sheep can be seen as tenants, or fish as prey, are more accidental circumstances than that they have fins and fleeces: the noun qualifies the adjective.

Though diction predates the neo-classical era, discussion of it during the eighteenth century appears to have been influenced by a concurrent philosophical debate concerning the relation between substances and modes. Its advent came with Locke's consideration of substance in the *Essay Concerning Human Understanding* (1690).[44] Locke's main thesis was that the world is constituted by Ideas (simple or complex) drawn from sense impressions, so that our Idea of a horse, say, arises from our impression of the properties coinhering in it: its size, shape, colour and behavioural traits. But Locke did not accept that a horse could be thought to be identical with its several properties, for he postulated the existence of an underlying substratum, or substance, as a medium in which predicates had necessarily to inhere. Substance itself, he contended, was not an Idea, in that it was not susceptible to being known through the senses; yet it still provided the basis on which all entities possess the attributes which distinguish them.

Locke's theory unsurprisingly met with derisive opposition, and from two separate camps. Berkeley charged it with unnecessary duplication in its assertion of the existence both of perceived material entities and of an imperceptible Substance underlying them; and he queried how Locke could possibly know that Substance existed, granted that no sense impression could be had of it. Another philosopher dismissive of the notion was Hume, who argued that entities should be thought of simply as collections of predicates, there being no logical requirement that these inhere in some underlying Substance.[45] What seemed most malformed about the Lockean theory was its stark incompatibility with the rigorous phenomenology of the rest of the *Essay*; yet the slight hint of non-phenomenalism contained in the notion of Substance rankled with several Christian theologians, who felt that the religious repercussions of the concept called for it to have been developed further. Soon after the *Essay*'s appearance, Benjamin Stillingfleet, Bishop of Worcester, entered into a controversialist correspondence with Locke, arguing against his belief that Substance could not be known but only postulated, and pointing out that even the mere supposition of Substance could hardly follow naturally from Locke's own principles.[46] A further confutation of the Lockean theory was given by Isaac Watts in his *Logick* (1726), who asserted that

> It must be confest, when we say ... *Matter is an extended solid Substance*, we are sometimes ready to imagine that *Extension* and *Solidity* are but meer *Modes* and *Properties* of a certain unknown *Substance* or Subject which supports them, and which we call *Body* ... But I rather think this to

be a meer Mistake, which we are led into by the
grammatical Form and Use of Words; and our *logical* Way
of thinking by *Substances* and *Modes*, as well as our
grammatical Way of talking by *Substantives* and *Adjectives*,
delude us into this supposition.[47]

One of Watts's assertions is that Locke's error in not understanding the consubstantial relation between entities and their
predicates could have been fostered, in part, by the taxonomic
rift between substantive and adjective. It would be vain to
suggest that the live philosophical debate about substances
and modes maps neatly on to the dyad of noun and adjective;
for example, in a noun-phrase such as 'black cat', the Lockean
position would insist that not just blackness but felineness, as
a whole, be seen as attributes of underlying Substance. Yet,
whereas adjectives in modern poems tend to the nature of
shafts of light, capriciously let fall on individual facets of
entities, eighteenth-century dictional epithets take heed of the
constitutive relation between things and their properties: a
mindfulness largely brought about by the debate over Lockean
Substance.

   That eighteenth-century culture was enamoured of generalization has itself been an unhelpful one, yet Augustan poetic
diction indisputably owed much to a generalizing habit.
Critics, as a rule, placed a high premium on writing which
addressed what were seen as the inherences rather than the
accidentals of life. Criticism of Shakespeare, in particular, ever
a litmus of larger intellectual dispositions, regularly invoked
this same dichotomy, though towards variable ends. Rymer's
notorious *A Short View Of Tragedy* (1692) impugned Shakespeare's conception of Iago's character as 'a close, dissembling,
false, insinuating rascal, instead of an open-hearted, frank,
plain-dealing Souldier': the artistic felony being Shakespeare's
arbitrary fixing on the inessential feature of one particular
specimen rather than on the inherent attributes of soldiery.[48]
Opposite, though related, was Johnson's much later recommendation of Shakespeare on account of his 'always mak[ing]
nature predominate over accident'.[49] The poetic practice of
diction conforms to the same values as those expressed in
Johnson's observation; and just as Johnson makes Shake-

speare's 'nature' paramount, so diction is perhaps best considered as a poetic notation specifically attuned to the predomination of nature over accident.

II

What, then, of Gray? At the outset, it should be admitted that Gray's extant papers are dispiritingly unopinionated about poetry, and while he often sent poems and criticisms of poems to friends, only the early letters exchanged with the soulful West see him goaded into any protracted elaboration of viewpoint. It is clear, moreover, that Gray took pains to avoid seeming to pontificate about literature, once concluding a letter to Mason thus: 'I have wrote a long letter of *poetry*, wch is tiresome, but I could not help it'.[50] Even his *Common-Place Book*, the one place where his writing can have been largely untroubled by the spectre of a future audience, hardly sheds more light. Far from throwing up any morsels of authorial self-commentary, it shows Gray submerging his creative self within the labour of impersonalized scholarship. It would be wrong to say that Gray's career as a working scholar impeded his writing of poetry, for his grasp of the genealogy of phrases and his handling of mythological material owed everything to a scholarly mentality. Yet the silent zeal of Gray's studying, allied with a general aversion to publicity, probably did much to ensure an effacement of his actual practice as a poet.

Something of what Gray disliked in poetic style can be gathered from part of the *Common-Place Book* given over to drafts for an envisaged literary history of Britain, and specifically devoted to Lydgate. The passage praises Dryden as the poet having done most since the Medieval period to refine the poetic tongue and urges that his example should be mobilized to redress certain abuses 'that time & ill custom have introduced'. These abuses are fourfold: 'the poverty of rhime, the crowd of monosyllables, the collision of harsh consonants, & the want of picturesque expressions'.[51] By 'poverty of rhime', Gray was hinting at numerous originally French polysyllabic words which, in the process of Anglicization, had had the final stress pushed back on to their penultimate syllable, thus making them useless for rhyming; while beneath the label 'harsh consonants', he was exercising a particular grudge against elided preterite forms such as 'stood'st' or 'gav'st'. Setting aside his urging of picturesque expression, the other items making of Gray's bill of complaint give an accurate impression of the fastidious detail with which he habitually responded to poetry. This is consistent with the intensely minute criticism he expended on the poems which Mason self-punitively entrusted to his judgement, poems which were ruthlessly combed for what Gray termed 'inaccuracies of style'.[52]

There is obviously well-founded truth in Gray's remark, made in the course of criticizing Mason's *Caractacus*, that expression was 'always the great point with me'; yet what he allowed to be good expression, and how he believed it might be achieved, are less predictable.[53] For one thing, in spite of Johnson's smear that he was a 'mechanical poet', his method of composing seems not to have been unduly toilsome. His practice apparently was to compose, to some degree of finality, in his head, then setting his lines down in a single stream. He upbraided Mason's habit when words failed to come to him of leaving gaps in his lines and plugging them later with afterthought. Gray alluded to this practice as composing 'at leisure', thinking it dissipated the energy of the writing, and countered it by declaring abruptly that: 'what I say, is true *in my head, whatever it may be in prose*'.[54] The remark calculatedly takes against 'prose', as being a medium always likely to put a cold drench on any stirrings of imaginative life; but there is also an intimation of Gray's ability to carry a poem in his head before getting it down on paper. Ultimately, not enough evidence, as surviving foul papers or corrected proofs, has come down for Gray's practices to be reliably reconstructed; however, the predictable assumption that his allusive style must have made writing ponderously slow should be set against his obvious interest, evident mainly in 'The Bard', in a figure of the poet not just as prophet but as inspired extemporizer. Gray seems to have invested personally in the withdrawn, estranged poet-figure of the earlier work, so it is plausible that he also identified with the bard of the later poem. In any event, one comic side-light is thrown on the technique of extempore recitation by Gray's natty line in impromptu comic epigrams, preserved among the British Museum papers.

On 18 January 1759 Gray wrote to Mason, enclosing corrections of his *Caractacus* and impressing on him some general principles of lyric:

> the true Lyric style with all its flights of fancy, ornaments & heightening of expression, & harmony of sound, is in its nature superior to every other style. wch is just the cause, why it could not be born in a work of great length, no more than the eye could bear to see all this scene, that we constantly gaze upon, the verdure of the fields & woods, the azure of the sea & skies, turn'd into one dazzling expanse of gems.[55]

The idea that a poem's most embellished passages should be interspersed amongst more jejune ones was a commonplace of poetic theory, evident in Dryden's remark on the variability of Milton's epic style, that there are 'flats amongst his elevations'.[56] Yet Gray's wording, over and above this, is pricked by unease about a possible extremity of lyrical aggrandisement, an unease mediated through the run of small taxonomic reinforcements: '*true* Lyric style ... *all* its flights ... *in its nature* superior' (my emphases). In addition to the idea that the lyricism of long poems should be curtailed into discrete passages, the secondary sense is that unabridged lyricism ('with all its flights') might regardless of duration be suspect and unhealthy. The tenor of a surprising number of Gray's recorded remarks is towards extolling poetry that remained free of any surfeit of ornamentation. He could even claim the term 'easiness' as expressive of the stylistic regimen he most admired: 'easiness' had been fairly ubiquitously adopted during the Augustan period as a label for a poetry distinguished by fluency and limpidity, yet also tended to attach to styles that were colloquial and low.

Some indication of Gray's attitude towards the more extreme features of lyric comes from opinions he expressed about Lord Lyttelton's *Monody* (1747). As Lonsdale's edition records, Gray and Lyttelton were to be adventitiously looped together by the mistaken association of Smollett's tactless parody of the *Monody*, under the title *A Sorrowing Ditty; Or, the Lady's Lamentation for the Death of her Favourite Cat*, with Gray's poem of similar subject-matter. The inhumanity of Smollett's electing to parody the poem gives some idea of the provocative nature of the kitsch ornaments of style with which Lyttelton chose to arabesque his wife's memory. The poem's merits were much debated, and it is easy now to see it as occasioning a crux of taste fundamental to mid-century poetics, concerning the need to square the increased vogue for a more private poetic subject-material with the priority still given to impersonally ornamented rhetorical forms. Probably the most stern endorsement of the claim of feeling over that of style was given by Johnson, someone whose own poetry was hardly at the sharp end of the new poetic techniques, when he criticized Milton's *Lycidas* on the grounds that 'passion runs not after remote allusions and obscure opinions'.[57] Gray received a copy of Lyttelton's *Monody* from Walpole and wrote back confessing some pleasure at it, though with the qualification that 'Nature and sorrow, and tenderness, are the true genius of such things' whereas 'poetical ornaments are foreign to the purpose'.[58] Subsequently, he wrote to Wharton, inquisitive about whether he had seen the poem, and remarked that 'there are Parts of it too stiff & poetical; but others truly tender & elegiac, as one would wish'.[59] That Gray should so readily depress 'poetical' to the level of a rebuke, collocating it unabashedly with 'stiff', seems surprising for a poet whose own writing has often been accused of archness and poeticality. Yet the letters of literary correction that Gray sent to friends habitually show him urging avoidance of excesses for which his own poetry has often been taxed. Just one such letter, containing criticisms on Mason's *Caractacus*, gives some impression of the sticking-places of his taste. Gray advises at least one correction on each of the following accounts: images providing unhelpful associations, tautology, repetition, faulty sense of verbal register, false solemnity, shortfall of syllables in a line, surfeit of allegorical figures and ungainly expression.[60] Admittedly, not all of these indicate the enforcement of a definable taste, but the stern monitoring of several forms of poetic affectation belies a poet whose own technique endured such a fraught relation with contemporary canons of literary taste.

Gray believed that the 'true lyric style', a style emboldened
with figurative flights, rhetorical ornamentation and elevated
diction, should be moderated by the interspersal of more
relaxed passages. He urged, for instance, that Mason should
drop from *Caractacus* some of the work's headily personified
abstractions (as 'Resignation', 'Peace', 'Revenge'), recom-
mending that 'a little simplicity ... in the expression would
better prepare the high & fantastic strain ... that follow[s]'.[61]
He also advocated the virtue of conciseness, a quality at odds
with the billowy circumstance generally associated with the
high lyrical vein, contending that 'extreme conciseness of
expression, yet pure, perspicuous, & musical, is one of the
grand beauties of lyric poetry'.[62] Norton Nicholls, moreover,
records a conversation in which Gray attributed Pope's mastery as a poet to the 'art of condensing a thought', an insight
which may have been tinged with wistfulness, for Gray's
epistolary remark on the necessity of concise expression in lyric
tapers off with the abject confession that 'this I have always
aim'd at, & never could attain'.[63]

From the evidence of the letters, it might surprise that
Gray's poems should have proved stylistically controversial,
yet probably no other major poet can in his own day have had
his poetic technique so much quizzed and attacked. Nor did
such criticism begin and end with the late *Odes* (1757), where
Gray by discounting public opinion unwisely made his two
poems a hostage to it. Johnson's robust debunking of Gray's
posthumous reputation began with the 'Ode on the Spring',
seen as marred by its luxuries of style, and also took in the Eton
College ode, where Johnson pinpointed the poet's principal
misapprehension as thinking 'his language more poetical as it
was more remote from common use'.[64] While Johnson
approved of the *Elegy*, Oliver Goldsmith prefaced its inclusion
in his *Beauties of English Poesy* (1767) with the remark that 'This
is a very fine poem, but overloaded with epithet'; and Joseph
Cradock was much later to record in his *Literary and Miscellaneous Memoirs* a skit by Goldsmith on the same poem, which
consisted of the omission of supposedly otiose words:

    The curfew tolls the knell of day,
      The lowing herd winds o'er the Lea;

The plowman homewards plods his way,
      And—[65]

The abuse of epithets amounted to a personal peeve of
Goldsmith's, with much of his animus being patently directed
at Gray. His review of Gray's *Odes* in the *Monthly Review* (1757)
picked out the 'hazardous epithet' as a blemish misguidedly
inherited from Pindar, and he also denigrated the 'pompous
epithet' in a stronger, though unspecific, rebuke, inserted in *An
Enquiry into the Present State of Polite Learning* (1759).[66] The
Pindaric *Odes* unsurprisingly lent themselves to criticism of a
different fervour and magnitude. Benjamin Stillingfleet, later
to come into Gray's acquaintance, writing to a friend shortly
after the poems' publication, denounced them as 'mere
clinquant! verbiage!', and adverted to their 'bombast' and
'gallimawfry style'; while the charge most commonly levelled
against them, that of wanton obscurity, became the principal
ground for a parody, in the style of the 'Burlesque-Sublime',
composed by Robert Lloyd and George Colman.[67]

It is a withering litany of critical aggrievance. Moreover,
these criticisms were not obviously driven by any testy literary
sectarianism (except in the case of Johnson, who evidently had
an aversion to what he knew of Gray's personality). Yet some
accusations, especially those made against the earlier poetry,
ought properly to be rebutted. While one recent critic has
drawn attention to a rhetorical shiftiness in Gray's use of verbs
in the *Elegy*, Goldsmith's concentration on the poem's modifiers (the words left out in the skit) seems more germane to its
technical singularity.[68] This having been said, though, the
simple translation of the period's general suspicion about
epithets on to those in the *Elegy* fails to convince as a grounded
criticism. The words Goldsmith let drop from the *Elegy*'s
opening lines ('parting', 'slowly', 'weary') are, in a strict sense,
semantically dispensable: 'knell' comes already fully invested
with what derives from 'parting', while 'wind' could hardly be
other than 'slowly'. Yet to conclude that what is dispensable is
therefore slack risks misjudging how the *Elegy* works through
skilfully texturing and fortifying a limited repertoire of effects.
The tranquillizing effect of the poem stems not just from the
reiterated certainty of the iambic quatrains but also from the

co-operative nature of the poem's lexis: words of like association being clustered to produce a concerted effect. The
technique is itself complemented by a tight-knit acoustical
pattern produced by alliteration.

Quite how much Goldsmith's criticism was meant to broach
the other major ground for criticizing modifiers, that they were
a soft option for filling out metre, remains unclear; but the
Elegy once more seems readily proof against such an accus-
ation. The disposal of epithets, in fact, provided Gray with an
important means of diversifying cadence. Take the poem's
second stanza:

> Now fades the glimmering landscape on the sight,
> And all the air a solemn stillness holds,
> Save where the beetle wheels his droning flight,
> And drowsy tinklings lull the distant folds.

> (ll. 5–8)

Again, Gray's adjectives are those of semantic reinforcement:
'fades' and 'sight' in the first line together induce that an apt
adjective should be 'glimmering', a word compact of both
ideas. The stanza's nouns and noun phrases actually run as
follows: epithet + noun, noun; noun, ep. + noun; noun, ep. +
noun; ep. + noun, ep. + noun. Such a sequence is not abstract
but meaningfully mimetic, in that a slight imbalance is
actuated in the first three lines through the internal situating of
noun against noun phrase, then giving way, in the last line, to a
calmative settling and balance: a syntactical effect feigning the
poem's overt drift from the world of diurnal fretfulness into
meditative tranquillity. Other examples could easily be given
of Gray's studied positioning both of epithets and of other
parts of speech as a means of modulating cadence. The first
line-ending of the poem, for example, 'parting day / The lowing
herd . . .', conjoins two participial adjective + noun combinations, making the cadence flex back on itself: the syntax's
own self-reiteration feeding into the stanza's overt sense of a
weary culmination being brought to day's routine pattern.

III

The remainder of this essay will defend Gray's poetic diction, as evident in poems up to 1747, in terms consistent with those used of the single part of speech: I will suggest that what might appear merely as a compositional rote becomes instead a flexible medium of poetic drama. The word 'defend' I use advisedly, for the *quality* of Gray's poetry remains an issue, and not merely because of his mixed contemporary reception and his subsequent subjection to the Romantic denigration of the poetic generation preceding their own. What troubles Gray's current reputation continues to be his engrossed allegiance to diction, something that nowadays can easily look like a misplaced faith. Granted the low esteem in which dictional poetry is generally held today, Gray tends to be seen as a poet who transcends the limitation intrinsic to his technique. The proximity of Gray's own *oeuvre* to what contemporaneously was poetically bad has, in fact, been addressed too little, and this omission is likely to be sustained by our current squeamishness about judgemental criticism. Yet by the mid-eighteenth century, diction did not just connote an august antecedent tradition but also a present mediocrity: it had become the badge of an enfeebled belles-lettrism. Gray would have been familiar with the mostly tepid affectations of Shenstone, Gilbert West, Lord Lyttelton and the like, but the body of third-rate verse he knew best belonged to William Mason. From 1751 until his death, Gray entered into a very reciprocal literary camaraderie with Mason, whose work he read and from whom he elicited criticism, in spite of Mason's palpable poetic inferiority. It was a liaison across the talent divide that could hardly have been conceived of in the fractious meritocracy of Scriblerian London. Mason's *Elegies*, indeed, make for a monument to the particular precipices of artistic failure over which, as a dictional poet, Gray himself trod. The common picture of Gray's contribution to literary history has been of his taking a tradition of high stylization and refining it into decadence, but his artistic success can also be seen as an alchemizing of the bad. Whereas, in the hands of Mason, diction becomes a recipe for the stilted and shop-worn, Gray's early poems assimilate it as an unlikely strength, creating their distinctive effect: we wonder quite why they should impress us, and suspect that their graces are, perhaps, only ever saving ones.

Diction, as well as being a repertoire of stylistic devices, also bespoke a mentality, both artistic and broader than the merely artistic. It is clarified by an epitaph composed by Mason after the death of his wife in 1767, a poem especially interesting for its dictional stylizing of grief:

> TAKE, holy earth! all that my soul holds dear:
>> Take that best gift which Heav'n so lately gave:
> To Bristol's fount I bore with trembling care
>> Her faded form: she bow'd to taste the wave,
> And died. Does Youth, does Beauty, read the line?
>> Does sympathetic fear their breasts alarm?
> Speak, dead MARIA! breathe a strain divine:
>> E'en from the grave thou shalt have power to charm.
> Bid them be chaste, be innocent, like thee;
>> Bid them in Duty's sphere as meekly move;
> And if so fair, from vanity as free;
>> As firm in friendship, and as fond in love.
> Tell them, though 'tis an awful thing to die,
>> ('Twas ev'n to thee) yet the dread path once trod,
> Heav'n lifts its everlasting portals high,
>> And bids 'the pure in heart behold their GOD.'[69]

Mason suffered the indignity, having sent a first draft to Gray, of finding the conclusion scrubbed out ('That will never do for an ending'), and replaced with four lines of Gray's, now standing at the end. Not all parts of the poem's rhetorical orchestration concern diction, but all effects strain for a radiantly pious commemoration. The poem divides about two rhetorical invocations 'TAKE, holy earth!' (l. 1) and 'Speak, dead MARIA!' (l. 7). Other architectonic ploys are the rhetorical questions of lines 6–7 and the anaphora 'TAKE ... Take' (ll. 1–2), 'Bid ... Bid' (ll. 9–10). What can be attributed to diction are the extended periphrases circumlocuting his deceased wife: 'all that my soul holds dear', 'that best gift which Heav'n so lately gave' (ll. 1–2); the incidence of dictional words as 'fount', 'bore', 'taste', 'wave', 'breasts'; and the presence of epithet-noun compounds where the modifier adduces some invariable quality in the substantive, as 'trembling care' and 'sympathetic fear' (ll. 3, 6). The epitaph gives the impression of having been cooked up by recipe, but is also culpable of only imperfectly realizing the experience it purports to describe. 'Taste the wave', for instance, is slack not merely because of its near-annexing of two dictional terms, but because the effect of those terms blurs whether Mrs Mason went to Bristol to bathe in the waters or to drink them: biographical evidence, in fact, says the latter, in which case 'wave' for 'water' is a misnomer. Sadly, this is not the sole instance where diction actually baulks what the poem halfheartedly imagines, or prods the reader into constructions that are luridly inapposite. Take 'To Bristol's fount I bore . . . / Her faded form': 'bore' is chosen here because of its soft heroicizing and its avoidance of the ungainliness of travel details; but the word's physicality, reinforced by mention of his wife's 'form', only allows to flicker the inapt image of a physical lugging. Worse still is 'she bow'd to taste the wave, / And died', where not just 'bow'd' and 'taste' but the facilely histrionic line-drop ('And died') dictate a sense of Mrs Mason's having expired verily between the cup and lip of her final draught.

The poem's aggregative effects make for a sentimental whitewash. Mrs Mason's death speaks to 'Youth' and 'Beauty', though she was not very young and Gray once remarked cruelly that the Masons' match had been made on the grounds that Mrs Mason had a nose as big as her husband's.[70] Mason's 'Epitaph' epitomizes two attitudes which generally characterize the application of diction. First, it records experience in essentially aesthetic terms: not just is the poem's central device an envisaged prosopopoeia, where the dead wife is inspirited into moralizing for the benefit of the living, but its phraseology, too, is detachedly artistic. Mrs Mason's parlous health deteriorated terminally during the winter of 1766–67, inducing Mason to write to Gray about the harsh weather's baleful effect: 'It nipt her as it would have done a flower half witherd'.[71] The cool figuring of her dying seems dispassionate, but it bespeaks a sensibility for which a brand of aestheticism, even *in extremis*, was second-nature. The epitaph's preciosity, however, has nothing to do with a sensitivity that was rarefied or even especially individual. Mason had earlier responded to the death of a close friend by declaring to Gray 'O Mr Gray how dreadful is it to sit besides a Dying Friend!'; and the tendency to generalize a sentiment, to put aside the personal contingencies of a case, figures also in the 'Epitaph'.[72] The eclipsing from it of any detail as to the nature of Mrs Mason's illness or dying was meant to make the poem affective on the same ground as that on which Johnson praised Gray's 'Elegy', namely that 'every bosom returns an echo'.[73]

Significantly, Gray's ending quatrain, though itself a posy verse, strikes a different note: ''tis an awful thing to die,/ ('Twas ev'n to thee)'. The bracket is a daring acknowledgement of how easily the anguish of the dying can become parenthetical to the lessons their deaths teach us. Moreover, the parenthesis, with its short, wrested intimacy between living and dead, is the mirror image of what the entire epitaph might have been—but falls short of. Gray's own dealings with death were likely to make him distrustful of the tidy sanctimony of Mason's 'Epitaph', and tell us much about how diction figures in his early poems. In particular, he had been harshly schooled in the untidiness that affairs of mortality could assume. He was mortified to have heard of his beloved West's death only through browsing upon a poetic obituary by their mutual friend, Thomas Ashton, and complained that his own letter had been returned unopened without any indication that the intended recipient had died.[74] Gray was evidently shaken by having unwittingly sent correspondence to a dead man, and, when asked by Walpole in 1747 to compose a poem on the death of one of his cats, he wrote back a poignantly comic letter on the need for accurate information about mortalities: 'As one ought to be particularly careful to avoid blunders in a compliment of condolence, it would be a sensible satisfaction to me ... to know for certain, who it is I lament'.[75]

Mason's epitaph epitomizes most of diction's biases: towards tableau, flourish, pathetic sentimentality, the reification of surface at the expense of depth, and an avoidance of pluralism or irony. In Mason's hands, it is a way of writing that foregoes certain conditions of mind: complexity, ambivalence, quizzicality, self-irony. Where Gray differs from Mason is that rather than employing diction to curtail a range of experience, he habitually uses it to record, and inhabit, his own ambivalence. Gray had a peculiar ability to situate himself on the very cusp of an incertitude, to balance on the horn of a dilemma; and this temperamental facet more than anything governs the orchestration of his poems. One of his finest pieces, neither a poem nor dictional, illustrates my point: this is his letter to Mason on his wife's death. Yet it was not exactly a condoling letter, for Gray wrote it in ignorance of whether Mrs Mason still lived:

> I BREAK in upon you at a moment, when we least of all are permitted to disturb our Friends, only to say, that you are daily & hourly present to my thoughts. if the *worst* be not yet past: you will neglect & pardon me. but if the last struggle be over: if the poor object of your long anxieties be no longer sensible to your kindness, or to her own sufferings: allow me (at least in idea, for what could I do, were I present, more than this?) to sit by you in silence, & pity from my heart not her, who is at rest; but you, who lose her. may He, who made us, the Master of our pleasures, & of our pains, preserve & support you! Adieu
>
> I have long understood, how little you had to hope.[76]

The mere sending of the letter, while the matter was so in doubt, was a fine thing; and the letter's mastery of its task is equally a triumph of humanity. It expresses both the due propriety of condolence platitudes (as being 'with someone' in their grief) and also their shortfall (for what is meant or served by saying such?), of the claim of etiquette (the need not to intrude on a grief) and the higher claim of friendship. But the risk of the letter was not to comply with grief but to tease it out of itself, by stressing its paradoxicality: to insist that Mason's wife, while 'no longer sensible to [his] kindness' was now released also from 'her own sufferings', that to bereave is not to pity the dead but to pity the living, therefore becoming a form of self-pity. Nor were these anodynes glibly handed down, for Gray had come to a recognition of grief's futile self-fixation when himself bereft over the death of West: 'My lonely Anguish melts no Heart, but mine; / And in my Breast the imperfect Joys expire'. Gray's letter, on its own, substantiates a claim for his literary stature; but, more particularly, it reveals a mental constitution that also embodied itself in the use made of diction in his early poetry. What characterizes the letter is a wariness of cheap consolatory adages, a finical weighing of the currency of condolence, and a scrupulous observance of what might be said on each side of the case. Yet from the shuffling tip-toe of dubieties and retractions ('if . . . but if . . . if . . . at least in Idea . . . not her . . . but you') emerges a sternly vigilant sympathy. Some of Gray's early poems are also of this order: showing a proclivity to 'situate' opinions without firmly endorsing them; and in such poems, the provisional status of viewpoints is often registered by diction.

For some time, it has been a commonplace of Gray criticism that his poems work dialogically; such poems as 'Ode on the Spring', 'Ode on a Distant Prospect of Eton College' and 'Sonnet on the Death of Richard West' are dramatic by dint of counterpoising viewpoints.[77] This format is another arguable shortcoming of Gray's poetry. His poems, however fearless in facing up to dubieties, are often non-committal, being merely concerned to accredit the existence of viewpoints rather than to opt for one or the other. In the early poems, where diction occurs only in one part, it dramatizes the distance between the rival outlooks a poem encompasses. One such poem is 'Ode on the Spring', a fifty-line work, comprising thirty lines attributed to a 'Contemplation' figure, a hinge-passage of twelve lines belonging to the narrator, and eight concluding lines voiced by the 'sportive kind'. The opening stanza suggests effects endemic throughout the first thirty:

> LO! where the rosy-bosom'd Hours,
> Fair VENUS' train appear,
> Disclose the long-expecting flowers,
> And wake the purple year!
> The Attic warbler pours her throat,
> Responsive to the cuckow's note,
> The untaught harmony of spring:
> While whisp'ring pleasure as they fly,
> Cool Zephyrs through the clear blue sky
> Their gather'd fragrance fling.
>
> (ll. 1–10)

The style is thickly enamelled, and rich in specific allusion. Dictional traits are the exclamatory opening; the compound epithets 'rosy-bosom'd', 'long-expecting'; the periphrases 'purple year' (for spring), 'Attic warbler' (for nightingale); and the occurrence of individual dictional words, such as 'train', 'Disclose' and 'Zephyrs'. After line 30, when the Contemplation figure's viewpoint ceases to be represented, dictional traits get thinner on the ground: one simple quantification being that there are six compound forms in the first thirty lines and none thereafter. Poetic diction is used to elaborate the opinion that human activity should be seen as futile against the brute fact of human temporality. This is then countered by an alternative viewpoint, not one that is actually its mirror-opposite, that a life spent inactively has small claim to be considered any less futile. The poem begins by eliding diction with a fatalism seen as self-indulgent, the contemplative cynic himself confessing to a smug recumbency: '(At ease reclin'd in rustic state)' (l. 17). Diction, in one sense, acts as a set of attitudinal quotation marks, separating the words of the contemplative voice from the rest of the poem; but diction also has an aptness to the cosy, truistical pessimism being voiced, the small petrifactions of style complementing the petrified cynicism of Contemplation's thought.

The poem, like other early ones, never troubles to decide between its two perspectives: it is not the case that the second supersedes, or even rounds out, the first. For one thing, the 'sportive kind' contribute only ephemerally at the end ('Poor moralist! and what art thou? / A solitary fly!' (ll. 43–44)), and the mockery of the contemplative position in terms suggestive of authorial self-mockery also tells against the assumption that the poem's ending categorically puts to rout what has passed earlier on. Moreover, the fatalistic tone established at the poem's outset is never queried, so that the greater buoyancy of the end still only reads like a loss-cutting exercise. This is characteristic also of 'Ode on a Distant Prospect of Eton College', which never questions whether adult life might hold anything other than horrors but merely queries whether children should be told of the dreadful things in store. That Gray's poems stay unresolved implies that their ordering is dispassionately diagrammatic, but the letter on the death of

Mason's wife suggests that a vigilant indecision, a cautious deferral of opinion, could itself be consolatory: that the mind might be tranquillized by its own unresolve.

Gray seems not to have associated diction with the elaboration of any fixed viewpoint but merely as a sign of an opinion's contingent status. *Ode on ... Eton College* again splits between alternative viewpoints: the first reflecting nostalgically on childhood innocence, and the second brooding over the litany of miseries which childhood inherits. That the poem divides in attitude exactly around its mid-point (l. 51) indicates the scrupulous balance Gray tried to maintain between its rival conceptions. As Steve Clark has remarked,[78] the poem's first half contains some of the most studied diction in all of Gray:

> Say, Father THAMES, for thou hast seen
> Full many a sprightly race
> Disporting on thy margent green
> The paths of pleasure trace,
> Who foremost now delight to cleave
> With pliant arm thy glassy wave?
> The captive linnet which enthrall?
> What idle progeny succeed
> To chase the rolling circle's speed,
> Or urge the flying ball?
> (ll. 21–30)

The harder task would be to say what elements are not dictional. The stanza embraces elaborate periphrases: 'rolling circle's speed' (a hoop), 'glassy wave'; the revival of a Latin root-meaning in 'pliant'; archly dictional words, such as 'race', 'Disporting', 'enthrall', 'progeny'; and one good example of the switching of natural place between epithet and noun, 'green bank' becoming 'margent green'. The aggrandizements of style so much exceed the subject of their expenditure as to border on mock-heroic. Moreover, just as heroi-comical poems tended to alight on artefacts as fixed points against which their stylistic dilations could be measured, so Gray seizes on the boys' hoop for a bravura periphrasis of his own, 'rolling circle's speed'. The tone, with its flickering of mock-heroic, recalls Gay's *Trivia*, with its own genteel coinages, such as 'harden'd Orbs' (II. 329) for snowballs.

Though the poem's second half does contain a string of personifications ('Misfortune', 'Anger', 'Fear' etc.), its style is generally plainer, the drop of register being immediately evident:

> Alas, regardless of their doom,
> The little victims play!
> No sense have they of ills to come,
> Nor care beyond to-day:
> Yet see how all around 'em wait
> The Ministers of human fate,
> And black Misfortune's baleful train!
>
> (ll. 51–57)

The curtness mimics an unnerving gratulation ('see how all around 'em wait'); while 'regardless of their doom, / The little victims play!' rings unhappily like the tacit confederacy of adults in some ghastly initiation rite. Unlike 'Ode on the Spring', diction elides with the more optimistic view given in the poem, its adornments of style registering a sense of the glassy fragility of an idyll. Style and argument tend to be closely dovetailed in Gray's poems, such that it might be seen to compromise the poem's success with diction that the arguments it helps to describe often seem crude or immature. 'Ode on . . . Eton College' seems vitiated by the fact that the initial rendering of childhood is tainted by adult sentimentality, and its subsequent forewarnings of traumatic adulthood are hysterically childish. The first part smacks of a virulent form of moist-eyed, ex-schoolboy nostalgia, while the rampant bogeymen conjured up in the poem's second half seem like the figments of a child's imagining.

The poems of Gray's which have interested me in this essay are those early ones where diction is confined to a single elaborated viewpoint, and where it invests the poems with a structure of disputation. These, though, are not the only poems where diction is used. 'Ode on the Death of a Favourite Cat' (1747) is a mock-heroic, distinguished by heavily schematized grandiloquences of style and allusion. Gray's two Pindaric *Odes* (1757) provide another case again, being poems constituted along the lines of a specific, though widely misunderstood, poetic kind. In 1752, Gray gave notice to Walpole of the

possibility of 'The Progress of Poesy' being ready for inclusion
in Dodsley's *Miscellany*, saying that 'I don't know but I may
send him very soon (by our hands) an ode to his own tooth, a
high Pindarick upon stilts'.[79] Forced by public incompre-
hension to add to the 1768 edition of the *Odes* an extensive
commentary, Gray noted that Poesy's progress had the effect of
'enriching every subject (otherwise dry and barren) with a
pomp of diction and luxuriant harmony of numbers'.[80] For
several reasons, though, the late *Odes* fall outside the narrower
ambit of this essay. For one thing, they are poems within which
the heroic is not merely a spectre raised by style but a
constitutive reality; while the contingency of the Pindaric form
itself, Gray's arguable concern to revive ancient Welsh metrical forms, the self-conscious breeding of 'florid expressions',
and, crucially, the fashioned inaccessibility of the poems (an
ingredient antithetical to traditional diction) all distance the
poems from those of Gray's earlier career.

I want to conclude, instead, by commenting on Gray's most
controversial exercise in diction, his 'Sonnet on the Death of
Richard West':

> In vain to me the smileing Mornings shine,
> And red'ning Phoebus lifts his golden Fire:
> The Birds in vain their amorous Descant joyn;
> Or chearful Fields resume their green Attire:
> These Ears, alas! for other Notes repine,
> A different Object do these Eyes require.
> My lonely Anguish melts no Heart, but mine;
> And in my Breast the imperfect Joys expire.
> Yet Morning smiles the busy Race to chear,
> And new-born Pleasure brings to happier Men:
> The Fields to all their wonted Tribute bear:
> To warm their little Loves the Birds complain:
> I fruitless mourn to him, that cannot hear,
> And weep the more, because I weep in vain.

Despite Roger Lonsdale's perception of 'the satisfying unity
and balance of the poem's form', the sonnet's constitution
seems curiously maladroit.[81] It institutes two separate issues:
first, the relation of the mourning poet to nature (ll. 1–6, 9–12);
second, the futility always incident to grief, because the object

of a person's mourning is no longer sensible to it. The intertwining of the two is syntactically hapless. Line 9, for example, states a contra-distinction ('Yet . . .') which can only become intelligible if the reader leaps back across the immediately previous sentence to the opening one about the poet's indifference to nature: 'I may be indifferent to the spring, *yet* it still comes around.' When Wordsworth criticized the poem's diction, the lines he exempted from reproach were 6–8 and 13–14. Although the detail could easily be quibbled over ('fruitless mourn' in line 13 has a Miltonic substitution of adjective for adverb, with inversion of natural word-order), this division of the poem's style is in rough accord with its two distinct subjects. Like other early poems, the 'Sonnet' is made up of opinions that are differentiated by style but not ultimately decided between. Roger Lonsdale rejects that the dictional passages might be 'ironic', curiously thinking this incompatible with Gray's use of diction being 'serious', and suggests instead that the cheery anthropomorphic epithets are ultimately justified as an antidote to grief.[82] Yet for a poet so ready as Gray to embrace complexities, the 'serious' and 'ironic' were invariably one. As elsewhere in Gray, the 'Sonnet' tries to succour the mind by suspending it between alternatives. The lure of diction is for a rhetorical self-estrangement: a constructed but, at the same time, self-alienated image of a grief. The lines composed in diction reflect the dismay that can compound a grief, when a mourner recognizes the world's blank indifference to any one individual's plight. But the possibility of indifference, of the dead's indifference to our sentiments about them, then becomes a countering consolation. It is diction that helps the mind better to know, and to mark, the possibilities for response, and, by division, better to heal itself.

NOTES

1. *Lyrical Ballads*, ed. R. L. Brett and A. R. Jones (London, 1965), 'Preface' (1800), p. 252.

2. *Correspondence*, 27August 1756, II, 477.

3. See Roger Lonsdale, 'Gray and "Allusion": The Poet as Debtor', in

Studies in the Eighteenth Century IV, ed. R. F. Brissenden and J. C. Eade (Canberra, 1979), pp. 31–55.

4. *Lyrical Ballads*, pp. 241–72. See also 'Appendix on Poetic Diction'(1802), pp. 314–18; and *Biographia Literaria*, Chapter 18, in *The Collected Works of Samuel Taylor Coleridge: 7*, ed. J. Engell and W. J. Bate, Bollingen Series LXXV (London and New York, 1983), ii, 73–76.

5. See 'Poetry in the Eighteenth Century', in *The New Pelican Guide to English Literature Vol. 4: From Dryden to Johnson*, ed. B. Ford(London, 1982), pp. 228–29.

6. *Rambler* 168 (26 October 1751), in *The Yale Edition of the Works of Samuel Johnson* (New Haven, 1958–), V, ed. W. J. Bate and Albrecht B. Strauss (1969), p. 124.

7. *Lyrical Ballads*, p. 251. For general treatment of diction, see Winifred Nowottny, *The Language Poets Use* (London, 1962), pp. 26–48.

8. 'Preface' to *Sylvae: or the Second Part of Poetical Miscellanies* (1685), in *Of Dramatic Poesy and other Critical Essays*, ed. G. Watson, 2 vols (London, 1962), II, 31.

9. 'Preface' to *Fables Ancient and Modern* (1700), in Watson, ed., II, 275; *The Advancement and Reformation of Modern Poetry* (1701), in *The Critical Works of John Dennis*, ed. Edward Hooker (Baltimore, 1939), I, 215; *Remarks upon Mr. Pope's Translation of Homer* (1717), in ibid., II,123.

10. 'Preface' to the *Iliad* (1715), in *The Poems of Alexander Pope*, ed. J. Butt *et al.*, 13 vols (London, 1938–68), VII, 10.

11. *Critical Works*, I, 215.

12. Joseph Trapp, *Lectures on Poetry*, trans. W. Bowyer and W. Clarke (1742), p. 42.

13. James Beattie, 'Essay on Poetry', Sect. II. 'Natural language is improved in poetry by the use of Poetical words', in *Essays on Poetry and Music* (1783), p. 514.

14. 'On Poetry, As Distinguished from Other Writing', *British Magazine*, 1761–63, erroneously attributed to Goldsmith and printed in *Works* (Turk's Head Edition, 1908), VII, 338–51; 'Life of Collins', in *Lives of the English Poets*, ed. G. Birkbeck Hill, 3 vols (Oxford, 1905), III, 341.

15. *Lives*, I, 420.

16. See 'Notes on *The Pleasures of Imagination*', 'L': 'This similitude is the foundation of almost all the ornaments of poetic diction', in *The Poetical Works of Mark Akenside*, ed. Rev. George Gilfillan (Edinburgh, 1857), p. 53.

17. See 'Advertisement' to *The Castle of Indolence* (1748), in *James Thomson: 'Liberty', 'The Castle of Indolence' and Other Poems*, ed. J. Sambrook (Oxford, 1986), p. 173: 'THIS Poem being writ in the Manner of *Spenser*, the obsolete Words, and a Simplicity of Diction in some of the Lines, which borders on the Ludicrous, were necessary to make the Imitation more perfect'. See also Pope's letter to Ralph Bridges, 5 April 1708: 'The great Beauty of Homer's Language, as I take it, consists in that noble simplicity, which runs through all his works; (and yet his diction, contrary to what one would imagine consistent with simplicity, is at the same time very Copious.)'. Cited from *The Correspondence of Alexander Pope*, ed. G. Sherburn, 5 vols (Oxford, 1956), I, 44.

18. *The Miscellaneous Works of Joseph Addison*, ed. A. C. Guthkelch, 2 vols

(London, 1914), I, 8; see David Hansen, 'Addison on Ornament and Poetic Style', in *Studies in Criticism and Aesthetics 1660–1800: Essays in Honor of Samuel Holt Monk*, ed. Howard Anderson and John J. Shea (Minneapolis, 1967), pp. 94–127.

19. *Classical Literary Criticism*, trans. T. S. Dorsch (London, 1965), p. 111.

20. *Guardian*, 28 March 1713, in *The Guardian*, ed. J. C. Stephens (Kentucky, 1982), pp. 84–85; *Correspondence*, November 1747, I, 289.

21. Watson, ed., II, 252.

22. *Correspondence*, c. 12 April 1742, I, 195.

23. 'Postscript' to the *Odyssey*, in *Poems*, X, 390.

24. *Correspondence*, 4 April 1742, I, 190.

25. Ibid., 8 April 1742, I, 192.

26. *Thomas Gray's Common-Place Book*, 3 vols, Pembroke College Library (unclassified), II, 745.

27. *Essays*, p. 515.

28. Ibid., pp. 518–25.

29. John Aikin, *An Essay on the Application of Natural History to Poetry* (1777), pp. 5–6.

30. Ephraim Chambers, *Cyclopaedia: Or, Universal Dictionary of Arts and Sciences* (1743), under 'Epithet'.

31. 'Postscript' to the *Odyssey*, in *Poems*, X, 387.

32. *Lectures*, pp. 69, 76.

33. *Correspondence*, Appendix Z, 'Norton Nicholls's Reminiscences of Gray', III, 1293–94.

34. Cited from *John Gay: Poetry and Prose*, ed. V. A. Dearing and C. E. Beckwith, 2 vols (Oxford, 1974).

35. 'Life of Dryden', in *Lives*, I, 420.

36. John Arthos, *The Language of Natural Description in Eighteenth-Century English Poetry* (Ann Arbor, 1949). See also V. L. Rubel, *Poetic Diction in the Early Renaissance from Skelton through Spenser* (New York, 1941).

37. Arthur Sherbo, *English Poetic Diction from Chaucer to Wordsworth* (Michigan, 1975), p. 165; Donald Davie, *Purity of Diction in English Verse* (London, 1952). See also Thomas Quayle, *Poetic Diction: A Study of Eighteenth Century Verse* (London, 1924); Bernard Groom, *The Diction of Poetry from Spenser to Bridges* (Toronto, 1955); Geoffrey Tillotson, *Augustan Studies* (London, 1961); and P. W. K. Stone, *The Art of Poetry 1750–1820* (London, 1967).

38. F. W. Bateson, *English Poetry and the English Language: An Experiment in Literary History* (Oxford, 3rd ed., 1973), p. 55.

39. Ralph Cohen, *The Art of Discrimination: Thomson's 'The Seasons' and the Language of Criticism* (London, 1964), pp. 327–28. Also pp. 315–80, passim.

40. See Ian Michael, *English Grammatical Categories and the Tradition to 1800* (Cambridge, 1970), pp. 295–97.

41. Robert Lowth, *A Short Introduction to English Grammar* (1762), pp. 40–41.

42. *Lectures*, p. 72.

43. Ibid.

44. See *Essay concerning Human Understanding*, Book II, Chapter XII, Section 6; see Peter Alexander, 'Locke on Substance-in-General: Part 1', *Ratio*, XXII (December 1980), 91–105.

45. George Berkeley, *A Treatise concerning the Principles of Human Understanding* (1710), Part I, Sections 16 and 17; David Hume, *A Treatise of Human Nature* (1739), I.i.6 'Of Modes and Substances'.

46. See John Yolton, *John Locke and the Way of Ideas* (Oxford, 1956), pp. 132–40.

47. Cited from ibid., p. 147.

48. *The Critical Works of Thomas Rymer*, ed. Curt A. Zimansky (New Haven, 1956), p. 135.

49. 'Preface' to *Shakespeare* (1765), in *Works*, ed. Arthur Sherbo, VII, 65.

50. *Correspondence*, June 1757, II, 507.

51. *Common-Place Book*, II, 745.

52. *Correspondence*, 14 February 1768, III, 1007.

53. Ibid., 28 September 1757, II, 528.

54. Ibid., 13 January 1758, II, 552.

55. Ibid., 18 January 1759, II, 608.

56. Watson, ed., II, 32.

57. *Lives*, I, 163.

58. *Correspondence*, November 1747, I, 289.

59. Ibid., I, 293.

60. Ibid., 18 January 1759, II, 605–10.

61. Ibid., II, 608.

62. Ibid., 13 January 1758, II, 551.

63. Ibid., III, 1292; II, 551.

64. *Lives*, III, 435.

65. *Collected Works of Oliver Goldsmith*, ed. A. Friedman, 5 vols (Oxford, 1966), V, 320.

66. Ibid., I, 114, 317.

67. See R. W. Ketton-Cremer, *Thomas Gray: A Biography* (Cambridge, 1955), pp. 154, 176–77.

68. George Watson, 'The voice of Gray', *Critical Quarterly*, XIX (Winter 1977), 51–57. See also W. Hutchings, 'Syntax of Death: Instability in Gray's *Elegy Written in a Country Churchyard*', *Studies in Philology*, 81 (Fall 1984), 496–514.

69. Cited from *Poems by William Mason, M.A.*, 4th ed. (1774), p. 65.

70. See *Correspondence*, 25 October 1764, II, 848.

71. Ibid., III, 950.

72. The friend was Dr Marmaduke Pricket; ibid., 23 September 1753, I, 382.

73. *Lives*, III, 441.

74. *Correspondence*, 17 June 1742, I, 213.

75. Ibid., *c*. 22 February 1747, I, 271.

76. Ibid., 28 March 1767, III, 953.

77. See F. Doherty, 'The Two Voices of Thomas Gray', *Essays in Criticism*, 13 (July 1963), 222–30; and P. M. Spacks, *The Poetry of Vision* (Cambridge, Mass., 1967), pp. 90–118.

78. S. H. Clark, '"Pendet Homo Incertus": Gray's Response to Locke. Part One: "Dull in a New Way"', *Eighteenth-Century Studies*, 24 (Spring 1991), 287.

79. *Correspondence*, August? 1752, I, 364.

80. *The Poems of Gray, Collins and Goldsmith*, ed. Roger Lonsdale (London, 1969), p. 161.

81. Ibid., p. 67.

82. Ibid., p. 66.

Gray's Humorous and Satirical Verse

T. W. CRAIK

'Gray never wrote anything easily but things of humour: humour was his natural and original turn.' Walpole's remark recalls Johnson's pronouncement that Shakespeare, unfettered by rules or traditions, 'indulged his natural disposition, and his disposition ... led him to comedy. In tragedy he often writes with great appearance of toil and study, what is written at last with little felicity; but in his comick scenes, he seems to produce without labour, what no labour can improve.' This in its turn recalls Johnson's objection to Gray's odes ('His art and his struggle are too visible, and there is too little appearance of ease and nature'); but Johnson shows no corresponding indulgence to Gray's lighter works, of which he mentions only two, 'an odd composition called *A Long Story*, which adds little to Gray's character', and the 'poem on the Cat', which, he says, 'was doubtless by its author considered as a trifle, but it is not a happy trifle'.[1]

Not that much more of Gray's humorous and satirical verse was available for Johnson's attention. At the time of Gray's death in 1771, nothing further of this kind had been published except (in 1769, without his authorization) the satirical quatrains 'On Lord Holland's Seat near Margate, Kent'. Mason's biography and edition of 1775 added only two pieces, the 38-line fragment known as 'Hymn to Ignorance' and the six-line 'Sketch of His Own Character'. The vigorous satire on the Earl of Sandwich, 'The Candidate', of which Walpole sent Mason a text in 1774, presumably arrived too late to be included, but in February 1777 it was published in the *London Evening Post*, where Johnson could have read it. The rest of Gray's extant humorous and satirical verse, all published after the appearance of Johnson's *Lives of the Poets*, amounts to little more than 150 lines. According to his Oxford editors of 1966, 'Mason saw fit to destroy much of this verse and thus has obscured the toughness of soul and satirical, often ribald, humour that Gray's more serious works do not reveal'.[2] How destructive of Gray's lighter verse Mason was I do not know (his irresponsible treatment of Gray's correspondence is notorious), but it seems unlikely that anything he destroyed can have differed substantially from what survives.

Gray's light verse was usually of a topical and occasional character. Such was his earliest extant original poem, inappropriately known as 'Lines Spoken by the Ghost of John Dennis at the Devil Tavern' and forming part of a reply to a versified letter that he had received from Walpole. Gray begins his letter as follows:

> I (tho' I say it) had too much modesty to venture answering your dear, diverting Letter, in the Poetical Strain myself: but, when I was last at the DEVIL [i.e. the Devil Tavern in Fleet Street, though Gray writes from Cambridge], meeting by chance with the deceased Mr Dennis there, he offer'd his Service, &, being tip'd with a Tester, wrought, what follows—[3]

Dennis had died recently enough (eleven months before) for his ghost to be topically invoked; he was for Gray and Walpole, as he had been for Swift and Pope, the type of the literary hack—and hence ready to compose 51 lines for sixpence. The seventeen-year-old Gray may seem heartlessly merry at the expense of the seventy-seven-year-old Dennis. Perhaps his self-disparagement (for being only able to write Walpole a hack's poem) excuses him; perhaps his self-approval (for writing so well in the hack vein) does not. At any rate, there are touches that recall the Dryden of *MacFlecknoe* ('Where ghostly Rats their habitations keep, l. 20) and the Pope of *The Rape of the Lock*: Dennis's soul arrives in 'a mead of Asphodel':

> Betwixt the Confines of ye light & dark
> It lies, of 'Lyzium ye St James's park:
> Here Spirit-Beaux flutter along the Mall,
> And Shadows in disguise scate o'er ye Iced Canal.

It is a token of Gray's high spirits in this verse-letter that after signing off, in three couplets, he adds a supplement:

> P.S. Lucrece for half a crown will shew you fun,
> But Mrs Oldfield is become a Nun.
> Nobles & Cits, Prince Pluto & his Spouse
> Flock to the Ghost of Covent-Garden house:
> Plays, which were hiss'd above, below revive;
> When dead applauded, that were damn'd alive ...

and so on for four more lines. The Oxford editors to the contrary notwithstanding, the topsy-turvy humour of the first couplet quoted depends on our taking 'Lucrece' and 'Nun' in their obvious senses alone, rather than toying with the colloquial ironical sense of 'Nun' (and, as they also allege, of 'Lucrece') as 'prostitute'.

Gray's next work in this category, an untitled fragment of 38 lines known as 'Hymn to Ignorance', celebrates his reluctant resumption of residence at Cambridge in 1742, as a fellow-commoner, after his return from the Continental Tour that he made with Walpole:

> Thrice hath Hyperion roll'd his annual race,
> Since weeping I forsook thy fond embrace.

He had in fact been away from Cambridge for four years, but he needed 'Thrice' for the metre. The metre is again the heroic couplet, and the matter is that of *The Dunciad*, with Ignorance replacing Dullness as the presiding goddess. As in *The Dunciad*, there is a strong infusion of *Paradise Lost*, particularly in the opening lines:

> Hail, Horrors, hail! ye ever gloomy bowers,
> Ye gothic fanes, and antiquated towers,
> Where rushy Camus' slowly-winding flood
> Perpetual draws his humid train of mud:
> Glad I revisit thy neglected reign,
> Oh take me to thy peaceful shade again.[4]

Having delivered this ironical salute to Cambridge, Gray begins to run out of steam. He exhorts Ignorance to maintain her power, in terms that recall Pope's and Dryden's more memorable ones:

> If any spark of Wit's delusive ray
> Break out, and flash a momentary day,
> With damp, cold touch forbid it to aspire,
> And huddle up in fogs the dangerous fire.[5]

Then, feeling that some independent stroke is called for, he interrupts his own address:

> Oh say—she hears me not, but careless grown,
> Lethargic nods upon her ebon throne.
> Goddess! awake, arise, alas my fears!
> Can powers immortal feel the force of years?

Pope's Dullness had put the world to sleep; Gray's Ignorance has put herself to sleep—with awkward implications for the allegory. Turning a blind eye to them, he proposes to picture Ignorance in her heyday, the Dark Ages, when 'all was Ignorance, and all was Night'; but the very first picture fades away:

> High on her car, behold the Grandam ride
> Like old Sesostris with barbaric pride;
> * * * * a team of harness'd monarchs bend
> $\qquad\qquad\qquad\qquad\qquad$ * * * *

The rest is silence.

In his 'Ode on the Death of a Favourite Cat, Drowned in a Tub of Gold Fishes' Gray achieves independence as a humorous poet. The poem's occasion is well known, and so is Gray's letter to Walpole (22 February 1747) in which, 'as one ought to be particularly careful to avoid blunders in a compliment of condolence', he asks which of Walpole's two cats it was, the tortoiseshell ('Selima, was it? or Fatima') or the tabby (Zara), that met with the accident.[6] Instead of the heroic couplet Gray chooses Chaucer's 'Sir Thopas' stanza, the verse-form known as *rime couée* or tailed rhyme, a circumstance which may have influenced his choice. Seven stanzas are enough both to relate the story and to decorate it (it is important that such a poem should not go on too long); and the decoration, rather than making the poem 'one of the hardest and most unfeeling pieces of clever writing',[7] serves to distance the unpleasant physical fact of the drowning.

It is impossible not to recognize that Gray had a proper appreciation of cats and their ways:

> Demurest of the tabby kind,
> The pensive Selima reclin'd,
> Gaz'd on the lake below.

> Her conscious tail her joy declar'd;
> The fair round face, the snowy beard,
> The velvet of her paws,
> Her coat, that with the tortoise vies,
> Her ears of jet, and emerald eyes,
> She saw; and purr'd applause.

He does not make the cat go directly after the fish, as the poem's title might lead us to expect, but contemplate her own image: this second stanza celebrates her beauty. When the two goldfish swim into her ken, they are creatures of beauty too, and objects of wonder:

> Still had she gaz'd; but 'midst the tide
> Two angel forms were seen to glide,
> The Genii of the stream:
> Their scaly armour's Tyrian hue
> Thro' richest purple to the view
> Betray'd a golden gleam.

'From morbid self-admiration' (writes a modern critic) 'the cat/woman turns to cupidity.' But is it not truer to say that Gray has transmuted these base passions? The moral comments, such as they are in this essentially amoral poem, burst in with calculated incongruity:

> What female heart can gold despise?
> What Cat's averse to fish?

> Presumptuous Maid! ...

> A Fav'rite has no friend!

> From hence, ye Beauties, undeceiv'd,
> Know, one false step is ne'er retriev'd,
> And be with caution bold.

> Not all that tempts your wand'ring eyes
> And heedless hearts, is lawful prize;
>   Nor all, that glisters, gold.

'If what glistered had been "gold"' (wrote Johnson) 'the cat would not have gone into the water; and, if she had, would not less have been drowned'.[8] Precisely.

The interplay of story and moral, animal and human, actual and epic, is cleverly handled. The figurative warning, 'Know, one false step is ne'er retriev'd', is prompted by the literal statement, 'The slipp'ry verge her feet beguil'd, / She tumbled headlong in'. 'Gray vividly portrays' (wrote an examination candidate) 'the whiskers and claws of the nymph'—an expression that might have pleased the poet. The actual drowning, which has to be narrated but which could have ruined the poem if narrated in the wrong way, makes the most of all three kinds of interplay:

> Eight times emerging from the flood
> She mew'd to ev'ry wat'ry God,
>   Some speedy aid to send.
> No Dolphin came, no Nereid stirr'd:
> Nor cruel *Tom*, nor *Susan* heard.
>   A Fav'rite has no friend!

'No Dolphin came': subliminally upon the reader's inward eye there flashes an image of a dolphin sporting in Walpole's china vase, an image of a cat riding Arion-like on a dolphin's back. Richard Bentley's contemporary design illustrating the poem is thoroughly in tune with Gray's imaginative treatment of the events: the inquisitive cat, the two goldfish, half of the vase, and half of an ornate cabinet are seen through a massive entablature flanked by caryatids representing a river-god stopping his ears and Destiny (the 'Malignant Fate' of the preceding stanza) about to cut the nine threads of Selima's life.[9]

Bentley also illustrated, with equal skill and taste, 'A Long Story'. This is yet another occasional poem, and, as Gray recognized, a particularly fugitive one. He caused it to be omitted from the 1768 edition of his poems, and told a correspondent that it 'was never meant for the publick, & only suffer'd to appear in that pompous edition because of Mr Bentley's designs, wch were not intelligible without it'; Mason added in his *Memoirs* that Gray foresaw 'that he risked somewhat by the publication of it', a statement which Johnson may have had in mind in saying that the poem 'adds little to Gray's character'.[10] Of course, a major reason for including it in the 1753 edition, and for getting Bentley to illustrate it, was to enlarge what remained a very small collection of poems.

If the poem made Bentley's designs intelligible, it was itself not intelligible, outside the small social circle for which it was written, without annotation. Gray provided in 1753 only five minimal explanatory notes, even fewer than he had added to his earliest extant holograph of it; and, no doubt intending to preserve an effect of mystery and caprice, he offered no account of the poem's occasion, which was as follows:

> The Dowager Viscountess Cobham, whose father had bought the Manor House at Stoke Poges, when she learned that the author of the *Elegy* was a neighbour, sent two friends, Miss Henrietta Jane Speed (later the Countess de Viry)and Lady Schaub, the French wife of Sir Luke Schaub, to call on Gray. Since he was not at home, they left a note, and Gray returned the call. A friendship quickly developed, and as a result Gray wrote this poem.[11]

'A Long Story' is indeed, as Johnson called it, an odd composition. It resembles Pope's *Rape of the Lock* in elaborating a trivial event, and in humorously invoking the supernatural. It resembles Prior's 'The Dove' in introducing the search of a room as a principal incident, and in employing the same octosyllabic quatrains.[12] But in its bifocal use of Georgian and Elizabethan images it is quite original. The old Manor House, Gray feigns, was built by 'Fairy hands' for the Huntingdons and Hattons. Sir Christopher Hatton, Elizabeth's Lord Chancellor, danced there, and ghostly ladies of Mary Tudor's court still haunt its passages. One morning there issue from it a pair of evidently contemporary beauties, 'rustling in their silks and tissues'. 'My Lady' has sent them to apprehend 'A wicked Imp they call a Poet', who is locally suspected of witchcraft. In searching the house he inhabits, they wonder whether he may be lying hidden 'under a tea-cup'. He has in fact been smuggled

by the Muses into 'a small closet in the garden'. Not finding
him, they fly 'out of the window', leaving on the table a magic
spell which compels him to present himself at the Manor
House, where his awe renders him 'as mute as poor *Macleane*'
('A famous Highwayman hang'd the week before.'—Gray's
note, 1753); 'The Peeress', however, scandalizing the Marian
ghosts by her affability, invites him to dinner. '*Here 500 Stanzas
are lost*', but a concluding stanza exists:

> And so God save our noble King,
> And guard us from long-winded Lubbers,
> That to eternity would sing,
> And keep my Lady from her Rubbers.

In his uninhibitedly self-reflexive narrative Gray anticipates
Byron: after four stanzas he reproaches himself, in a fifth
stanza, for wasting time ('Can you do nothing but describe?'),
and resumes with 'A House there is, (and that's enough)'. His
rhymes anticipate *Don Juan* too—and recall *Hudibras*: 'doublet',
'trouble it'; 'Apparatus', 'Great-house'; 'old-tree', 'poultry'. If
he meant the 'old-tree', under whose shade the story's Poet
admits to having penned a sonnet or two, to be the same as
'yonder nodding beech / That wreathes its old fantastic roots so
high' in the *Elegy*, it adds an extra touch of humour—and if he
did not, then it doesn't matter. One can see the fancies forming
as he writes: the Poet, rumour ran, was one

> Who prowl'd the country far and near,
> Bewitch'd the children of the peasants,
> Dried up the cows, and lam'd the deer,
> And suck'd the eggs, and kill'd the pheasants.

This stanza begins with a conventional list of witchlike doings
(perhaps, too, with a glance at Herne the Hunter[13]—Stoke
Poges being only a stone's throw from Windsor, and from Eton
where Gray went to school), but in the fourth line the activities
become those of a rat or a weasel, thus pointing forward, in the
next stanza, to 'To rid the manour of such vermin' (on which
the editorial tradition of notes about old statutes directed
against vagrant minstrels is highly inappropriate).

We come now to a group of Cambridge poems, written at
various times during the next fifteen or so years. An eight-line

inscription written to accompany Mason's caricature of the Rev. Henry Etough, a trouble-making clergyman whose name Gray roughly anagrammatizes as Tophet (as who should say the Rev. Mr Hellmouth), and who had been a dissenter before entering the Church of England, ends:

> Our Mother-Church with half-averted sight
> Blushd as she blesst her griesly proselyte:
> Hosannahs rung thro Hells tremendous borders
> And Satans self had thoughts of taking orders.

The poem beginning

> O Cambridge, attend
> To the Satire I've pen'd
> On the Heads of thy Houses,
> Thou Seat of the Muses!

has nothing to do with University politics or personalities. The presiding genius is Skelton, Gray taking the hint from a couplet of Pope's, and the technique from, for example, *Philip Sparrow*:

> Know the Master of Jesus
> Does hugely displease us;
> The Master of Maudlin
> In the same dirt is dawdling;
> The Master of Sidney
> Is of the same kidney;
> The Master of Trinity
> To him bears affinity;
> As the Master of Keys
> Is as like as two pease,
> So the Master of Queen's
> Is as like as two beans; ...[14]

In the last couplet—

> P.S. As to Trinity Hall
> We say nothing at all.—

he neatly solves the problem of rounding off so unprogressive a catalogue.

The lines called 'Sketch of His Own Character' make an interesting companion-piece to the 'Epitaph' at the end of the *Elegy*:

> Too poor for a bribe, and too proud to importune;
> He had not the method of making a fortune:
> Could love, and could hate, so was thought somewhat odd;
> No very great Wit, he believ'd in a God.
> A Post or a Pension he did not desire,
> But left Church and State to Charles Townshend and Squire.

—on whom see the *Dictionary of National Biography* and the explanatory notes of editors.

'The Candidate', otherwise known as 'Jemmy Twitcher', or 'The Cambridge Courtship', is Gray's contribution to the election contest for the High Stewardship at Cambridge in 1764. He represents Lord Sandwich, popularly nicknamed Jemmy Twitcher because of a phrase in Gay's *Beggar's Opera* which was topically being applied to his betrayal of his old friend John Wilkes, as paying court to the Cambridge electorate, personified as the three sisters Physic, Law, and Divinity. Physic dislikes his appearance, Law his morals:

> Divinity heard, between waking and dozing,
> Her sisters denying, and Jemmy proposing;
> From dinner she rose with her bumper in hand,
> She stroked up her belly, and stroked down her band.
>   What a pother is here about wenching and roaring!
> Why David loved catches, and Solomon whoring.
> Did not Israel filch from th' Aegyptians of old
> Their jewels of silver, and jewels of gold?
> The prophet of Bethel, we read, told a lie:
> He drinks; so did Noah: he swears; so do I.
> To refuse him for such peccadillos, were odd;
> Besides, he repents, and he talks about G--.
>   Never hang down your head, you poor penitent elf!
> Come, buss me, I'll be Mrs. Twitcher myself.
> D--n ye both for a couple of Puritan bitches!
> He's Christian enough, that repents, and that --------.

Gray superimposes on the personified Divinity the physique
and circumstances of a Cambridge divine, and puts into her
mouth a speech of nicely-turned cynicism ('He drinks; so did
Noah: he swears; so do I'). As in the 'Sketch of His Own
Character', the word 'God' makes a good clinching end to a
couplet. The resolution, if less logically satisfying than the
Judge's 'Put your briefs upon the shelf! / I will marry her
myself!' in *Trial by Jury* (for Jemmy Twitcher cannot marry
three ladies at once, though he is asking them all to accept
him), serves well enough. The last couplet, and in particular
the last word, gave Walpole and Mason trouble. A manuscript
copy in Walpole's hand reads clearly *stitches*, meaning 'copu-
lates'. He considered this 'too gross' to be read by any decent
woman; Mason agreed; and both of them drafted alternative
versions which evade the point, namely that Jemmy Twitcher's
repentance and his sexual ability combine to qualify him as a
suitor.[15]

In July 1765 Gray, who had just been visiting Mason at
York, where he was Precentor and a Residentiary Canon, sent
him a poem headed 'William Shakespeare to Mrs Anne,
Regular Servant to the Revd Mr Precentor of York'. Shakespeare writes as embodied in a volume of his collected works
which Mason has had interleaved with blank sheets on which
to indulge in textual criticism. He complains:

> Much have I born[e] from canker'd Critick's spite,
> From fumbling Baronets, and Poets small,
> Pert Barristers, & Parsons nothing bright:
> But, what awaits me now, is worst of all!

(From the recent history of Shakespearean scholarship it was
easy to identify the offenders.) He urges Mason's servant to
make use of the leaves as kitchen paper:

> Better to bottom tarts & cheesecakes nice,
> Better the roast-meat from the fire to save,
> Better be twisted into caps for spice,
> Than thus be patch'd, & cobbled in one's grave!

> So York shall taste, what Clouet never knew;
> So from *our* works sublimer fumes shall rise:

> While Nancy earns the praise to Shakespear due
> For glorious puddings, & immortal pies.[16]

There was example for it: John Warburton (1682–1759, antiquary and Somerset Herald, and no relation of William Warburton, the 'parson nothing bright' who had edited Shakespeare in 1747) had revealed that his cook, appropriately named Betsy Baker, had destroyed fifty-five old plays, including unique copies of works by Chapman, Massinger, and Ford, in exactly this way. Gray appended to this poem the sentence 'Tell me, if you don't like this, & I will send you a worse'.[17]

'On Lord Holland's Seat near Margate, Kent', his last known satirical poem, is one of his best poems of any kind. Like the piece just mentioned, it is written in the same stanza as the *Elegy*, a fact which shows to what different uses Gray could apply a single metrical form. In the 'Shakespeare' lines he introduces humorously archaic diction ('But stint your clack for sweet St Charitie').[18] In the *Elegy* he is sober and sententious. In the present poem he writes with a highly-charged irony which recalls the manner of Pope in his *Moral Essays*. As usual, present circumstances stimulated him to composition. Henry Fox (1705–74, created Baron Holland in 1763, on whose career see the *Dictionary of National Biography* and the notes of Gray's editors) had in 1767 written and privately printed a poem, 'Lord Holland Returning from Italy', in which he denounced his former political associates. In the following year Gray paid a visit to his friend the Rev. William Robinson at Denton, Kent, not far from Kingsgate, where Lord Holland had recently built himself a villa in imitation of Cicero's at Baiae and had erected artificial ruins in its grounds. No doubt a sight of the poem in 1767, and of the villa and ruins in 1768, produced Gray's lines.[19]

> Old and abandon'd by each venal friend
>   Here H[olland] took the pious resolution
> To smuggle some few years and strive to mend
>   A broken character and constitution.
> On this congenial spot he fix'd his choice,
>   Earl Godwin trembled for his neighbouring sand;
> Here Seagulls scream and cormorants rejoice,
>   And Mariners tho' shipwreckt dread to land;

Here reign the blustring north and blighting east,
    No tree is heard to whisper, bird to sing,
Yet nature cannot furnish out the feast,
    Art he invokes new horrors still to bring;
Now mouldring fanes and battlements arise,
    Arches and turrets nodding to their fall,
Unpeopled palaces delude his eyes,
    And mimick desolation covers all.
Ah, said the sighing Peer, had Bute been true
    Nor Shelburn's, Rigby's, Calcraft's friendship vain,
Far other scenes than these had bless'd our view
    And realis'd the ruins that we feign.
Purg'd by the sword and beautifyed by fire,
    Then had we seen proud London's hated walls,
Owls might have hooted in St Peters Quire,
    And foxes stunk and litter'd in St Pauls.

Gray seizes on the idea of desolation and inflates it inventively. The situation of the villa, so bleak that it might as well have been built on the Goodwin Sands, is congenial only to the disposition of a Timon (Shakespeare's, not Pope's) prepared to make 'his everlasting mansion / Upon the beachèd verge of the salt flood'. The ruins of London, seen in the misanthropic mind's eye, evoke the feelings of a Coriolanus. The echoes of Pope amplify the satiric mood: 'Arches and turrets nodding to their fall'; 'And mimick desolation covers all'; 'Owls might have hooted in St Peters Quire, / And foxes stunk and litter'd in St Pauls'.[20] Was it deliberate on Gray's part to introduce Lord Holland's family surname into the last line of the poem?

'Gray avait de la gaieté dans l'esprit et de la mélancolie dans le caractère', wrote his young friend Bonstetten in his memoirs.[21] His humorous and satiric poems testify often enough to the gaiety; perhaps also occasionally, and in an undertone, to the melancholy.

NOTES

1. Horace Walpole, letter to William Cole in *Correspondence of Horace Walpole*, ed. W. S. Lewis and others (New Haven, 1937–), I, 367. Samuel Johnson, Preface to edition of Shakespeare (1765), *The Yale Edition of the Works*

of Samuel Johnson (New Haven, 1958–), VII, ed. Arthur Sherbo (1968), 69.
Samuel Johnson, 'Life of Gray', in *Lives of the English Poets* (1781), ed. G.
Birkbeck Hill, 3 vols (Oxford, 1905), III, 425, 434.

   2. *Complete Poems*, p. x.

   3. Letter to Walpole, 8 December 1734, *Correspondence*, I, 9.

   4. Cf. *Paradise Lost*, I, 250–51 ('hail horrors, hail / Infernal world') and
VII, 305–06 ('where rivers now / Stream, and perpetual draw their humid
train'). [Quoted from *The Poems of John Milton*, ed. John Carey and Alastair
Fowler (London, 1968).] In the next quotation but one, the appeal 'awake,
arise' is also from *Paradise Lost* (I, 330).

   5. Cf. *The Dunciad*, IV, 634–35, and *MacFlecknoe*, ll. 21–24.

   6. *Correspondence*, I, 271.

   7. W. P. Ker, quoted by Arthur Johnston(ed.), *Selected Poems of Thomas
Gray and William Collins* (London, 1967), p. 11.

   8. *Lives*, III, 434.

   9. *Designs by Mr. R. Bentley, for Six Poems by Mr. T. Gray* (London, 1753).
See Irene Tayler, 'Two Eighteenth-Century Illustrators of Gray' [the other is
Blake], in *Fearful Joy. Papers from the Thomas Gray Bicentenary Conference at
Carleton University*, ed. J. Downey and B. Jones (Montreal and London, 1974),
pp. 119–35.

   10. Gray, letter to James Beattie, 24 December 1767, *Correspondence*, III,
982. Mason, *Memoirs*, quoted in *Correspondence*, I, 364, n. 7. Johnson, *Lives*,
III, 425.

   11. *Complete Poems*, p. 224. The *Elegy* was not published until February
1751, but Walpole had communicated it in manuscript to several friends. 'A
Long Story' was written in 1750.

   12. Venus having lost her favourite dove, Cupid suspects Cloe of stealing
it, and leads a posse to her house, where he finds her in bed. She denies the
charge and defies Cupid to search her room.

> Her Keys He takes; her Doors unlocks;
>   Thro' Wardrobe, and thro' Closet bounces;
> Peeps into ev'ry Chest and Box;
>   Turns all her Furbeloes and Flounces.
>
> (ll. 97–100)

Not finding the dove, he returns to the bed, where Cloe 'Begins to treat Him
with Disdain' (l. 104):

> I marvel much, She smiling said,
>   Your Poultry cannot yet be found:
> Lies he in yonder Slipper dead,
>   Or, may be, in the Tea-pot drown'd?
>
> (ll. 105–08)

Cupid, however, declares, 'He's hid somewhere about Your Breast' (l. 110),
and the poem ends with sexual innuendo as he searches her. Quoted from *The
Literary Works of Matthew Prior*, ed. H. Bunker Wright and Monroe K. Spears,
2 vols, 2nd ed. (Oxford, 1971).

13. *The Merry Wives of Windsor*, IV.iv.29–30: 'And there he blasts the trees, and takes the cattle, / And makes milch-kine yield blood . . .' (ed.T. W. Craik, Oxford, 1990).

14. Pope, *The First Epistle of the Second Book of Horace*, ll. 37–38: 'Chaucer's worst ribaldry is learn'd by rote, / And beastly Skelton Heads of Houses quote'. Quoted from *The Poems of Alexander Pope*, ed. John Butt (London, 1963). *John Skelton's Complete Poems*, ed. P. Henderson (London, 1931, rev. and repr. 1966), pp. 81 ('Of Marcus Marcellus / A process I could tell us') and 63–64 ('Sometime he would gasp / When he saw a wasp; / A fly or a gnat / He would fly at that; / And prettily he would pant / When he saw an ant. / Lord, how he would pry / After the butterfly! / Lord, how he would hop / After the gressop!').

15. *Complete Poems*, p. 239. Walpole's version is 'Damn you both! I know each for a Puritan punk. / He is Christian enough that repents when he's drunk'. This has the merit of implying that the repentance is merely a drunken one. Mason's version is 'Damn ye both for two prim puritanical saints! / He's Christian enough that both whores and repents! (or) that drinks, whores and repents'.

16. Clouet was the French cook of the Duke of Newcastle, who was at that time Chancellor of Cambridge University.

17. *Correspondence*, II, 880. Mason, rising to the occasion, replied, 'As bad as Your Verses were, they are Yours, and therefore when I get back to York I'll paste them carefully in the first page of My Shakespeare to inhance its Value for I intend it to be put in My Marriage Settlement as a Provision for my Younger Daughters'. He was about to be married, a circumstance to which Gray had also referred in the poem.

18. Cf. Chaucer, *Canterbury Tales*, The Miller's Prologue: 'The Reve answerde and seyde, "Stynt thy clappe!"' (l. 3144; *The Works of Geoffrey Chaucer*, ed. F. N. Robinson, 2nd ed., London, 1966). The venereal sense of clap made the word no longer available to Gray. In *Hamlet*, IV.v.57, Ophelia's song includes the line 'By Gis, and by Saint Charity' (ed. G. R. Hibbard, Oxford, 1987).

19. For further details see *Correspondence*, III, 1259–62 (Appendix T).

30. Cf. *Essay on Man*, IV, 129 ('Or some old temple, nodding to its fall'); *The Dunciad*, IV, 656 ('And universal Darkness buries All'); *Windsor Forest*, ll. 71–72 ('The Fox obscene to gaping Tombs retires, / And savage Howlings fill the sacred Quires'). With the rhythm of the last-quoted line cf. *Elegy*, l. 8 ('And drowsy tinklings lull the distant folds'), probably an unconscious reminiscence on Gray's part.

21. Charles Victor de Bonstetten, *Souvenirs* (Paris, 1831), quoted in *Correspondence*, III, 1111, n. 1.

Thomas Gray's Travel Writing

WILLIAM RUDDICK

Without ever intending it, Thomas Gray was destined to become one of the first significant British travel writers. Like his poetry, the total mass of his prose concerned with travelling (whether abroad or in his own country) was small in extent, and as with the poetry its small compass includes material produced over a considerable number of years. But unlike the poetry it was all published at once (albeit in a heavily edited and somewhat doctored form) and from the time of its first appearance, in William Mason's *Memoirs of the Life and Writings of Mr. Gray* (1775), its influence was to be both widespread and lasting. In particular, Gray's manner of writing about mountain landscapes and the way he responded to them was to affect both poets and prose writers until at least the time of the second-generation Romantics; into the 1820s or even later.

Gray's own opportunities for travel mostly occurred in middle life, in the 1750s and 1760s. Earlier he had the good fortune to be invited to accompany his school friend Horace Walpole on the Grand Tour to France and Italy between 1739 and 1741, but after his quarrel with Walpole and solitary return to England, Gray's relatively narrow circumstances and family commitments ensured that his holidays for several years were almost uniformly spent either in London or at Stoke Poges. Then, as later, he either wrote little about his travels, or else the correspondence has not survived. But throughout his life it seems to have been the case that Gray needed to experience the double stimulus of new places combined with the sense of having a congenial friend as a correspondent, whose participation in the visual and emotional discoveries which travelling brought could be so strongly desired as to be imaginatively grafted on to the original experience, before he chose (or perhaps was able) to write at length about his journeyings. Gray did, at times, keep travel records, particularly concerning his longer excursions in later life, but they tend to take the form of notes, and to be chiefly factual.[1] Even in the 1760s, when Gray's summer tours were becoming increasingly enterprising and reflected a growing contemporary interest in travel itself (particularly to those parts of the country which could show the sublimity of mountains, or the picturesque), which was matched by an evident eagerness to read about such places on the part of those who were unable to afford the time or the money for journeying,[2] he never thought of writing up any of his travel notes for publication: a point which seems all the more striking when contemporary library records show that he was a lifelong reader of travel narratives of all sorts.

Yet ironically Gray was to become almost the first of the truly influential travel writers of the second half of the eighteenth century, both enlarging the emotional range and helping to codify the modes of response of following generations. Most significantly of all, for later authors (and readers) still, he showed topographical writers how to combine the formally codified 'sublime and beautiful' reactions to landscape and the pictorialism which was increasingly a feature of the late eighteenth and early nineteenth centuries with specifically and naturalistically-observed descriptions of phenomena which, in their turn, led towards more psychologically exact and truthful analysis of individual responses to nature. Gray's prose provided a model for the age of Gilpin and the picturesque tourists; it also exercised a benevolent influence upon that phase which is exemplified by the naturalism of Dorothy Wordsworth's *Journals*, the Lakeland sections of Coleridge's *Notebooks*, some parts of Wordsworth's descriptive poetry, and, very recognizably, certain aspects of his *Guide to the Lakes*.

From the moment of their publication in Mason's *Life*, the power and aesthetic adventurousness of Gray's early letters describing his and Walpole's visit to the Grande Chartreuse and crossing of the Alps in 1739 were recognized. But a close reading of Gray's letters shows something which was to be a feature of his travel writing always: he is master of two distinct (though closely-related) styles, the first directly and vividly descriptive (and hardly to be improved on as such) and the second still precisely visualized, but also exploratory of the emotional, psychological and even spiritual stimuli which novel aesthetic experiences derived from a direct contact with natural forces could bring to him.

Gray's first manner can be found in his letters home to his parents. To his mother, for example, he describes the road leading to the Grande Chartreuse:

> ... It is six miles to the top; the road runs winding up it, commonly not six feet broad; on one hand is the rock, with woods of pine-trees hanging over head; on the other a monstrous precipice, almost perpendicular, at the bottom of which rolls a torrent, that sometimes tumbling among the fragments of stone that have fallen from on high, and sometimes precipitating itself down vast descents with a noise like thunder, which is still made greater by the echo from the mountains on each side, concurs to form one of the most solemn, the most romantic, and the most astonishing scenes I ever beheld.[3]

Other letters to his parents describing Alpine scenery maintain the same controlled response to sublime nature; the epithets required to characterize it are always ready to fall into place, and his own *Journal* of the ascent to the Grande Chartreuse offers the same measured preciseness, even though he ends by allowing that the 'beauties of so savage and horrid a place', contrasting with 'the solemn Sound of the Stream that roars below', do 'concur to form one of the most poetical Scenes imaginable'.[4] The landscape of Gray's poem 'The Bard' and other passages dealing with natural sublimity in his poems of the 1750s would show the lasting effect of this recognition.

Walpole's response to the road leading up to the Grande Chartreuse, as described in a letter to West, had shown more enthusiastic emotions, offering, as Ketton-Cremer says, the suggestion that they had been 'moving through a magnificent picture, some incomparable canvas of Salvator Rosa'.[5] But as Ketton-Cremer also senses, Gray's companion letter to West reveals what his letters to his parents had not shown; that 'that unforgettable ride was of far deeper significance to him':[6]

> In our little journey up to the Grande Chartreuse, I do not remember to have gone ten paces without an exclamation

that there was no restraining: not a precipice, not a torrent, not a cliff, but is pregnant with religion and poetry. There are certain scenes that would awe an atheist into belief, without the help of other argument. One need not have a very fantastic imagination to see spirits there at noon-day: You have death perpetually before your eyes, only so far removed, as to compose the mind without frighting it. I am well persuaded St. Bruno was a man of no common genius, to choose such a situation for his retirement; and perhaps should have been a disciple of his, had I been born in his time.[7]

The letter is full of remarkable insights: it offers, for example, one of the classic definitions of the Sublime, almost twenty years before Burke's *Origin of our Ideas of the Sublime and the Beautiful* (1757). But in one respect it surprises by a lack of reference. The letter is written by a scholar-traveller well up in literature concerned with the Alps and with mountain sub-limity (and ready to stir his friend's recollections of the same) but, unlike Walpole, Gray shows no direct acquaintance with those schools of seventeenth-century landscape painting which were to be referred to, almost as touchstones, by the vast majority of later British writers on mountain scenery. Walpole, of course, had had the advantage of familiarity with his father's great collection of paintings at Houghton (which Gray had yet to see). At this date Gray still chiefly relies upon Latin poetry (in which West and he were equally well read) for associations and images to help him clarify and express his sense of wonder at the psychological and aesthetic shocks which had stirred him.

One other aspect of the letter to West deserves attention. W. P. Jones has established the fact that Gray read travel narratives of all kinds, but he notes that, although Gray might at times draw upon his reading for the enrichment of his poetry, in general 'the spirit is that of the boy reading about the discovery of brave new worlds, not of the scholar following the changes of Oriental dynasties' (or whatever else the books chanced to be concerned with).[8] Jones makes the further point that when Gray does draw closely upon his reading, to combine it with actual travel observation, it is because he wishes to enable a friend to share the excitement of a powerful, and generally a new, experience.

In describing the ascent to the Grande Chartreuse, Gray has both West and their shared literary and historical culture in mind:

> You may believe Abelard and Heloise were not forgot upon this occasion: If I do not mistake, I saw you too every now and then at a distance among the trees ... You seemed to call to me from the other side of the precipice, but the noise of the river below was so great, that I really could not distinguish what you said; it seemed to have a cadence like verse.[9]

Gray's feelings are lightened (and sharpened) by a persistent accompaniment of banter in the most imaginative passages of this letter ('il me semble, que j'ai vu ce chien de visage là quelque part'), but there is no mistaking his deep involvement in the attempt to find meaning in a powerful experience now at last recollected in tranquillity.[10] After the last tour of which Gray left a significant account, his visit to the Lake District in 1769, there was also to be a time lapse before he wrote up his immediate travel notes for transmission as a connected narrative for his friend, and intended companion, Thomas Wharton.

West died young, and it was to be many years before Gray found another correspondent whose shared interest in natural scenery drew him out of himself to explore his responses on paper. In the meantime, the extent to which the Alps had affected his sensibilities and his imagination is evident from the increasing part (after an interval of ten years or so) which sublime mountain scenery was to play in 'The Bard', 'The Progress of Poesy' and other poems. But it need not be thought, however, despite the presence of 'sublime' or 'gothic' elements in this later verse, that Gray ceased to be responsive to, or had ever been less than highly aware of, the other chief constituent of the pleasure to be gained from landscape (as eighteenth-century poets saw it), the beautiful.

British artists and writers had adopted the custom of analysing natural scenery in terms of the sublime and the beautiful well before Burke's classic treatise of the 1750s, and equally established was the practice of resorting to the names of Salvator Rosa on the one hand and Claude Lorrain and Gaspard Poussin on the other as chief exemplars of the two qualities in visual art: merely to quote their names was to offer a thumbnail sketch of the aesthetic responses they were expected to elicit from a reader. So Dr John Brown (whom Gray seems to have known slightly) speaks of 'the full perfection of Keswick' as possessing qualities which it would require 'the united powers of Claude, Salvator and Poussin' to evoke in his pioneering and highly influential *Description of the Lake at Keswick* ..., first published (in part) in *The London Chronicle* in 1766, and in its entirety as an often-reprinted pamphlet the following year.[11] But Gray's somewhat tardy education in the visual arts coincided with a period when a significant change in ways of responding to both the sublime and the beautiful was coming about. An early letter to Walpole, dated August 1736, shows him playing with the two concepts by using them in a burlesque fashion to describe the unremarkable countryside surrounding the home of his uncle, Jonathan Rogers, at Burnham. First comes the sublime, applied to an all-too-evidently tame landscape:

> ... I spy no human thing in it but myself; it is a little Chaos of Mountains and Precipices: Mountains, it is true, that don't ascend much above the Clouds, nor are the Declivities quite so amazing as Dover-Cliff; but just such hills as people, who love their Necks as well as I do, may venture to climb, & Crags, that give the eye as much pleasure, as if they were more dangerous.[12]

This essay in the mock-sublime is not without its literary reference, to Gloucester and Dover Cliff; but when the beautiful gets its turn, it appears only as the literary backdrop to a traditional picture of Gray himself as the poet in a traditional poet's landscape, while most of the suggestions of rural beauty are made through a series of literary allusions:

> At the foot of one of these ['venerable Beeches'] squats me I; il Penseroso, and there grow to the Trunk for a whole morning ... like Adam in Paradise, but commonly without an Eve, & besides I think he did not use to read Virgil, as I usually do there: in this situation I often converse

with my Horace aloud too, that is talk to you; for I don't
remember, that I ever heard you answer me; I beg pardon
for taking all the conversation to myself; but it is your own
fault indeed.[13]

As in the somewhat later letter to West already examined,
Gray involves his absent friend as a sounding board for his own
emotional explorations; but the significant difference here is
that the context is overwhelmingly literary, and the emotions
well under control, as is almost invariably the case when Gray
writes of the beautiful, as distinct from the sublime, until the
sudden breakthrough to his direct involvement with beauty in
several passages in the later *Journal* of his tour in the Lakes. The
visual range of the early letter to Walpole is severely restricted,
and its reference to Walpole's unresponsiveness to Gray's
imagined attempts at dialogue (quite unlike West's to Gray's
similar thoughts in the Alps) only serves to emphasize the
writer's loneliness. Given a darker emotional range, there is
much here which foreshadows the situation and the descriptive
limits of the 'Ode on the Spring' of a few years later: indeed the
latter part of the *Elegy* also seems not entirely unrelated to it.

Leaving aside the early tour with Walpole, it can be said that
the period of Gray's major tours really begins when the deaths
of his near relatives freed his movements in summertime, and a
network of Cambridge friends in various parts of the country
enabled him to combine extended visits to them with shorter
tours to places of scenic or historic interest. After his first trip to
the North and visit to Durham in 1753, Gray was to explore the
Midlands (1754), the South Coast (1755), Suffolk and Norfolk
(1761), York and Old Park (1762), the Channel Coast again in
1764, leading on to a further tour to Salisbury and Stonehenge,
York and the North East Coast in 1765, followed by a further
tour as far as Glamis Castle and some parts of the Highlands:
then, as Gray's appetite for mountain scenery clearly increased
with feeding, tours to the Peak District in 1767, leading to his
first attempt to visit the Lakes in the company of Thomas
Wharton (it had to be cut short when Wharton developed
asthma at Keswick); and, after the sublime had alternated
with the beautiful in another summer visit to the South Coast
in 1768, Gray joined up with Wharton again in 1769 to visit the

Lakes. This second attempt was even more disastrous for Wharton than the first, since he developed asthma once more at Brough and Gray made the tour alone; but Wharton's loss was to be posterity's gain, as it was for the sake of the disappointed traveller that Gray wrote up his travel notes into the narrative which has always been inaccurately but conveniently referred to as his *Journal* of the visit. In 1770 Gray sought sublimity again by visiting the Welsh Borders, but unfortunately left little record of this final extended tour.[14] In May 1771, less than a month before his death, he wrote to Wharton about his plans for a summer visit and declared that 'travel I must, or cease to exist'.[15] Ironically, hostile readers of Gray's Lakeland *Journal* later did much to spread the idea that he was a timorous and unadventurous traveller. In actual fact he travelled widely by the standards of his time, exploring areas which were only just beginning to receive attention in the books and periodical literature of the day, and making particularly good use of the improved road system which the Turnpike Acts were bringing into existence in the North of England during the 1760s.[16]

Sadly, Gray seems to have left almost no record of several of his later tours either in letters to his friends or elsewhere. But even from brief comments, at the time of his first tours in the 1750s, a fresh viewpoint can be discerned when he chooses to describe the beautiful. He had informed West in a letter from Rome in 1740 that he agreed with Walpole that 'our memory sees more than our eyes in this country ... since, for realities, London or Richmond Hill, is infinitely preferable to Albano or Frascati'.[17] As if to prove his point, the bulk of his description is indeed taken up by references to places familiar to West and himself from the Classics: and he soon veers off to transcribe a Roman sepulchral inscription. Thirteen years later, however, describing his first journey back from Durham to Stoke for Wharton, his recent host, Gray turns to literature of a very different sort, and develops his argument in a very different way, for he uses an initial reference to John Evelyn's *Sylva* to introduce a catalogue and discussion of the characteristic trees of the region which he had seen in the North. But his keen-eyed account of them is not solely classificatory in its purpose:

At York Walnuts ripe, 20 for a penny, from thence, especially South of Tadcaster, I thought the Country extremely beautiful, broke into fine hills cover'd with noble woods, (particularly toward the East) & every thing as verdant almost as at Midsummer, this continued to Doncaster; the Hazle & White-thorn were turning yellow in the hedges, the Sycamore, Lime, & Ash (where it was young, or much exposed) were growing rusty, but far greener than in your Country. The old Ash, the Oak, & other Timber shew'd no signs of winter.[18]

Perhaps the most significant feature here is the fusion of exact observation with a spatial and potentially pictorial sense of natural beauty in a landscape which Gray does not seem to have possessed as a younger man. Two years later, in 1755, writing to Wharton after a visit to the South Coast on which 'I wished for you often', he launches effortlessly into a prospect description as ample and composed as could have been expected from any professed admirer of Claude Lorrain at that period:

... from Fareham to Southampton, where you are upon a level with the coast, you have a thousand such Peeps and delightful Openings, but would you see the whole at once, you must get upon Ports-Down 5 mile on this side Portsmouth. it is the top of a ridge, that forms a natural Terass 3 Mile long, literally not three times broader than Windsor-Terrass with a gradual fall on both sides & cover'd with a turf like New-Market. to the North opens Hampshire & Berkshire cover'd with woods, and interspersed with numerous Gentlemen's Houses & Villages. to the South, Portsmouth, Gosport, &c: just at your foot in appearance, the Fleet, the Sea winding, & breaking in bays into the land, the deep shade of tall Oaks in the enclosures, wch become blue, as they go off to distance, Portchester-Castle, Carshot-Castle, & all the Isle of Wight, in wch you plainly distinguish the fields, hedgerows, & woods next the shore, & a back-ground of hills behind them. I have not seen a more magnificent or more varied Prospect.[19]

Thereafter the characteristic fusion of the composed pictorial effect with the constantly specific is Gray's to command:
but it only occurs in letters to a correspondent whose interest in
topography and picturesque natural scenery he knows
matches his own. Essentially the sole (and the ideal) sharer of
Gray's fully-developed response to landscape beauty or sublimity is Wharton. More than once in his letters Gray laments
Wharton's absence when he visits a beautiful spot, or one rich
in the sense of history which they also shared. In 1758, for
instance, he declares that when enjoying the delights of
Hampton Court and Twickenham, '. . . I never saw in so small
a spot so much variety and so many natural advantages, nor
ever hardly wish'd more for your company to partake of
them'.[20]

Clearly, Wharton was the ideal recipient for Gray's travel
letters, sharing his interest in antiquities, natural history,
scenic beauty and (perhaps increasingly on both their parts)
picturesque landscape. In the later 1760s the friends also
became would-be explorers of the kind of natural scenery
which had first stirred Gray's imagination in his youth: the
mountainous sublime.

Gray's summer tours of the middle and late 1760s seem,
whether consciously or otherwise, to have followed on a larger
scale the common eighteenth-century tendency to alternate
experiences of the beautiful with the sublime. In 1765 he
ventured to Scotland, seeing Glamis Castle and something of
the Highlands. The novelty of all things Scottish, whether
antiquarian or scenic, caused his account of the tour for
Wharton to form, on the whole, a masterly series of compressed notes or thumbnail sketches of what he had seen and
felt. But he was evidently much impressed by what he saw of
the Highlands ('in short since I saw the Alps, I have seen
nothing sublime till now').[21] Probably as a result of this, Gray
and Wharton set out together on their first unsuccessful
attempt to explore the Lake District in 1767, when they only
saw its northern fringes before Wharton's illness struck.
Wharton's illness at an even earlier stage of the 1769 tour
meant that he was destined to play the part of the wished-for
but absent companion with whom (as in the letters to West of

years before) Gray would imagine himself sharing his discoveries and impressions from day to day as he went along.

By an accident of publication, Thomas Gray's narrative of the few days which he spent in the Lake District between 30 September and 8 October 1769, together with his account of the journey homewards by Kendal and Lancaster, Settle and Skipton, as far as Leeds, was to become his best-known and most influential piece of writing in the travel mode. Since Mason published it (shorn of introductory and concluding epistolary materials and lightly edited) in 1775, it has never lacked appreciative readers. But neither has it lacked its persistent detractors, who have fastened on to particular aspects of the narrative (especially Gray's somewhat heightened account of his reactions on a walk into Borrowdale and the sense of terror with which it inspired him) to ridicule his supposed timidity as a tourist and his inadequacies (and above all his gullibility) as a factual witness.[22]

The criticisms should be looked at, but they are generally not difficult to counter. Gray was travelling alone, the season was advanced, and so he probably chose not to do a number of things (such as ascend Skiddaw: he mentions one day as being of the right sort for an ascent) which he might well have attempted if Wharton had been his companion. But the things which he chose not to do were, in general, those which the infant tourist industry was already offering to visitors as desirable, and the literature which had created that industry had stressed as being almost *de rigeur*. In another year or two, to ascend a mountain and to make the circuit of Derwentwater and Ullswater by boat were virtually obligatory features of a Lakeland tour. Arthur Young had done the latter in 1768: the Hutchinson brothers did both in 1773, and the tone of their books suggest in each case that these were experiences not to be missed.[23] Gray may well have felt nervous about venturing on the water, as his early detractors claimed, but it seems equally likely that he did not relish the prospect of submitting himself to the attentions of the Keswick boatmen, who would have given him what had already developed into the stock ride round the lake, stopping off at recognized places to savour the correct impressions of sublimity (on the way out towards the head of the lake and Borrowdale) and beauty (on the return).[24]

An eagerly-anticipated experience of discovery would have turned into what we might now think of as a 'theme park' experience, just as Arthur Young's proposal to open up easy pathways to the best viewpoints for walkers was to do when embodied in the Rev. Thomas West's long-standard *Guide to the Lakes* with its catalogues of carefully-characterized, pictorially-effective 'Stations'.

Instead of taking a boat and feeing a party of boatmen, Gray enjoyed the company of his landlord *gratis* on a walk along the side of Derwentwater and into Borrowdale. In doing so he broke all the rules which had so rapidly become codified in the second half of the 1760s. The modern reader of Gray's *Journal* is unlikely to appreciate how quickly the publicity created by the first accounts of the Lake District in the *Gentleman's Magazine* in the late 1740s and 1750s, the appearance of the first large prints of the Lakes by William Bellars and Thomas Smith of Derby (Gray mentions the latter),[25] the publication of John Dalton's *Descriptive Poem* on Keswick in 1755 and the still-more-influential *Description of the Lake of Keswick* by John Brown in 1766 led to the emergence of a recognizable tourist industry in the Lakes.[26] Circumstances were favourable for the growth of tourism. As Gray was to note, the Turnpike Acts had effected important improvements in the road system and the area was suddenly far more accessible. The native population, whose traditional industries were declining, welcomed a new source of income. Even in 1769, Keswick (which Brown and Dalton had made the chief centre of attention) offered organized guides and boatmen. They knew what visitors who had read the literature about the region expected to see, and were not lacking in acumen of their own in adding to at any rate the sublime excitements. By later standards the delights on offer in 1769 were relatively modest: the Duke of Portland's barge, with brass cannon and french horns at the ready, so that visitors could enjoy having the wild echoes set flying while they lunched on the lake (as the Hutchinson brothers did on Ullswater in 1773), does not seem to have plied this early (there was also another ducal barge on Derwentwater by the time of the Hutchinsons' visit); and the museums, guide books, summer regattas and architectural fantasies still lay ahead. But nevertheless it is quite clear that, when Arthur Young made his flying visit to the Lakes in 1768, gathering material for his *A Six Month's Tour through the North of England* (1770), the places he visited and the experiences he sought out were those which Dalton's and Brown's texts had canonized. Indeed, the difference in style and tone between the episodes when he is being ferried round Derwentwater, pausing at the 'correct' sites and struggling for a succession of brief epithets to characterize the expected visual and emotional responses, and those where he abandons the tourist route (as when he finds a 'station' overlooking Windermere) or gains a little time to react for himself (as at Lodore, where he made some sketches) is strikingly apparent.

As a picturesque tourist in a hurry, Arthur Young is mostly rather coarse-grained in his responses. Sailing round Derwent-water and gradually leaving the beautiful behind him as he approaches Lodore and Borrowdale, he registers emotions which interestingly foreshadow Gray's in the following year:

> From hence you coast a dreadful shore of fragments, which time has broken from the towering rocks, many of them of a terrible size; some stopped on the land by larger than themselves, and others rolled into the lake, through a path of desolation, sweeping trees, hillocks, and every thing to the water; the very idea of a small shiver against the boat strikes with horror.[27]

A year later, Thomas Gray approached the same area on foot, and, set against Young's lumbering passage, his often-derided nervousness seems altogether less remarkable; while the quality of his prose speaks for itself:

> ·.. the crags, named *Lodoor-banks* now begin to impend terribly over your way; & more terribly, when you hear, that three years since an immense mass of rock tumbled at once from the brow, and bar'd all access to the dale (for this is the only road) till they could work their way thro' it. luckily no one was passing at the time of this fall; but down the side of the mountain & far into the lake lie dispersed the huge fragments of this ruin in all shapes & in all directions.[28]

Both the clumsy prose of Arthur Young, turning his conducted tour of Derwentwater into a series of instructions concerning places and responses for an imagined friend ('Leaving the hill you walk down to your boat, and are struck with the limpid transparency of the water...') and the more deeply-stirred responses of Gray are, in fact, strongly conditioned by both Dalton's poem and (most of all) Brown's *Description*. In the vicinity of Lodore, Dalton offers

> Rocks to the lake in thunders borne,
> Or such as o'er our heads appear
> Suspended in their mid career.

Brown supplies

> ... rocks and cliffs of stupendous height, hanging broken over the lake in horrible grandeur, some of them a thousand feet high, the woods climbing up their steep and shaggy sides, where mortal foot never yet approached. On these dreadful heights the eagles build their nests; a variety of water-falls are seen pouring from their summits, and tumbling in vast sheets from rock to rock in rude and terrible magnificence: while on all sides of this immense amphitheatre the lofty mountains rise round, piercing the clouds in shapes as spiry and fantastic as the very rocks of Dovedale.[29]

It is not difficult to see how memories of Brown's prose, working upon a sensibility eager to re-experience a vividly-remembered Alpine sublimity, and an imagination ready to re-embody it, launched Gray into the often-derided description of Borrowdale, in which the well-known pathway over Stye-Head becomes a mysterious Alpine route only approached with dread by secretive peasants in the summer season, while memories of avalanches add terror to the scene. Norman Nicholson (who rightly suspects a resurgence of the dash of humour which adds spice to the Grande Chartreuse letter to West) surely gets to the heart of the matter when he remarks that

> ... it shows the thoughts which were in his mind— thoughts which to him were part of the pleasure of the

scene. For in his tentative, tremulous way he was a seeker
for sensation. He delighted in the idea of danger so long as
it remained only an idea, and he delighted, too, in a sense
of obscurity and strangeness. It pleased him to think of
secret passes among the mountains, and he would even
assume for a moment a primitivism which was not quite in
his nature ... He anticipated more than one feature of the
later Picturesque.[30]

The early visitors to Keswick were eager to experience those
sublime thrills which Dalton, Brown and the earliest prints
published from pictures of the area promised them. Gray was
no exception. He was conditioned in relation to what he should
seek out, and (to some extent) in his expectations concerning
how he should respond, by his predecessors in the area. But he
should also be credited with having often taken an independent
line in seeking out sublime and beautiful stimuli, and in the
quickness with which he responded to unexpected opportunities or strokes of luck. So, for example, the melodramatics of
Gray's account of his walk into Borrowdale are tempered and
humanized by the enclosed narrative of how he met the young
farmer from Grange who took him and his landlord home and
gave them excellent country fare to augment the cold tongue
which they had brought with them. This young man could
offer a first-hand account of the annual attempt to rid the vale
of eagles. Gray was keen to learn about this since he had met
with the creatures already in Dalton's poem, where they:

> ... floating on the billowy sky,
> With full expanded pinnions fly,
> Their flutt'ring or their bleating prey
> Thence with death-dooming eye survey.[31]

In place of the gothic, Gray gives a good, plain indication of the
young farmer's talk, characteristically ending with an exact
specification of the kind of eagle involved and its Latin
classification by Linnaeus. The whole episode seems all the
more remarkable when one recollects that the accounts of early
visitors to the Lakes are almost wholly lacking in any mention
of the inhabitants: landscapes may be sublime or beautiful, but
they are almost always unpeopled.

Such seizings of, or being surprised by, opportunity are a constant feature of Gray's *Journal*. He arrived in the area expecting to find the sublime and the beautiful, and armed with the means to identify pictorial features through the use of a Claude-glass, tinted to give the correct tones of sunshine or sunset glows. He used the glass constantly, taking evening strolls to find the hues of Claude or his disciple Richard Wilson:

> From hence I got to the *Parsonage* a little before Sunset, & saw in my glass a picture that if I could transmitt it to you, & fix it in all the softness of its living colours, would fairly sell for a thousand pounds. this is the sweetest scene I can yet discover in point of pastoral beauty. the rest are in a sublimer style.[32]

But an earlier visit to the Parsonage had resulted in a near-accident (omitted by Mason in his tidied-up *Journal* text) which, in retrospect, seems to take on an emblematic quality:

> Dined by two o'clock at the Queen's Head, & then straggled out alone to the *Parsonage*, fell down on my back across a dirty lane with my glass open in one hand, but broke only my knuckles: stay'd nevertheless & saw the sun set in all its glory.[33]

Gray's mind was too well stored to settle long within a single convention. Nature, botanical novelties, the vagaries of light and shade in Lakeland weather, the sounds of water and experiences which affect his other senses (most early tour writers only offer a few stock effects, generally to do with rushing waters), human contacts ... these, as well as literary echoes and pictorial conventions, all crowd in to enrich Gray's *Journal* narrative, so that it rarely settles into a single mode or medium for more than the briefest snatch of time. And above all, the sharp preciseness of statement which had been his to command since the days of his early letters home from the Alps never fails him. As Peter Bicknell rightly comments:

> Like Wordsworth's *Guide*, which was to follow forty-two years later, Gray's journal stands out from the rest of the literature of the Lakes as the work of a poet.[34]

Wordsworth himself, much aware of the fact that Gray's *Journal* was written in the last part of his life, notes how

> The journal of Gray feelingly showed how the gloom of ill-health and low spirits had been irradiated by objects, which the Author's powers of mind enabled him to describe with distinctness and unaffected simplicity.[35]

He then goes on to praise Gray's description of Grasmere Vale as a 'little unsuspected paradise', thus making more explicit what his own poetry so often reveals: that Gray's vision of a rural Elysium, a fit place for poets to inhabit, contains the germ of the Wordsworthian idea that civilized man coming to visit, or reside within, the Lake District must live in studied submission to (and with respect for) the natural alliance between the glories of nature and the works of the indigenous population, evolved through centuries of the closest and most harmonious contact. Gray's prose provides, in fact, one of the starting points for Wordsworth's own *Guide to the Lakes*.

The story of how Gray's *Journal* came to be so influential remains to be told. Essentially it was a matter of chance. In 1778 the Rev. Thomas West published the first edition of his *Guide to the Lakes*, in which he frequently engages in a running debate with Gray while he indicates to visitors the best picturesque viewpoints, or 'stations' from which the scenery should be viewed. West died in the following year and the task of seeing his planned second edition through the press was entrusted to a local man, William Cockin, who added a substantial *Appendix* containing earlier accounts of the region, amid which Gray's *Journal* occupies a prominent place. In this form, West's *Guide* remained the standard book for the next forty years, until supplanted by Wordsworth's and other later guide books in the 1820s and 1830s. So generations of visitors to the Lakes experienced Gray's prose both directly and obliquely as part of West's main narrative: furthermore successive writers were affected by it. Wordsworth's description of the encircling vale and the lake in *Home at Grasmere* is clearly influenced by both Gray and West, and its visual perspective derives from them. De Quincey, describing his first sight of Grasmere from Red Bank in his *Recollections of the Lake Poets*, is equally conditioned by both what he sees and the way

Gray and West had taught him to describe and interpret it.[36] Many lesser writers were similarly affected.

But most lasting of all, perhaps, is the way Gray demonstrated that the passion for the picturesque and the cult of the sublime and the beautiful (with its confining emotional imperatives) can coexist with a respect for actuality of all kinds. Gray's prose represents, in this regard, a notable precursor of the Romantic writers who were to engage in a profound exploration of the links between man and nature in the Lake District, discovering in their own function within this endangered harmony one which might ultimately be redemptive. For all his natural timidity, Gray was an independent explorer of Lakeland, not content with a range of prescribed experiences and responses which the work of other contemporary writers shows to have been hardening rapidly into dogma even at the time of his 1769 tour. And in Gray's constantly-reiterated need to show his discoveries to (indeed almost to make them in the company of) an absent but imaginatively-present companion, a brother self, he prefigures that longing for sharers in fresh revelations concerning nature and humanity which remains among the most distinguishing and attractive features of Romantic art.

NOTES

1. A full description of Gray's surviving manuscripts, including short travel journals and notes, is given by W. P. Jones in *Thomas Gray, Scholar* (New York, 1965), pp. 175–78.

2. A reading of copies of the *Gentleman's Magazine* from about 1745 onwards shows how quickly the taste for travel narratives developed beyond the antiquarianism of earlier travel notes.

3. *Correspondence*, I, 122.

4. Ibid.

5. R. W. Ketton-Cremer, *Thomas Gray: A Biography* (Cambridge, 1955), p. 35. Walpole's letter to West of 28 September 1739, is here quoted in part from *The Correspondence of Gray, Walpole, West and Ashton*, ed. Paget Toynbee (Oxford, 1915), I, 247.

6. Ketton-Cremer, op. cit., p. 35.

7. *Correspondence*, I, 128.

8. W. P. Jones, op. cit., pp. 79–80.

9. *Correspondence*, I, 128.

10. A month had elapsed between the writing of the more direct account to Mrs Gray and the composition of this letter to West.

11. Full details of original publication and rapid reprintings can be found in Peter Bicknell's *The Picturesque Scenery of the Lake District* (Winchester, 1990), pp. 23–24.

12. *Correspondence*, I, 46–48.

13. *Correspondence*, I, 48.

14. This summary omits lesser tours, chiefly in the Thames Valley and Norfolk, many of which were made over the years.

15. *Correspondence*, III, 1189 (24 May 1771).

16. On the Turnpike Acts, road improvements and the rapid opening up of the Lake District to tourism, see Edmund Hodge, *Enjoying the Lakes: From Post Chaise to National Park* (London, 1957) and R. Millward and A. Robinson, *The Lake District* (London, 1970).

17. *Correspondence*, I, 160–61.

18. *Correspondence*, I, 386.

19. *Correspondence*, II, 427–28.

20. *Correspondence*, II, 578.

21. *Correspondence*, II, 894.

22. A choice selection of early tall stories can be found in James Clarke's *A Survey of the Lakes*, 1787.

23. Arthur Young, *A Six Month's Tour through the North of England*, 1770. (Young's account of Derwentwater and the Keswick area can be found between pages 141 and 156 of volume 3); William Hutchinson, *An Excursion to the Lakes in Westmoreland and Cumberland*, 1776.

24. By the early 1770s competition among the local innkeepers and boatmen was getting them a bad name. Having praised the superior appointments of the Duke of Portland's barge ('a commodious vessel of four oars') which could be hired for the trip round Derwentwater, William Hutchinson bursts out thus: 'The innkeepers of the neighbouring stages are not ingenuous enough to point out to strangers this convenience;—an unhappy spirit still rages which was generated in the corruptions of contested elections;—and this partiality exposes travellers to this reverse; a nasty, leaking fishing boat, with an impertinent, talkative lying pilot.' (Hutchinson, op. cit., p. 176).

25. For an annotated list of these early prints see Bicknell, op. cit., pp. 21–23.

26. For editions and reprintings elsewhere of Dalton's poem, see Bicknell, op. cit., p. 22.

27. Young, op. cit., 3, 145–46.

28. *Correspondence*, III, 1080.

29. The key passages from Dalton and Brown were collected in the Appendix to West's *Guide* in the second and subsequent editions. They can now be consulted most conveniently in *The Lake District: An Anthology*, compiled by Norman Nicholson (London, 1977). This was republished by Penguin Books (Harmondsworth) in 1977 and has frequently been reprinted.

30. Norman Nicholson, *The Lakers: The Adventures of the First Tourists* (London, 1955), p. 58.

31. Nicholson, *The Lake District*, p. 94.

32. *Correspondence*, III, 1090.

33. *Correspondence*, III, 1079.

34. Bicknell, op. cit., p. 3.

35. *Wordsworth's Guide to the Lakes*, ed. E. de Selincourt (Oxford, 1970), p. 69.

36. I have followed through these connections in 'Painters, Poets and the Grasmere Landscape', published in *Interfaces: Image, Texte, Langage* (Cahiers du Centre de Recherche Image, Texte, Langage, Université de Bourgogne (Dijon, 1991), pp. 147–60.

Thomas Warton, Thomas Gray, and the Recovery of the Past

DAVID FAIRER

I

In his recent study of the literature between Pope and Wordsworth, provocatively entitled *Preromanticism*, Marshall Brown reinstates an outmoded and despised term.[1] He replaces the old model of preliminary flickerings and prefigurings—a gradual though uneven development towards a full-flowering 'romanticism'—with his own model of an inability to be romantic, based on the concept of the premature, the not-yet-ready-to-be-born. Replacing a story of gradual and increasing success with a paradigm of repeated though varied failure, Brown nevertheless remains tied to the old teleological model, assuming an end or completion.

For Brown, 'romanticism' (or his more intensive term 'high romanticism') is the thing that completes and finally delivers what the '*pre*-romantics' sought but had neither the literary forms nor poetic language to deliver. They are therefore *pre*-romantic virtually in proportion as they are failures, fashioners of 'empty vessels that only their successors were able to fill'; and he speaks of 'their unfulfilled ambitions, that is, their preromanticism'.[2] Far from wanting to escape from the teleology of the old pre-romanticism, Brown asserts that 'the real problem with earlier studies of preromanticism is that they are not teleological enough', and he happily develops this point by dismissing any notions of the gradual or developmental: 'Eighteenth-century writers either are romantics or they are not ... they cannot be both of their age and of a later one'.[3] Brown's approach therefore is also rigidly taxonomic: a work is either 'romantic' or it is not.

One wonders quietly at this point what this clearly demar-
cated category of the 'romantic' is, and whether Brown knows
he is taking as his own *telos* something that was itself constructed retrospectively: the term 'romanticism' (the goal of
these pre-mature figures) was after all developed by Victorian
writers looking back and finding one category for a very
disparate body of literature (and it is one of Brown's principles
that you cannot have the concept until you have the language
for it). It is a slight contradiction, then, for him to disconte-
nance any approach which in his words 'reads history backwards', since 'a telos is a goal in the distance'. True to his word,
Brown finds one of the great romantic achievements to be the
discovery of forward-looking hope, which for him is the only
active and productive time-sense. He says of Goldsmith:
'Goldsmith's imagination . . . looked nostalgically backward. It
needed the power of hope to turn it around and marry it to an
active and productive time sense'.[4]

What hope, then, for the two figures who form the subject of
this essay? Two writers whose scholastic and poetic work was
emphatically retrospective?

The earlier 'pre-romanticism' was essentially a narrative,
and in it Gray and Warton played important roles as 'pioneers'
of romanticism;[5] little attempt was ever made to contrast their
contributions. The trouble with the old narrative is that it *was*
teleological and therefore had little investment in opposing two
figures who seemed to be cooperating in the same enterprise. It
is such an opposition that I take as my subject here. My
argument is that Gray and Warton offer two contrasting
models for the relationship of a mid-eighteenth-century poet-
scholar to his literary past, and in placing it in the context of
what is sure to be a reopened debate about pre-romanticism, I
want to use this contrast to assert the significance of the
Wartonian model in challenging Brown's method and conclusions.

I am also attempting to work towards a view of literary
history which reinstates notions of development, growth, and
root-systems of literary influence, but freed from the teleology
of either the old or 'new' concept of 'pre-romanticism'. In this
enterprise I take as my cue the notion of a retrospect, a looking
back which becomes an attempt to recover the past; and what

Warton in particular offers is a language of the organic as a means of making this recovery: hence my use of the terms 'growth', 'root-systems' and other organic images drawn from Warton's work: springs and sources, sacred removed places where a mouldering text is still partly visible, or where an ancient language can yet be heard; a recovery of, and germination from, a hidden older text. Warton's images of interconnectedness through recovering voices and texts from the past will perhaps provide an alternative model for literary history as sustaining a precarious tradition, a development through retrospection repeated by the many poets of the last two decades of the eighteenth century who drew on Warton's work, and in turn by Wordsworth, Coleridge and Southey, who feed it into their own poetry. In this model the stress is on a locating of sources and an acceptance of influence as benign. In place of a Bloomian anxiety at a repressively looming father-figure, there is a nurturing parent encouraging articulateness. I argue that Warton's role in establishing this particular model was an important one, lost sight of in the taxonomies that have replaced the interwoven narratives of literary history.

II

An appropriate starting-point is 15 April 1770, when Thomas Gray sent Thomas Warton his outline sketch of a history of English poetry, a project he had enthusiastically taken up in 1753 but abandoned some ten years later.[6] A reworking of a similar sketch made by Pope,[7] Gray's scheme is a formal one, grouping poets under their various schools: the 'School of Provence', the First, Second and Third 'Italian Schools', and the 'School of France'. The 'Second Italian School', for example, contains Ariosto and Tasso, and in England Wyatt and Surrey, the great Spenser, followed by such figures as Drayton and Golding, and (as Gray writes) 'this school ends in Milton'; while the 'Third Italian School' ('full of conceit') begins in Elizabeth's reign, takes in Donne and Crashaw, reaches its height in Cowley, 'ending perhaps in *Sprat*'. His final 'School of France' is the familiar Johnsonian pantheon beginning with Waller, then Dryden and Pope, 'which', says Gray, 'has continued down to our own times'.

Gray's letter is a revealing and rather puzzling document. In 1660, were there *three* schools active at once, one coming to its climax in Cowley, one reaching its end in Milton, while another was being inaugurated by Waller? And where did Gray place his own work? Did he really believe that Milton had marked a closure? That there was no continuity during his own century from *The Faerie Queene* or *Paradise Lost?* And was he himself continuing the French school of Dryden and Pope? I don't believe Gray could have thought this. But it is symptomatic that his plan is not merely taxonomic (splitting off Milton, Cowley and Waller into different schools, for example), but that he could not find continuity between Spenser, Milton and himself. Yet we know that he would read Spenser before starting to compose.[8]

It is instructive at this point to set Gray's scheme of categories, discontinuities and endings, alongside Warton's response to this plan. When he received Gray's letter Warton was already well advanced with the first volume of his *History of English Poetry*,[9] and his reply to Gray attempts as diplomatically as possible to explain how his own work is generically different. Warton's language uses the ambulatory imagery of the picturesque traveller who stops to take in the view and absorbs what offers itself to his notice:

> I write chronologically in Sections; and continue, as matter successively offers itself, in a series of regular Annals, down to & beyond the Restoration ... I should have said before, that, although I proceed chronologically, yet I often stand still to give some general View, as perhaps of a *particular species* of poetry, &c. and even *anticipate* sometimes for this purpose. These *views* often form *one* Section; yet are interwoven into the Tenor of the work without interrupting my historical series. In this respect, some of my Sections have the effect of your *Parts* or *Divisions*.[10]

Warton's imagery is of interweaving. The manuscript of the letter shows that he originally wrote 'without interrupting my historical thread'. By crossing out 'thread' and substituting 'series' he is perhaps trying to recall himself from his metaphor of intertexture towards a stricter chronology. But again the manuscript is revealing: in his phrase describing the scope of his work as 'down to & beyond the Restoration', the phrase '& beyond' is an interlineation. He was at this stage, it seems, not certain where his journey would end.

The first volume of Warton's *History of English Poetry* appeared in 1774 after Gray's death, and in the preface Warton describes his task as one of digression and recapitulation, of gathering up what has been scattered:

> I have often deviated into incidental digressions; and have sometimes stopped in the course of my career, for the sake of recapitulation, for the purpose of collecting scattered notices into a single and uniform point of view ...[11]

And he turns in confessional mode to the schemes of Pope and Gray, now explicitly rejecting their taxonomic approach as a contrived system-building that imposes artificial categories on to the fulness and variety of literary history:

> To confess the real truth, upon examination and experiment, I soon discovered their mode of treating my subject, plausible as it is, and brilliant in theory, to be attended with difficulties and inconveniences, and productive of embarassment both to the reader and the writer. Like other ingenious systems, it sacrificed much useful intelligence to the observation of arrangement; and in the place of that satisfaction which results from a clearness and a fulness of information, seemed only to substitute the merit of disposition, and the praise of contrivance. The constraint imposed by a mechanical attention to this distribution, appeared to me to destroy that free exertion of research with which such a history ought to be executed, and not easily reconcileable with that complication, variety, and extent of materials, which it ought to comprehend.[12]

Warton sees his own task, therefore, as one of absorption and collection, a drawing of threads together, rather than distributing into categories. His rejection of the 'mechanical' presents his history, by implication, as an organic enterprise. Indeed the *History*, originally contracted for two volumes, grew over the years as Warton absorbed new discoveries, and the eighty pages of the fourth volume issued after his death took the narrative no further than the beginning of the seventeenth century.[13] And while it grew it became increasingly retrospective, as more material was accumulated from additional research and helpful correspondents. In the case of the *History*, Warton's difficulty in completing a narrative was radically different from Gray's. I shall go on to argue that in his poems, as in his scheme for a history of English poetry, Gray was unable to make a connection between past and present which would link up his own voice with those of his sources. Warton's dilemma, however, was the reverse one of wishing to recover his own sources, and the incompletion of the *History* seems symptomatic of his preference for working with the material that provided the fertile ground for his own poetry. His editing of Milton's early poems during the last eight years of his life[14] can be seen as reaching back along the thread to those texts that had inspired so much of his own earlier verse. In fact *The History of English Poetry*, when supplemented by *Observations on the Faerie Queene*[15] and the *Milton*, is largely complete in terms of Warton's own poetic ancestry.

But the pattern is not completed in the teleological sense. Warton's poetic retrospection reaches towards his sources; his substantial annotations to the *Milton* feed back into Spenser, his *Observations on the Faerie Queene* work from that poem to Spenser's roots in Chaucer and medieval romance. Warton's much-cherished lengthy footnotes are frequently in this sense retrospective narratives, offering him a means of presenting material recovered from oblivion and 'enriching the stock of our early literature'.[16]

Much of Warton's work was a recovery of the past in the terms which I have outlined, but in his more specifically historical writing there is the added ingredient of place. Each place and institution with which Warton was associated was the subject of his historical study, with a particular emphasis on its origins. As a fellow of Trinity College Oxford he wrote the life of its founder, Sir Thomas Pope, and of its most generous benefactor President Bathurst, and to this work he prefixed a Latin poem on the building of the college chapel, erected at Bathurst's expense, 1691–94.[17] Among the Trinity Warton manuscripts is an unpublished poem, 'Ode on the Monument of Sir Thomas Pope',[18] set in the college chapel at midnight while Warton is kneeling in prayer at the founder's tomb. The founding of Oxford University was celebrated in *The Triumph of Isis* (London, 1750), and in his humorous *Companion* to the official Oxford guide[19] he sketched in some of the unofficial history of the place, the Carfax conduit and the old clock overlooking it, as well as the venerable down-and-outs' bench nearby. His collection of humorous Oxford verse, *The Oxford Sausage* (1764), gathered and preserved much fugitive material, and Warton himself engraved the frontispiece of 'Mrs Dorothy Spreadbury, Inventress of the Oxford Sausage'. As Rector of Kiddington, near Woodstock, Warton published the history of the parish from its earliest settlement,[20] and his second home at Winchester College (where his brother Joseph was Headmaster) was commemorated in his *History and Description of Winchester* (1760). He also prepared for the press an edition of the fourteenth-century account roll of its founder, William of Wykeham, which he discovered in the muniment room in 1778.

Much of Warton's poetry is about the location and recovery of texts, of authentic lost voices; but they are revived not as something dead, but as a resource that can feed into the work of the modern poet. His 'Sonnet Written in a Blank Leaf of Dugdale's Monasticon' is specific:

> While cloyster'd Piety displays
> Her mouldering roll, the piercing eye explores
> New manners, and the pomp of elder days,
> Whence culls the pensive bard his pictur'd stores.
>
> (ll. 9–12)[21]

'New manners' is the shock, where we might expect the adjective 'old'. But Warton's reversal of regarding the 'old' as the 'new' is a typical function of his retrospectiveness: he searches for fresh things backwards in time, and here he finds the writings of the 'elder days' a source for the images of the modern poet.

Repeatedly in Warton's verse we encounter a lost text, worn

away by time, covered in mould, dimly discernible, and usually housed in a remote and concealed place. In the 'Ode Written at Vale-Royal Abbey'[22] he goes

> within the deep fane's inmost cell,
> To pluck the grey moss from the mantled stone,
> Some holy founder's mouldering name to spell.
>
> (ll. 74–76)

In his 'Ode on the Approach of Summer'[23] he enters a more mystical space, but with similar intent:

> As thro' the caverns dim I wind,
> Might I that holy legend find,
> By fairies spelt in mystic rhymes,
> To teach enquiring later times
>
> (ll. 249–52)

The texts are 'holy' because they are original and revelatory, and his search is for the founder of a native tradition. In his 'Sonnet on King Arthur's Round Table at Winchester'[24] he engages with another text waiting to be recovered:

> on the capacious round
> Some British pen has sketch'd the names renown'd,
> In marks obscure, of his immortal peers.
> Though join'd by magic skill, with many a rime,
> The Druid-frame, unhonour'd, falls a prey
> To the slow vengeance of the wisard Time,
> And fade the British characters away
>
> (ll. 6–12)

The table carries a text that is disappearing from view: it is literally a *poetic* language that is fading, taking with it the 'British characters'—both the words themselves and the men who once sat around that table. But they live on, Warton ends by saying, in the pages of Spenser. The world of Arthur, then, has not been entirely lost, and Warton's unspoken boast here is that he himself, in his *Observations on the Faerie Queene*, had established Malory as one of Spenser's chief sources.[25] The poem is completed with that silent link to his own work as poet, critic and scholar.

Warton's acts of recovery are the subject of a humorous

poem by his brother Joseph Warton, in which Joseph issues a fearful curse on his brother; it is a nightmare in which poor Thomas's texts all fade and elude him:

> But now may curses every search attend
> That seems inviting! may'st thou pore in vain
> For dubious Door-ways! may revengeful moths
> Thy ledgers eat! may chronologic spouts
> Retain no cypher legible! may Crypts
> Lurk undiscern'd! nor may'st thou spell the names
> Of Saints in storied Windows! nor the dates
> Of bells discover! nor the genuine site
> Of Abbots' Pantries!
>
> (ll. 18–26)[26]

In Warton's poems the doorways and hidden entries into the past regularly open, as empty and deserted places are peopled and filled with light and music.

Linked to these ruins are the many Wartonian secret places, some containing magic springs, which become sources from which the poet can draw. In his early 'Invocation to a Water-Nymph' (written before he was twenty)[27] the poet summons the nymph 'in secret Solitude' where she presides over a magic spring. As the poet seeks permission to drink from the 'silver Lake' he invokes not only Milton's Sabrina, but through her the young Milton himself. On Warton's part this was to be a life-long commitment. Significantly, Warton's final poem, the *Birthday Ode* of 1790,[28] concerns itself with springs, celebrating a series of health-giving waters: the 'mystic spring' of Bath, the 'dim retreat' in the cliffs at Matlock, the cavernous rocks at Hotwells, Bristol, and the 'rich veins' within the mountains at Malvern. Wartonian caves and nooks are filled with music, echoes, dim or reflected lights, the sounds of springs, whispers, murmurs or chanting choirs.

In a similar way, Warton's ruins are not merely dilapidated or empty, but are spaces waiting to be re-animated by the poet's imagination. An example of this procedure is an unpublished fragment, 'As o'er your domes'.[29] Here the poet enters into a scene of darkness and desolation, but as he sits on the turf and contemplates the history of the ruined abbey, it

becomes once more consecrated and spiritually alive, a place of
magic sounds and visionary light:

> Ah see! amid the crumbling waste
> In rubbish foul obscur'd, digrac'd,
> The precious Vase no longer flows,
> No more with ancient Lustre glows.
> Yet shall the Muse's piercing Eye
> The consecrated Spot descry;
> Her clue shall guide Me to persuade
> The midmost depth of the dun Shade,
> And each mild Eve with musing Pace
> I'll joy to seek the sainted place,
> And on the bare turf sadly sit
> In vision wild, and holy fit.
> While rapt I hear in thought profound
> That golden harp's ambrosial sound
> That sooth'd each Eve the Sage's Mind
> To rest on leafy couch reclin'd;
> While as the warbles by degrees
> Sink in a dying close, and cease,
> The gleams thick-glancing I behold
> Of parting wings bedropt with gold.
>
> (ll. 25–44)

In this poem Warton enters the world of Gray's churchyard (a
phrase earlier in the fragment, 'Beneath yon' yew-tree's awfull
Shade' [l. 17] is a specific echo); but the poem works
retrospectively, reaching beyond the figure of Gray's poet to
recover that earlier contemplative, Milton's Penseroso, and
drawing on his 'vision wild, and holy fit' to discover and re-
animate the 'consecrated Spot'.

There is a surfeit of holy texts in Gray's *Elegy*—storied urns,
frail memorials, artless tales, and uncouth rhymes—strewn
around and begging to be read, imploring the passing tribute
of a sigh. But the effect of Gray's speaker is not to recover and
re-animate them. Instead he builds up a sense of frustration, of
indignant possibility left interred and repressed, however
much the turf heaves about him. At the emotional climax of the
poem the various quiet sounds are gathered up into the 'voice
of Nature' (l. 91), which cries out from the tomb as if expecting

some personal benediction from the speaker. But at the point where we might look for the 'I' of the poem to accept this into his own present experience, the text is taken out of his hands, and he is given his own tombstone, not by an act of imaginative sympathy, but by the decree of a fatal and impersonal voice upon him.

In the poem's original ending the speaker had intervened to still the cries and offer through his own internalized voice a blessing that linked his present self with the dead of the graveyard:

> Hark how the sacred Calm, that broods around
> Bids ev'ry fierce tumultuous Passion cease
> In still small Accents whisp'ring from the Ground
> A grateful Earnest of eternal Peace
>
> No more with Reason & thyself at Strife;
> Give anxious Cares & endless Wishes room
> But thro' the cool sequester'd Vale of Life
> Pursue the silent Tenour of thy Doom.[30]

But in removing these lines from the final version, as Roger Lonsdale has said, 'the suffering present is ingeniously vacated'.[31] Part of the poem's enormous power comes, I think, from its denial of that recovery and re-animation inherent in the Wartonian model, where the speaker's imaginative sympathy interacts with the scene: Gray's terrifying concept of 'dumb Forgetfulness' could have no greater contrast than Warton's voicing of memory. Gray's 'ample page / Rich with the spoils of time' (ll. 49–50), that text which so delighted Warton, is never unrolled.

Another poem which draws power from its inability to recover the past and give it meaning in the present is Gray's 'Sonnet on the Death of Richard West', but here the first-person singular is trapped in the present, and in place of an elegiac imaginative retrospect is an endless cycle of present-tense activity in which the poet cannot join. In this poem there is no past to contemplate. Surrounding the poet is a busy scene of recovery and resumption (by the sun, fields and birds) which only serves to throw into ironic relief his own inability to stage any kind of imaginative retrieval from the past: 'I fruitless mourn to him, that cannot hear' (l. 13). In a different way from the *Elegy*, this poem too is haunted by dumb forgetfulness; here a gap between a present that cannot speak and a past that cannot hear.

In the *Ode on a Distant Prospect of Eton College* Gray's difficulties in negotiating between past and present are expressed through the gulf between youth and age, innocence and experience. The poet remains a silent voyeur who watches the children at play and is trapped in a knowledge he declines to share. In his analysis of the division of the self in Gray's poetry, Roger Lonsdale considers the *Eton Ode* in these temporal terms, seeing in it 'a gulf between past and present selves which cannot be explored or given meaning'.[32] In terms of my Warton–Gray contrast this gulf becomes especially ironic through the handling of old father Thames, and the role he does, and does not, play in Gray's poem.

In Warton's poetry, links with the past are regularly mediated through a parent-figure, specifically a benign foster-parent who carries away the infant and nurtures it in a secluded place. The model, from *The Pleasures of Melancholy* (1747) is the baby Contemplation,

> whom, as tradition tells,
> Once in his evening walk a Druid found,
> Far in a hollow glade of Mona's woods;
> And piteous bore with hospitable hand
> To the close shelter of his oaken bow'r.
> There soon the sage admiring mark'd the dawn
> Of solemn musing in your pensive thought;
> For when a smiling babe, you lov'd to lie
> Oft deeply list'ning to the rapid roar
> Of wood-hung Meinai, stream of Druids old.
>
> (ll. 306–15)[33]

This pattern is repeated through several poems of Warton's, where the baby becomes Poetry, nurtured by King Alfred in his Saxon cell; or the 'royal nursling' Edward the Black Prince, brought up by his foster-mother, the University of Oxford.[34] And in his brother Joseph's *The Enthusiast* (London,

1744) is the same motif, where Shakespeare is a smiling babe found by Fancy on the banks of the Avon, who takes him to her cavern, feeds 'the little prattler' and teaches him her songs.[35]

Such Wartonian fosterings express an organic growth from infancy to maturity, a development from childish prattlings to articulateness, under the guidance of a benign parent. There is no gulf dividing innocence from experience, no terrible discovery, but instead a loving routine of learning, listening and feeding. In the special removed place the idea can grow and find its own voice.

Turning back to Gray's *Eton Ode* we can see that such nurturing and teaching is doubly avoided. Alongside the playing fields 'Wanders the hoary Thames along / His silver-winding way' (ll. 9–10). This personified figure is too old and lazy to be a spring or a watery cave, or a Wartonian 'native stream',[36] and unlike Warton's matronly Isis, he is not interested in the youth educated on his banks. Instead, he quietly wanders away, refusing the role of wise counsellor or foster-parent. He does not respond to the poet's questions and contributes nothing further to the poem. In the river's absence, the speaker assumes the place of the allegorical parent-figure ready to impart a store of knowledge; but he realizes he can teach the children nothing except the misery of maturity, and so keeps silent. For him, knowledge is fate, and thought a fall from innocence. And so, the infant, the parent-figure and the poet, which in the Wartonian model would have converged, go their separate ways.

The one poem of Gray's which seems to be consciously attempting a retrieval of the past to re-animate the present is his ambitious Pindaric Ode, 'The Progress of Poesy' (1757). It takes for its theme, after all, the progress of lyric verse from the ancient Greece of Pindar, to Rome, and on to Albion's shore; and at first sight there appears within it a perfect example of the Wartonian fostering of a child of Nature, in this case the infant Shakespeare. Gray's passage in the third strophe is directly drawn from Joseph Warton's cameo in *The Enthusiast*, but it is the contrast between them which is, for my purposes, significant. These are Warton's lines from the version revised for Dodsley's *Collection of Poems*, 1748:

What are the lays of artful Addison,
Coldly correct, to Shakespear's warblings wild?
Whom on the winding Avon's willow'd banks
Fair Fancy found, and bore the smiling babe
To a close cavern: (still the shepherds shew
The sacred place, whence with religious awe
They hear, returning from the field at eve,
Strange whisp'rings of sweet music through the air)
Here, as with honey gather'd from the rock,
She fed the little prattler, and with songs
Oft sooth'd his wond'ring ears, with deep delight
On her soft lap he sat, and caught the sounds.

(ll. 168–79)

And this is Gray's version in 'The Progress of Poesy' of
Shakespeare's infancy:

Far from the sun and summer-gale,
In thy green lap was Nature's Darling laid,
What time, where lucid Avon stray'd,
To Him the mighty Mother did unveil
Her aweful face: The dauntless Child
Stretch'd forth his little arms, and smiled.
This pencil take (she said) whose colours clear
Richly paint the vernal year:
Thine too these golden keys, immortal Boy!

(ll. 83–91)

Where Joseph Warton's kindly foster-mother, Fancy, feeds
and soothes the infant Shakespeare in her lap while she sings to
him, Gray's figure is a slightly alarming 'mighty Mother' who
unveils her 'aweful face' before the baby, and in entrusting him
with the golden keys seems to be imposing a responsibility *upon*
him rather than awakening a divine gift *within* him. In face of
this, the 'dauntless' infant's stretching forth his little arms is as
much an act of courage as a response to maternal love.

The hints at sublime awe that have found their way into this
episode are present also at the end of the poem, where Gray
reaches the present day, having himself to be the climax of this
handing-on of poetic power. But the act of transfer is signalled
instead by a moment of loss, followed by a timid question—a

modesty *topos* that sits awkwardly after the earlier lyric flights.
He is talking of Dryden:

> Hark, his hands the lyre explore!
> Bright-eyed Fancy hovering o'er
> Scatters from her pictur'd urn
> Thoughts, that breath[e], and words, that burn.
> But ah! 'tis heard no more—
> Oh! Lyre divine, what daring Spirit
> Wakes thee now?
>   (ll. 107–13)

It is as if the 'Thoughts, that breath[e], and words, that burn'
have to cease (as they almost do through over-punctuation)
before Gray can bring himself forward; and even as he does so,
he disclaims the 'ample pinion' (l. 114) of Pindar, which is what
his poem has to this point been exemplifying. Gray's 'progress'
in this way beautifully collapses into self-questioning and
uncertainty.[37]

Earlier, in discussing Gray's sketch-plan for a history of
English poetry, I drew attention to his curious statement that
the tradition of Surrey and Spenser had ended with Milton,
and it is significant that in the middle of 'The Progress of
Poesy', at the very moment when he appears to be tracing a
tradition of writing, Gray added a footnote drawing on that
same fact (as he saw it) of *dis*continuity. His note to line 66
reads:

> Progress of Poetry from Greece to Italy, and from Italy to
> England. Chaucer was not unacquainted with the writ-
> ings of Dante or of Petrarch. The Earl of Surrey and Sir
> Tho. Wyatt had travelled in Italy, and formed their taste
> there; Spenser imitated the Italian writers; Milton
> improved on them: but this School expired soon after the
> Restoration, and a new one arose on the French model,
> which has subsisted ever since.[38]

This footnote (quite close to the plan he sent Warton) was
added for the 1768 edition, and it is perhaps with a slight shock
that we notice that his underlying image here is not one of a
thread of influence joining the various authors, but rather a

fan-shaped outline, where the poets individually drew on a set of Italian models. Perhaps this simple difference offers a clue as to why he could not formulate a linear pattern that might link his own work through Milton to Spenser. For Gray, perhaps, it was not 'the Tradition of Surrey, Spenser and Milton', but almost literally 'the Second Italian School', and Gray could see no place for himself in a school which had (in his words) 'expired' a century earlier.

Where Warton, in his *History of English Poetry* and his own verse, reached back into the past to establish continuities and recover a tradition of which he felt himself a part, Gray is at his most powerful and interesting when confronting discon-nections and loss, texts that find no sympathetic reader, voices that echo with a momentary chill, break off, or expire.

Gray's final problematic reaching into the past, 'The Bard', has an underlying irony, once again pointed to by Lonsdale:

> Gray has not merely provided his poet with flowing locks and bardic robes, but has invested him with everything he and his contemporaries could identify as a lost source of poetic power, as if hoping to channel into his poem the authentic springs of all the great poetry of the past ... Yet at the end the Bard ... has to commit suicide, and that spectacular plunge to death also marks the end of Gray's serious career as a poet at the age of forty.[39]

The first major discontinuity was in the writing of the poem. By August 1755 Gray had composed the bard's opening curse on King Edward and his lament for his fellow poets whom the King had executed, followed by their ghostly chorus prophesy-ing the disasters that would overtake Edward's Plantagenet successors. This came to a climax in the third strophe, where the Bard disappears:

> "Edward, lo! to sudden fate
> "(Weave we the woof. The thread is spun)
> "Half of thy heart we consecrate.
> "(The web is wove. The work is done.)"
> 'Stay, oh stay! nor thus forlorn
> 'Leave me unbless'd, unpitied, here to mourn:
> 'In yon bright track, that fires the western skies,

'They melt, they vanish from my eyes.'

(ll. 97–104)

It would seem that Gray broke off either at this point, or at the phrase 'The work is done' four lines earlier, and for twenty months could not bring himself to take the poem any further.[40] Throughout this time the ode remained suspended, either on an ironic note of completeness ('The work is done') or on a loss of vision ('they vanish from my eyes'), and both are oddly appropriate for the view of Gray which I have been taking in this essay.

From the 'original argument' of the poem in Gray's commonplace book it is clear that he had intended the bard to prophesy

> the noble ardour of poetic Genius in this Island, & that men shall never be wanting to celebrate true Virtue & Valour in immortal strains, to expose Vice & infamous Pleasure, & boldly censure Tyranny and Oppression.[41]

But William Mason believed that Gray had lost confidence in the idea that the later development of English poetry from Spenser to Addison could be seen as bearing out the bard's optimism.[42] If Mason was right, then Gray's problem of finding continuity in literary history was once again a crucial issue.

By a fortunate coincidence in the spring of 1757 Gray suddenly felt himself in touch with the genuine bardic tradition, when the blind Welsh harper, John Parry, performed at Cambridge, and (says Gray) 'scratch'd out such ravishing blind Harmony, such tunes of a thousand year old with names enough to choak you, as have set all this learned body a'dancing'.[43] The ode was duly finished, with the bard prophesying the glorious Tudors and, in ten awkward and obscure lines, looking forward to the poetry of Spenser, Shakespeare and Milton (we need Gray's own note to recognise the allusions):

> 'The verse adorn again
> 'Fierce War, and faithful Love,
> 'And Truth severe, by fairy Fiction drest.
> 'In buskin'd measures move

'Pale Grief, and pleasing Pain,
'With Horrour, Tyrant of the throbbing breast.
'A Voice, as of the Cherub-Choir,
'Gales from blooming Eden bear;
'And distant warblings lessen on my ear,
'That lost in long futurity expire.

(ll. 125–34)

Gray's note in defence of these last two lines is: 'The succession of Poets after Milton's time'. Mason was unhappy with them, and Gray wrote to him:

> why you would alter *lost* in long futurity I do not see, unless because you think *lost & expire* are tautologous, or because it looks as if the end of the prophecy were disappointed by it, & that people may think Poetry in Britain was some time or other really to expire: whereas the meaning is only, that it was lost to his ear from the immense distance. I can not give up *lost*, for it begins with an L.[44]

But we have seen Gray use the word *expire* in describing the termination of the poetic tradition of Spenser and Milton. Gray's humour cannot dispel a feeling that the sounds the bard hears from the future *may* die out before they can reach Gray himself.

In all these poems Gray's speaker has difficulty in retrieving something from the past and re-animating it so that it can find a response in the present (that thread between past and present which I have traced in Warton's work). In the *Elegy* the poet is pre-empted by a fate which intervenes to memorialize *him* in the past before he can draw the strands of his present contemplation together; in the West sonnet there *is* no voice from the past, only an objectless present; in the *Eton Ode* the speaker contemplates his own past innocence across an unbridgeable gulf, like Satan watching Adam and Eve; and in the two Pindaric Odes the poet finds it difficult to discern an unbroken tradition linking present and past. In their different ways these texts all pose a teleological problem: each finds it difficult to conclude, to find completion in the present.

At this point it is appropriate to turn back to Thomas

Warton, to a poem which can be seen in this context as his reworking of Gray's 'Bard'. 'The Grave of King Arthur' was first
published in Warton's 1777 collection of poems. The setting is
Cilgarran Castle, where Henry II is holding court, and, as if to
draw attention to his poetic act of re-animation, Warton adds
in his introductory note:

> The Castle of Cilgarran, ... now a most romantic ruin,
> stands on a rock descending to the river Teivi in Pembro-
> keshire: and was built by Roger Montgomery, who led the
> van of the Normans at Hastings.[45]

It is this ruin which Warton brings to life:

> Illumining the vaulted roof,
> A thousand torches flam'd aloof:
> From massy cups, with golden gleam
> Sparkled the red metheglin's stream:
> To grace the gorgeous festival,
> Along the lofty-window'd wall,
> The storied tapestry was hung:
> With minstrelsy the rafters rung
> Of harps, that with reflected light
> From the proud gallery glitter'd bright
>
> (ll. 9–18)

Inside the brilliantly-lit castle Henry is being entertained by
the Welsh bards, and as in Gray's poem they divide into a
chorus and a single ancient bard with white flowing hair. They
sing in turn to Henry about the legend of King Arthur,
supposedly waiting to return and save his country. In Gray's
poem the bard had cried out at his vision of the future:

> 'Ye unborn Ages, crowd not on my soul!
> 'No more our long-lost Arthur we bewail.
>
> (ll. 108–09)

Gray's speaker is uneasily poised between what has been *long-
lost* and what is yet *unborn*, and at this moment, for all his
ecstatic vision, he is a figure of disconnection. The bards in
Warton's poem, however, make the 'long-lost Arthur' the
theme of their song, and they attempt to recover him. They do

so in two different ways: first the chorus of bards sings how the elfin queen removes him

> "To her green isle's enamel'd steep,
> "In the navel of the deep.
> "O'er his wounds she sprinkled dew
> "From flowers that in Arabia grew:
> "On a rich, inchanted bed,
> "She pillow'd his majestic head;
> "O'er his brow, with whispers bland,
> "Thrice she wav'd an opiate wand;
> "And, to soft music's airy sound,
> "Her magic curtains clos'd around.
> "There, renew'd the vital spring,
> "Again he reigns a mighty king
>
> (ll. 51–62)

Warton reaches back through Milton's *Comus* to that mythical place of revivification, Spenser's Garden of Adonis.[46] But at this point the ancient bard himself steps forward and sings another kind of song, which moves from myth to history, from teleology to archaeology. To the assembled company he recounts how Arthur's body was carried off to Glastonbury:

> "In the fair vale of Avalon:
> "There, with chanted orison,
> "And the long blaze of tapers clear,
> "The stoled fathers met the bier:
> "Through the dim iles, in order dread
> "Of martial woe, the chief they led,
> "And deep intomb'd in holy ground,
> "Before the altar's solemn bound.
> "Around no dusky banners wave,
> "No mouldering trophies mark the grave:
> "Away the ruthless Dane has torn
> "Each trace that Time's slow touch had worn;
> "And long, o'er the neglected stone,
> "Oblivion's veil its shade has thrown:
> "The faded tomb, with honour due,
> "'Tis thine, O Henry, to renew!
>
> (ll. 117–32)

And the bard calls on Henry to retrieve and honour Arthur's physical remains. The poem ends with the King vowing on his return, not just to recover the body but to build a shrine in commemoration of him:

> O'er the sepulchre profound
> Ev'n now, with arching sculpture crown'd,
> He plans the chantry's choral shrine,
> The daily dirge, and rites divine.
>
> (ll. 177–80)

The place of death will be given life, and Arthur's tomb will be the location for poetry and music to voice the present's recovery of the past.

III

In an article in the *Quarterly Review* in 1824, Robert Southey singled out Thomas Warton as the decisive influence on what he thought of as the new generation of English poets: 'If any man may be called the father of the present race, it is Thomas Warton', and he spoke of the 'School of Warton' as 'the true English school'.[47] Elsewhere I have attempted to trace this 'school' in the work of William Lisle Bowles, Henry Headley, Thomas Russell, John Bampfylde, Henry Kett, Thomas Park, William Benwell and George Richards, and in the earlier poems of Charlotte Smith, Southey himself and his friend Robert Lovell; and through to Coleridge's River Otter and Wordsworth's Tintern Abbey.[48] In these writers the various Wartonian motifs I have attempted to gather together link up in subtle and fruitful ways: the recovery of invisible or fading texts; special removed places within which voices can be heard; neglected spaces that may be animated by imagination or retrieved through a specifically literary archaeology; springs from which the poet may learn an original, revelatory language; and behind these motifs the concept of the nurturing foster-parent. The Wartonian places are visited or revisited, discovered or granted, and there is consequently the underlying concept of the gift of language, the transfer of eloquence from one age or generation to another. If we are to use Southey's word 'school', then I think we have to do so with due circumspection, avoiding the institutional implications behind Gray's use of that word, and recovering the element of benign learning and discovery (the element powerfully avoided in Gray's *Eton Ode*) that these later poets found in Warton, and Warton himself found in Milton and Spenser. The pattern emerging here is not one of influence forwards, or development towards a conclusion, but a repeated retrospect, with a succession of poets linking themselves to a root-system which could recover something of value. Just as Warton delighted in the early Milton because he could recover through it the world of Spenser, and revelled in Spenser because of the more distant echoes of Malory and Chaucer, so those who followed Warton did so because they could work back through him to a native tradition of poetry.

It is grotesquely inappropriate to impose an anticipatory pattern on the retrospection of the later eighteenth century. A taxonomically-conceived 'pre-romanticism' simply will not do: it is ineffective in characterizing the organic model of literary history (which Warton exemplifies), and it allows no room for the kinds of distinction I have tried to make between two of the age's most influential poetic voices. The complex patterns and shapes of literary history (as Warton understood when writing his *History of English Poetry*) operate in many different ways, and we have to be careful about imposing categories on what Warton called its 'complication, variety, and extent of materials'. If we read literary history teleologically, whether according to the old notion of 'pre-romanticism' or Marshall Brown's revised version, we have to beware of assuming that any literary tradition or tendency can be completed, and even more of attaching greater value to something (in our own eyes) that *is* completed and finished.

Warton was not influenced by Spenser and Milton; he absorbed them, led his own poetry back through them: he was not influenced by a tradition, but placed his own work within it (writing, as it were, retrospectively), repeatedly working his way to its sources, the vital springs of his own 'native stream'. In place of an 'anxiety of influence' or 'the burden of the past', Warton substituted a willing absorption, recovery and re-animation of the past. His literary parent is a loving and nurturing one.

Set against Warton, Gray does indeed, from our vantage point, appear the more modern figure, a poet of anxieties and disconnections as opposed to Warton's reassuring connectedness. But what that contrast should really tell us is that any attempt to generalize about the literary history of the mideighteenth century, however 'brilliant in theory' (to use Warton's words), will 'like other ingenious systems ... sacrifice much useful intelligence to the observation of arrangement'.[49]

NOTES

1. Marshall Brown, *Preromanticism* (Stanford, 1991).

2. Ibid., pp. 6–7.

3. Ibid., p. 3.

4. Ibid., p. 9.

5. See, for example, Edmund Gosse, 'Two Pioneers of Romanticism: Joseph and Thomas Warton', *Proceedings of the British Academy*, VII (1915–1916), 145–63. Among influential works were W. L. Phelps, *The Beginnings of the English Romantic Movement* (Boston, 1893) and Henry A. Beers, *A History of English Romanticism in the Eighteenth Century* (London, 1899).

6. Gray–Warton, 15 April 1770 (Eton College MS 316). Part of this letter was printed in *Correspondence*, III, 1122–25. On Gray's project, see William Powell Jones, *Thomas Gray, Scholar* (New York, 1965), pp. 84–107.

7. Pope's skeleton scheme for a history of poetry is assessed by René Wellek, *The Rise of English Literary History* (Chapel Hill, 1941), pp. 162–63. The scribbled paper was found by William Warburton, who sent it to William Mason *via* Richard Hurd. From Mason it reached Gray, who made an exact transcript (see *Works of Gray*, ed. T. J. Mathias, 1814, II, vi–vii) and from it drew up his own plan. Hurd had already sent Warton a copy of Pope's scheme (see Hurd–Warton, 10 December 1763. British Library Add. MS 42560, fol. 123).

8. Norton Nicholls's 'Reminiscences' of Gray (1805), *Correspondence*, III, 1290.

9. *The History of English Poetry, from the Close of the Eleventh to the Commencement of the Eighteenth Century*, 3 vols (London, 1774–81). Warton had been gathering materials since 1754, but the decision to write the *History* was not made until 1762. In the Summer of 1769 he sat down to write 'in good Earnest', and by September 1770 he was telling Thomas Percy: 'My *Opus Magnum* goes on swimmingly. We shall go to Press in October.' The first volume was eventually published on 21 March 1774. See David Fairer, 'The Origins of Warton's *History of English Poetry*', *Review of English Studies*, N.S. XXXII (1981), 37–63, and Wellek, pp. 170–73.

10. Warton–Gray, 20 April 1770 (MS Trinity College Oxford: Bodleian MS Dep.c.638, fol. 42). Printed in *Correspondence*, III, 1128–30.

11. *History*, pp. iii–iv.

12. Ibid., p. v.

13. A further section remained in manuscript. See *A History of English Poetry: an Unpublished Continuation*, ed. Rodney M. Baine(Los Angeles, 1953). Augustan Reprint Society Publication no. 39.

14. *Poems upon Several Occasions, English, Italian, and Latin, with Translations, by John Milton*, ed. Thomas Warton (London, 1785; 2nd ed. 1791).

15. Thomas Warton, *Observations on the Faerie Queene of Spenser* (London, 1754; 2nd ed. in 2 vols, 1762).

16. *History*, I, viii.

17. *The Life of Sir Thomas Pope, Founder of Trinity College, Oxford* (London, 1772; 2nd ed. 1780); *The Life and Literary Remains of Ralph Bathurst, M.D.* (2 vols, London, 1761).

18. Bodleian MS Dep.c.638, fols 51 and 118.

19. *A Companion to the Guide, and a Guide to the Companion: Being a Complete Supplement to All the Accounts of Oxford Hitherto Published* (London, 1760).

20. *Specimen of a Parochial History of Oxfordshire* (n.p., 1782).

21. First printed in Warton's *Poems: A New Edition, with Additions* (London, 1777), p. 77. See *The Poetical Works of the Late Thomas Warton, B.D.*, ed. Richard Mant, 2 vols (Oxford, 1802), II, 150.

22. First printed in 1777 *Poems*, pp. 30–34 (Mant, I, 130–39).

23. First printed in Warton's anthology, *The Union; or, Select Scots and English Poems* ('Edinburgh', 1753). It was reprinted in Mant, II, 1–37.

24. First printed in 1777 *Poems*, p. 82 (Mant, II, 158–59).

25. See Arthur Johnston, *Enchanted Ground. The Study of Medieval Romance in the Eighteenth Century* (London, 1964), pp. 100–19.

26. 'Epistle from Thomas Hearne, Antiquary, to the Author of the *Companion* to the *Oxford Guide*', first printed in *The Oxford Sausage* (Oxford, 1764). See Mant, II, 189–91, and *Biographical Memoirs of the Late Revd. Joseph Warton, D.D.*, ed. John Wooll (London, 1806), pp. 159–60.

27. The poem appeared anonymously in *Poems on Several Occasions. By the Reverend Mr. Thomas Warton* (London, 1748), p. 21–22. This posthumous volume of the poems of their father, Thomas Warton the Elder, was edited by Joseph Warton. See David Fairer, 'The Poems of Thomas Warton the Elder?', *Review of English Studies*, N.S. XXVI (1975), 287–300 and 395–406 (pp. 296–97).

28. Mant, II, 135–42.

29. MS Trinity College Oxford: Bodleian MS Dep. c.638, fol. 113.

30. *Complete Poems*, p. 40.

31. Roger Lonsdale, 'The Poetry of Thomas Gray: Versions of the Self', *Proceedings of the British Academy*, LIX (1973), 105–23, p. 110.

32. Ibid., p. 116.

33. Mant, I, 95.

34. *The Triumph of Isis* (London, 1750), ll. 211–24 (Mant, I, 21–22); and 'On the Birth of the Prince of Wales', first printed in Oxford's *Gratulatio Solennis*, 1762 (Mant, I, 46–53).

35. Wooll, p. 120.

36. 'Sonnet to the River Lodon', first printed in 1777 *Poems*, p. 83. For a discussion of the wide influence of Warton's sonnet on the poets of the next generation, see J. B. Bamborough, 'William Lisle Bowles and the Riparian Muse', in *Essays and Poems Presented to Lord David Cecil*, ed. W. W. Robson (London, 1970), pp. 93–108.

37. Lonsdale (p. 120) remarks that Gray was 'expressing here not merely a sense of personal inadequacy, but a more general uncertainty about the capacity of his own over-civilized society to maintain the tradition'.

38. *Complete Poems*, p. 207.

39. Lonsdale, p. 120.

40. On Gray's delay and resumption, see *The Poems of Gray, Collins, and Goldsmith*, ed. Roger Lonsdale (London and Harlow, 1969), pp. 178–79.

41. MS Pembroke College, Cambridge, *CB* II, p. 933.

42. *The Poems of Mr. Gray. To which are prefixed Memoirs of his Life and Writings by W. Mason, M.A.*, 2nd ed. (London, 1775), pp. 89–90 (*Poems*).

43. Gray–Mason, [?24/31] May 1757 (*Correspondence*, II, 502).

44. Gray–Mason, [11] June 1757 (*Correspondence*, II, 504).

45. 1777 *Poems*, p. 62 (Mant, II, 51).

46. *Comus*, ll. 980–1001, and *The Faerie Queene*, III, vi, 29ff.

47. Review of Hayley's *Memoirs*, in *The Quarterly Review* XXXI (1824–25), 289.

48. David Fairer, '"Sweet native stream": Wordsworth, Coleridge, and the School of Warton', Wordsworth Summer Conference, Grasmere, 1989 (Wordsworth Trust Cassette).

49. *History*, p. v.

Gray, Akenside and the Ode

PAUL WHITELEY

I

'You are very particular, I can tell you, in liking Gray's Odes', Horace Walpole observed to George Montagu in a letter of 25 August 1757; 'but you must remember the age likes Akinside, and did like Thomson. Can the same people like both? Milton was forced to wait till the world had done admiring Quarles...'[1] Having printed Gray's 'The Progress of Poesy' and 'The Bard' at his own Strawberry Hill press, and having urged Gray unsuccessfully to add notes to help his readers, Walpole's response to Montagu's preference is understandable. He had earlier written to Horace Mann that the odes were 'a little obscure',[2] and we only need to look at Gray's correspondence from this period to show the misunderstanding and confusion that the works caused for some of their readers.

Yet Walpole's comment is also interesting in drawing a comparison between Gray and Mark Akenside, the poet-physician whose contemporary fame rested on his dialectic poem *The Pleasures of Imagination* (1744) and on his *Odes on Several Subjects* (1745); the latter work (with revisions) was to be reprinted by Dodsley, Gray's own publisher, in 1760. Though no critic would disagree that Gray's is the greater talent, the Milton to Akenside's Quarles, in the years after Pope's death it was Akenside who best seemed to embody the new spirit of English poetry. His odes were the essential example for Joseph Warton and William Collins, whose collections were published in 1746—two years before Gray's early odes first appeared in Dodsley's famous *Collection of Poems* (better known as Dodsley's 'Miscellany'). As a result, it seems odd that critics have not examined the relationship between the works of Gray and Akenside, especially with regard to the ode. Though Gray's reputation was to soar beyond Akenside's in the later decades of the eighteenth century, Walpole's comment to Montagu shows that, in the 1750s, Akenside's reputation was still formidable.

II

The major reason for this lack of comparison is, of course, a question of dates.Gray's early odes were written in 1742, when Akenside was composing *The Pleasures of Imagination* in New-castle; Akenside's own odes seem to have been composed between 1740 (the date given for 'On the Winter Solstice') and his return to England from Leyden in 1744 (as suggested by his 'On Leaving Holland'). Akenside could not have read Gray's odes until 1748, and there is no reference in Gray's correspon-dence to his having read Akenside's when they appeared in 1745. Probably he was influenced by his earlier perusal of *The Pleasures of Imagination*. As he wrote to Wharton on 26 April 1744:

> You desire to know, it seems, what Character the Poem of your young Friend bears here. I wonder to hear you ask the Opinion of a Nation, where those who pretend to judge, don't judge at all; & the rest (the wiser Part) wait to catch the Judgement of the World immediately above them, that is, Dick's Coffee-House, & the Rainbow: so that the readier Way would be to ask Mrs This & M^{rs} T'other, that keeps the Bar there. however to shew you I'm a Judge, as well as my Countrymen, tho' I have rather turn'd it over, than read it, (but no matter: no more have they) it seems to me above the middleing, & now & then (but for a little while) rises even to the best, particularly in Description. it is often obscure, & even unintelligible, & too much infected with the Hutchinson-Jargon. in short it's great fault is that it was publish'd at least 9 Years too early. and so methinks in a few Words, a la Mode du Temple, I have very pertly dispatch'd what perhaps may for several Years have employd a very ingenious Man worth 50 of myself.[3]

Like Dr Johnson, Gray seems to have been unable (or unwilling) to read Akenside's poem through; the obviously jocular note of the criticism makes one wonder about his real response to it, though his observation that *The Pleasures of Imagination* is 'too much infected with the Hutchinson-Jargon' suggests that he found Akenside's championship of the doctrines of the Third Earl of Shaftesbury and his followers distasteful. Like Dr Johnson later in the century, Gray probably deplored Akenside's 'unnecessary and outrageous zeal for what he called and thought liberty'.[4] No wonder he seems to have avoided reading Akenside's odes!

By the 1750s, when Gray's earlier poems had appeared in print and his reputation was assured through the *Elegy*, his references to Akenside become more critical. Writing to Wharton in 1754, Gray calls Akenside 'no Conjurer' (i.e., far from clever) in architecture; and in 1758 he tells Mason that Akenside is a sad fellow, a comment expanded in an earlier letter to Wharton:

> Then here is the Miscellany (Mr Dodsley has sent me the whole set gilt and lettered, I thank him). Why, the two last volumes are worse than the four first; particularly Dr Akenside is in a deplorable way. What signifies Learning and the Antients, (Mason will say triumphantly) why should people read Greek to lose their imagination, their ear, and their mother tongue?[5]

The final volumes of Dodsley's miscellany included Akenside's 'Hymn to the Naiads', his odes to the Earl of Huntingdon and the Bishop of Winchester, and several Inscriptions, and it is the first of these works that Gray seems to be attacking. He may have been still smarting from the criticism he records Akenside as making on 'The Progress of Poesy': 'Dr Akenside criticises opening *a source* with *a key*'.[6] This suggests that Akenside himself had read Gray's odes of 1757, though as a member of Dodsley's Pall Mall circle and a frequent visitor at his bookshop he probably knew Gray's other works as well. Akenside had not only acted as editor of Dodsley's periodical *The Museum* (1746–1747), but (as is shown by Dodsley's own correspondence) had aided him in compiling his miscellany.[7]

From the above evidence, it can be deduced that the relationship between Gray and Akenside was slight. Akenside left no correspondence comparable to Gray's, and we know his responses to contemporary writers only through the remarks of others. Though they shared the same publisher, there is no record that they ever met; and, from their respective lifestyles, one imagines they would have had little in common. Even Roger Lonsdale, in his edition of Gray, draws only a few parallels between his works and those of Akenside. With regard to the mid-century ode, what is in fact interesting about Gray and Akenside is the obvious difference between their respective approaches.

III

This difference can best be shown by comparing two of Gray's odes with two by Akenside: Gray's 'Ode on the Spring' (1742) with Akenside's 'Preface' to *Odes, Book I* (originally called 'Allusion to Horace' [1745]); and Akenside's 'On Lyric Poetry' with Gray's 'The Progress of Poesy' (1757).[8] Such a comparison is useful because the two former works both adopt the classical commonplace of the poet reclining in the shade from the noon-day sun to subtly different ends; while, as John Sitter has suggested, Akenside's 'On Lyric Poetry' is 'an interesting anticipation of Gray's *Progress of Poesy*'.[9] Moreover, these poems show their poets' use of the major models for the ode in the period: the Horatian and the Pindaric respectively.

Gray begins his 'Ode on the Spring', his first lyric effort in English, with a deliberate attempt to recreate earlier descriptions of the spring before moving to a description of the retired poet:

> LO! Where the rosy-bosom'd Hours,
> Fair VENUS' train appear,
> Disclose the long-expecting flowers,
> And wake the purple year!
> The Attic warbler pours her throat,
> Responsive to the cuckow's note,
> The untaught harmony of spring:

While whisp'ring pleasure as they fly,
Cool Zephyrs thro' the clear blue sky
Their gather'd fragrance fling.

Where'er the oak's thick branches stretch
A broader browner shade;
Where'er the rude and moss-grown beech
O'er-canopies the glade
Beside some water's rushy brink
With me the Muse shall sit, and think
(At ease reclin'd in rustic state)
How vain the ardour of the Crowd,
How low, how little are the Proud,
How indigent the Great!
(ll. 1–20)

The quasi-iconographic nature of the opening stanza, with its richness of allusion to Horace, Virgil, Lucretius and Milton, shows that Gray was not imitating any particular model but aiming to stir his audience's recollection of poetic commonplaces. And the obvious artifice and formality of the opening stanza provides a neat foil to the introduction of the poet with his Muse, 'at ease reclin'd in rustic state'. Though the description is more concrete and direct here, the literary allusiveness and elaborate artifice are no less obvious—the introduction of the Muse as a physical existence in the landscape emphasizes the conventionality of the final lines of the stanza as the poet draws the expected contrast between the pleasures of the retired or contemplative life and the problems of the busy world of ambition.

The obvious artifice and leisurely expansiveness of Gray's opening can neatly be contrasted with the opening stanza of Akenside's poem in its original form:

Amid the garden's fragrance laid
Where yonder limes behold their shade
    Along the glassy stream,
With Horace and his tuneful ease
I'll rest from crouds, and care's disease,
    And summer's piercing beam.
(ll. 1–6)[10]

This is much more deliberately an 'allusion' to Horace, yet it seems at once more particular and domestic than Gray's corresponding description. The humorous overtones are missing, as is the sense of deliberate artificiality. Yet Akenside later changed the stanza to read:

> On yonder verdant hilloc laid,
> Where oaks and elms, a friendly shade,
>   O'erlook the falling stream,
> O master of the Latin lyre,
> Awhile with thee will i retire
>   From summer's noontide beam.
>
> (ll. 1–6)

The language has become more formal, the situation more generalized. And the antithesis between the retired poet and the busy world of ambition has also been removed. Yet, even in its original version, this antithesis had little to do with Akenside's development of the commonplace he shares with Gray.

The deliberate artifice of Gray's poem is, as many critics have argued, dramatic in its approach. The studied movement from the formal depiction of the spring to the poet's moralistic reflections as he and his Muse recline in 'rustic state' symbolizes the definite uneasiness that Gray feels about the antithesis between the contemplative life and the busy world. This becomes more obvious as the poet moves in the following stanzas to observe the 'insect youth' (l. 25) whose 'busy murmur' brings into the stasis of the rural scene that sense of 'crouds, and care's disease' that such a poet traditionally seeks to avoid, be it in a natural setting or in the seclusion of Horace's *parva rura*. And, as the situation of the poet earlier sparked appropriate reflections, so now does the appearance of the 'insect youth':

> To Contemplation's sober eye
> Such is the race of Man:
> And they that creep, and they that fly,
> Shall end where they began.
> Alike the Busy and the Gay
> But flutter thro' life's little day,

In fortune's varying colours drest:
Brush'd by the hand of rough Mischance,
Or chill'd by age, their airy dance
They leave, in dust to rest.

(ll. 31–40)

So far Gray's poem well agrees with Dr Johnson's observation that 'the language is too luxuriant, and the thoughts
have nothing new'.[11] But this insistent artifice and contrivance
is part of the purpose of the poem, for in the last stanza the poet
takes up his metaphor of man as insect and turns it upon
himself:

Methinks I hear in accents low
The sportive kind reply:
Poor moralist! and what art thou?
A solitary fly!
Thy Joys no glittering female meets,
No hive hast thou of hoarded sweets,
No painted plumage to display:
On hasty wings thy youth is flown;
Thy sun is set, thy spring is gone—
We frolick, while 'tis May.

(ll. 41–50)

The dramatic nature of this reversal, the moralist moralizing
on the pose he has adopted, is not merely ironic but highly self-
conscious. Equally, as P. M. Spacks observes, it forces us to
look more closely at the relation between artifice and reality;
for 'artifice, perceived first as a device for arbitrarily shaping
one's perception of reality (towards optimism or toward
pessimism), ultimately provides new insight into reality'.[12]

And here the contrast with Akenside's approach is interesting, for Akenside uses a similar situation in an entirely different
way. He writes in the revised version of 1760:

And, lo, within my lonely bower,
The industrious bee from many a flower
    Collects her balmy dews:
"For me," she sings, "the gems are born,
"For me their silken robe adorn,
    "Their fragrant breath diffuse."

Sweet murmurer! may no rude storm
This hospitable scene deform
          Nor check thy gladsome toils;
Still may the buds unsullied spring,
Still showers and sunshine court thy wing
          To these ambrosial spoils.

Nor shall my Muse hereafter fail
Her fellow-labourer thee to hail;
          And lucky be the strains!
For long ago did nature frame
Your seasons and your arts the same,
          Your pleasures and your pains.

(ll. 7–24)

There is a very different kind of artifice here, and one more
obviously literary in its intention. Akenside's retirement is with
his book of Horace's odes; his 'lonely bower' emphasizes his
essential seclusion from the external world; and the 'industrious bee' is quickly associated with the poet's own Muse.
Retirement, in Akenside's ode, becomes the statement of a
poetic manifesto:

Like thee, in lowly, sylvan scenes,
On river-banks and flowery greens
          My Muse delighted plays;
Nor through the desart of the air,
Though swans or eagles triumph there,
          With fond ambition strays.

Nor where the boding raven chaunts,
Nor near the owl's unhallow'd haunts
          Will she her cares imploy;
But flies from ruins and from tombs,
From superstition's horrid glooms,
          To day-light and to joy.

Nor will she tempt the barren waste;
Nor deigns the lurking strength to taste
          Of any noxious thing;
But leaves with scorn to envy's use
The insipid nightshade's baneful juice,
          The nettle's sordid sting.

From all which nature fairest knows,
The vernal bloom, the summer rose,
    She draws her blameless wealth;
And, when the generous task is done,
She consecrates a double boon,
    To pleasure and to health.

                        (ll. 25–48)

In Akenside's poem, unlike Gray's, the objective appearances
of nature become literary metaphors, contained within the
central metaphor which equates the bee and the Muse. And,
though the antithesis between retirement and ambition obviously underlies the poem, it is far less important than it is for
Gray. For Akenside's poet, within his 'lonely bower', the choice
between retirement and engagement can be largely avoided.
As long as his Muse imitates the 'industrious bee', the
unpleasant qualities of the world cannot rise up to challenge
the poet's position. By isolating himself, and by proclaiming a
poetic mission that avoids both 'fond ambition' and 'super-
stition's horrid glooms'—the latter neatly conceived in terms
deriving from the 'graveyard' poets—Akenside suggests that,
though the outside world may be harsh and hostile, it can be
negated by the poet's remaining true to his proper allegiances.
The emulation of Horace will produce a poetry synonymous
with 'pleasure' and with 'health', physical and mental. In
relation to Gray's stance, therefore, Akenside remains
throughout the poem the poetic contriver. His use of metaphor
is not a means of revealing reality, rather it is a means of
escaping from it.

IV

Gray's 'Ode on the Spring' and Akenside's prefatory ode are
thus both concerned with the role of the poet and the purpose
of poetry, but they offer contrasting visions of that role and
purpose. In Akenside's ode, the view of poetry's purpose is
ultimately consolatory and the role of the poet an essentially
'public' one, despite his obvious isolation. Poetry (the Muse)
allows one to shape reality in an optimistic way. For Gray, the
converse is surely true. The purpose of poetry seems only to

reveal the real dilemma of the individual, his own insecurity and frustration. And the position of the poet 'does not help the man to solve his private dilemma: it only reveals that dilemma to him'.[13]

The purpose of poetry and the role of the poet are central concerns of Gray's 'The Progress of Poesy' and Akenside's 'On Lyric Poetry', which may explain why John Sitter sees in the latter 'an interesting anticipation' of the former. But, while both odes are Pindaric in form, they work to different ends. Akenside's 'On Lyric Poetry', the last poem in his *Odes on Several Subjects* of 1745, is a further poetic manifesto—it attempts to synthesize the entire Greek lyric tradition and adopt it for modern needs. Gray's 'The Progress of Poesy' is, as its title suggests, a 'progress' poem—a tracing of the steps by which poetry was conceived to have deserted Greece for England.

Akenside's 'On Lyric Poetry' predates Gray's own experiments with the Pindaric ode as it had been established by Congreve in 1706—not the irregular form popularized by Cowley and others, but a form consisting of three stanzas—the strophe, antistrophe and epode. The metre and stanzaic form of the strophe was duplicated precisely in the antistrophe, while in the epode the poet created another, contrasting, stanzaic form. Both Gray and Akenside follow this pattern, but they make very different use of it. This can best be seen by looking at the first three stanzas of Akenside's ode in comparison with Gray's:

> Once more i join the Thespian choir,
> And taste the inspiring fount again:
> O parent of the Grecian lyre,
> Admit me to thy powerful strain—
> And lo, with ease my step invades
> The pathless vale and opening shades,
> Till now i spy her verdant seat;
> And now at large i drink the sound,
> While these her offspring, listening round,
> By turns her melody repeat.
>
> I see Anacreon smile and sing,
> His silver tresses breathe perfume;

His cheek displays a second spring
Of roses taught by wine to bloom.
Away, deceitful cares, away,
And let me listen to his lay;
Let me the wanton pomp injoy,
While in smooth dance the light-wing'd Hours
Lead round his lyre it's patron powers,
Kind laughter and convivial joy.

Broke from the fetters of his native land,
Devoting shame and vengeance to her lords,
With louder impulse and a threatening hand
The Lesbian patriot smites the sounding chords:
Ye wretches, ye perfidious train,
Ye curs'd of gods and freeborn men,
Ye murderers of the laws,
Though now ye glory in your lust,
Though now ye tread the feeble neck in dust,
Yet Time and righteous Jove will judge your dreadful
cause.

(ll. 1–30)

Only extensive quotation reveals the argument that forms the
basis of Akenside's ode, for the invocation of Melpomene,
'parent of the Grecian lyre', transports the poet to an imagined
landscape in which the Muse of lyric poetry is discovered
surrounded by her poetic 'offspring'. Through Anacreon and
Alcaeus (the 'Lesbian patriot') Akenside is able to exemplify
the qualities of lyric poetry—in this case 'kind laughter and
convivial joy' and patriotic fervour. And these poets are
followed by Sappho and Pindar, introducing ideas of love and
divine aspiration.

Akenside's characterizations of the Greek lyric poets have
some parallels with Gray's personifications of Shakespeare and
Milton, but, while Akenside is content to enumerate the Greek
poets as a means of providing his poetic credentials (in a
similar way to his introduction of Horace in the earlier ode),
Gray's approach is to characterize his subject by more powerful images:

Awake, Aeolian lyre, awake,
And give to rapture all thy trembling strings.
From Helicon's harmonious springs
A thousand rills their mazy progress take:
The laughing flowers, that round them blow,
Drink life and fragrance as they flow.
Now the rich stream of music winds along
Deep, majestic, smooth, and strong,
Thro' verdant vales, and Ceres' golden reign:
Now rowling down the steep amain,
Headlong, impetuous, see it pour:
The rocks, and nodding groves rebellow to the roar.

(ll. 1–12)

The difference between Akenside's conception and Gray's is obvious from this one stanza—like Pindar, Gray unites subject and simile, seeing the various sources of poetry as springs flowing from Mount Helicon, home of the Muses. Where Akenside is concerned with one particular kind of poetry, Gray is concerned to outline its whole nature, and to do so in vivid images with swift transitions between them.

The reason for this contrast becomes obvious when we look at the purpose of the poems as a whole. For Gray, outlining the nature of poetry is also to show its progress from Greece to England, with the suggestion implicit in such 'progress poetry' that the true virtues of poetry 'had not merely been transmitted to Britain but had thrived there as never before'.[14] As Gray illustrates the nature of poetry—its enrichment of its subject, its ability to control the cares and passions, the intensification of emotion, its compensation for human misery, and so on—we expect that this vision of poetry will be shown to have a realization in the present. But the ode ends with no such promise:

Hark, his hands the lyre explore!
Bright-eyed Fancy hovering o'er
Scatters from her pictur'd urn
Thoughts, that breath[e], and words, that burn.
But ah! 'tis heard no more—
Oh! Lyre divine, what daring Spirit

Wakes thee now? tho' he inherit
Nor the pride, nor ample pinion,
That the Theban eagle bear
Sailing with supreme dominion
Thro' the azure deep of air:
Yet oft before his infant eyes would run
Such forms, as glitter in the Muse's ray
With orient hues, unborrow'd of the Sun:
Yet shall he mount, and keep his distant way
Beyond the limits of a vulgar fate,
Beneath the Good how far—but far above the Great.

(ll. 107–23)

P. M. Spacks points out how the 'Good/Great' antithesis seems oddly irrelevant to the rest of the poem since its subject is the nature of poetry rather than the role of the poet.[15] Yet looking back to the 'Ode on the Spring', we can see that for Gray this was a central conflict he could not fully resolve. And its appearance here would seem to suggest an ambiguous resolution to the question of poetic progress that the line, 'But ah! 'tis heard no more', emphasizes. For Gray, it seems, the past is irrevocably past and cannot be recaptured in the present—the spirit that grasps the lyre now cannot emulate Shakespeare or Milton.

For Akenside, however, the possibilities of the past *are* to be realized in the present:

Propitious Muse,
While i so late unlock thy purer springs,
And breathe whate'er thy ancient airs infuse,
Wilt thou for Albion's sons around
(Ne'er had'st thou audience more renown'd)
Thy charming arts imploy,
As when the winds from shore to shore
Through Greece thy lyre's persuasive language bore,
Till towns and isles and seas return'd the vocal joy?

(ll. 52–60)

The message of these lines is similar to Akenside's desire in *The Pleasures of Imagination* to 'tune to Attic themes the British lyre'

(I, 604); to recapture through the evocation of the Greek poets
the spirit of their poetry. And at this point Akenside, like Gray,
brings in the question of the role of the poet. Although in the
past 'pleasure's lawless throng' polluted lyric verse with
'impious revels dire' (ll. 61–64)—an echo of Gray's vision of the
enemies of poetry (ll. 77–80)—Akenside begs his Muse that
such discord be not allowed to invade the poetic landscape he
has created. And, after associating the Muse with nature and
the passions, he then turns to his own desires:

> When midnight listens o'er the slumbering earth,
> Let me, o Muse, thy solemn whispers hear:
> When morning sends her fragrant breezes forth,
> With airy murmurs touch my opening ear.
>   And ever watchful at thy side,
>   Let wisdom's awful suffrage guide
>   The tenor of thy lay:
>   To her of old by Jove was given
> To judge the various deeds of earth and heaven;
> 'Twas thine by gentle arts to win us to her sway.

> Oft as, to well-earn'd ease resign'd
> I quit the maze where science toils,
> Do thou refresh my yielding mind
> With all thy gay, delusive spoils.
> But, o indulgent, come not nigh
> The busy steps, the jealous eye
> Of wealthy care or gainful age;
> Whose barren soul thy joy disdain,
> And hold as foes to reason's reign
> Whome'er thy lovely works ingage.

> When friendship and when letter'd mirth
> Haply partake my simple board,
> Then let thy blameless hand call forth
> The music of the Teian chord.
> Or if invok'd at softer hours,
> O! seek with me the happy bowers
> That hear Olympia's gentle tongue;
> To beauty link'd with virtue's train,

> To love devoid of jealous pain,
> There let the Sapphic lute be strung.
>
> But when from envy and from death to claim
> A hero bleeding for his native land;
> When to throw incense on the vestal flame
> Of liberty my genius gives command,
>   Nor Theban voice nor Lesbian lyre
>   From thee, o Muse, do i require;
>   While my presaging mind,
>   Conscious of powers she never knew,
> Astonish'd graps at things beyond her view,
> Nor by another's fate submits to be confin'd.
>
> (ll. 81–120)

Again, only extensive quotation can show the difference between Akenside's and Gray's conceptions in these poems. What is especially notable here, of course, is the way in which Akenside wants to out-Pindar Pindar—he needs no 'Theban voice' to sing the praise of liberty. These final lines, according to Charles Bucke, relate to Akenside's ambition to write an epic poem on Timoleon: 'Akenside told Warton, that he alluded, in the last line, to the LEONIDAS of GLOVER, which he looked upon as a failure'.[16]

Even if this was not Akenside's intention, these final stanzas of 'On Lyric Poetry' have an importance in relating the power of the Muse to his own situation. Not only does Akenside invoke the spirit of the Grecian lyric, but he also desires it to have an active presence in his life. The various aspects of Melpomene, personified by the poets who are her offspring, are to answer the poet's varying moods. And, yet again, we have a sense of Akenside being more concerned to create a poetic refuge, to withdraw from the real world into the world of Greek lyric (probably in as concrete a form as the copy of Horace he introduced in his prefatory ode) than to face the conflict that lurks behind Gray's ode. Though Gray is quick to dismiss the ills that await man,

> Labour, and Penury, the racks of Pain,
> Disease, and Sorrow's weeping train,

And Death, sad refuge from the storms of Fate!
(ll. 43–45)

he is at least willing to accept that they exist, and that the
'heav'nly Muse' may not be totally able to banish them.

V

'As a lyric poet', Charles Bucke argues, 'Akenside yields, on the
whole, to Gray and Collins. He is defective in pathos; his
images occasionally want warmth, and his verse melody; but
his lyrical productions, nevertheless, exhibit a fine glow of
sentiment, an ardent admiration of the great and good, an
enthusiastic love of true liberty, an utter detestation of tyranny,
and a fine sensibility to all the best and noblest feelings of the
heart.'[17]

One cannot say that the poems examined really show the
Akenside that Bucke admires—Akenside as a public poet,
expressing his zeal for Whiggish liberty. Yet his argument that
Akenside 'yields' to Gray must be qualified. Gray's sensibility
and his approach to the ode are far less Augustan than
Akenside's, for all the latter's seeming autobiographical qualities. Where Gray found difficulty in relating his own personal
tensions to conventional forms, Akenside was able to avoid the
harsh realities of the real world through his response to
surrogate muses. Whereas Gray's poems, despite their conventional and allusive qualities, become the expression of a
uniquely personal voice, Akenside is content with his allegiances to the figures of the past that he invokes. It is little
wonder that, as the century drew to its close, Horace Walpole's
words became prophetic.

NOTES

1. *Horace Walpole's Correspondence*, ed. W. S. Lewis and others (New Haven
and Oxford, 1937–), IX, 215.
2. Ibid., XXI, 120.
3. *Correspondence*, I, 223–24.
4. Dr Johnson, 'Life of Akenside', in *Lives of the English Poets*, ed.
G. Birkbeck Hill, 3 vols (Oxford, 1905), III, 411–12.

5. *Correspondence*, II, 566. For letter of 1754 see I, 407, and for letter of 1758, II, 568.

6. Ibid., II, 526.

7. For Akenside's association with Dodsley, see C. T. Houpt, *Mark Akenside: A Biographical and Critical Study* (New York, 1944), pp. 94–125.

8. There is no readily accessible edition of Akenside's *Odes on Several Subjects* of 1745, and these odes were much revised during Akenside's lifetime. I accordingly quote Akenside from *The Poems of Mark Akenside, M.D.* (London, 1772), except where noted.

9. J. Sitter, *Literary Loneliness in Mid-Eighteenth-Century England* (Ithaca and London, 1982), p. 115.

10. Ibid.

11. 'Life of Gray', III, 434.

12. P. M. Spacks, *The Poetry of Vision: Five Eighteenth-Century Poets* (Cambridge, Mass., 1967), p. 95.

13. Ibid.

14. *The Poems of Gray, Collins and Goldsmith*, ed. Roger Lonsdale (London, 1969), p. 160.

15. *The Poetry of Vision*, p. 110.

16. C. Bucke, *On the Life, Writings, and Genius of Akenside* (London, 1832), p. 73.

17. Ibid., p. 89.

The 'Wonderful Wonder of Wonders': Gray's Odes and Johnson's Criticism

ANNE McDERMOTT

The lack of warmth in the relationship between Gray and Johnson has been often noticed. Gray was one of the few writers of his generation whom Johnson never met, and the Rev. Norton Nicholls, a close friend of Gray's, reported that Gray 'disliked Doctor Johnson, & declined his acquaintance'.[1] There is nothing unusual in two notable contemporaries heartily disliking each other, but in this case the reasons are interesting. Johnson's hatred was normally reserved for those of radical political or unorthodox religious views. Certainly Gray differed from Johnson in politics, being closely associated with the Walpole circle and possessing the principles of 'every true & rational Whig',[2] while Johnson was a steadfast Tory, but the antipathy between the two writers seems, unusually for literary disputes, to have stemmed almost wholly from a difference of literary principles. Johnson and Gray had fundamentally opposed views on what poetry should be trying to do, or more precisely, on what poetic language should be trying to do, and this difference tells us a great deal about the shift in poetic attitudes in the middle of the eighteenth century.

The difference between them had been simmering under the surface, but came out into the open after the publication of Johnson's 'Life of Gray'. The withering scorn with which Johnson described Gray's two Pindaric odes as the *wonderful Wonder of Wonders* met with puzzled disbelief in some quarters where Gray was regarded as the greatest living poet and his sister odes as the pinnacle of his achievement. In the face of the virtually universal acclaim with which Gray's poems had been received, Johnson's views looked dogmatically prejudiced, insensitively dismissive, and hidebound by outmoded attitudes. The anonymous author of a letter printed in the *Gentleman's Magazine* asked 'Shall the superlative merit of Gray himself be overlooked and forgot, because the jealousy of Johnson would not suffer him to see much merit in his contemporaries?', and Edmund Cartwright in the *Monthly Review* thought that Johnson was displaying 'a dogmatic spirit of contradiction to received opinions'.[3] Yet Johnson's judgements have to a large extent been ratified by subsequent opinion. Gray's *Elegy*, which Johnson praised as 'abound[ing] with images which find a mirror in every mind, and with sentiments to which every bosom returns an echo', is now regarded as Gray's finest achievement, and of the two Pindaric odes, as R. W. Ketton-Cremer says, 'there is much to be said in favour of Johnson's critical severities'.[4] The peculiar thing is that the features of Gray's verse which prompted Johnson to challenge the general acclaim were precisely those valued most highly by Gray's admirers.

Most assessments of Gray's verse end by confronting the issue of his language, critics such as Johnson finding it obscure, and admirers finding in it a mystical suggestivity which is not reducible to ordinary sense. It is not surprising that Johnson, as writer of the *Dictionary*, should find objections to the latter point of view, but the criticisms voiced in his 'Life of Gray' indicate a larger antipathy to a whole range of poetic developments, and demonstrate a shift in the habits of linguistic thought of a generation. When the two Pindaric odes were first published in 1757 they had a mixed reception, but even the most effusive admirers complained of their semantic obscurity. As Gray wrote to Wharton, 'we are not at all popular, the great objection is obscurity, no body knows what we would be at'.[5] The nature of this obscurity is what is interesting in assessing the reaction to Gray's poetry. Gray proclaimed in his epigraph to the Pindaric odes that they were intended to be 'vocal to the intelligent alone'. The problem was that even the intelligent found that they did not understand them. In itself this did not seem to bother some early supporters of Gray who thought the obscurity of the odes part of their charm. Walpole enthused, 'they are Greek, they are Pindaric, they are sublime—consequently I fear a little obscure', and criticized Johnson for not appreciating the graces of the Grecian ode and for requiring them to be 'indited in as Dunstable prose as a bill in Chancery'.[6]

This is the nub of the issue: does the language of poetry have to mean in the same way as the language of prose? Clearly Johnson thought it did, as his appeals to the common reader amply demonstrate, but others thought that the sublimic effect of poetry was actually enhanced if its literal meaning could not be fully discovered. Mrs Thrale thought that Johnson had 'no Taste for Modern Poetry' and she reports him as complaining of Gray's 'unmeaning and verbose Language'.[7] Coleridge makes a similar point when, speaking of his own early reaction to Gray's odes, he writes: 'Feelings created by obscure ideas associate themselves with the one *clear* idea ... Poetry gives most pleasure when only generally & not perfectly understood. It was so by me with Gray's *Bard*, & Collins' odes—*The Bard* once intoxicated me, & now I read it without pleasure'. The language of Gray's odes had fallen out of favour again by the time Coleridge wrote this, but the association of obscure meaning with something sublime and numinous continued. Coleridge wondered 'whether or no the too great definiteness of Terms in any language may not consume too much of the vital & idea-creating force in distinct, clear, full made Images & so prevent originality'.[8] This is the full development of a view of poetic language, the complete antithesis of Johnson's, which was beginning to form at the time Johnson wrote his criticisms of Gray.

Gray seems never to have had the common reader in mind for his poetry, claiming that his 'ambition was terminated by that small circle' [of the intelligent] and desiring that his 'Progress of Poesy' should be shown to 'very few, & especially not to mere Scholars, that can scan all the measures in Pindar, & say the Scholia by heart'. He objected to the insertion of notes to explain his meaning: 'I do not love notes ... They are signs of weakness and obscurity. If a thing cannot be understood without them, it had better be not understood at all.' Yet he inserted some notes out of a kind of contemptuous exasperation: '... as to the notes, I do it out of spite, because the Publick did not understand the two odes (wch I have call'd Pindaric)'.[9] Nonetheless, the common reader seems to have been content to admire Gray's Pindaric odes without fully understanding them, regarding their obscurity as 'mysterious' and 'sublime'. Robert Potter, for example, thought that 'The Bard' was 'the grandest and sublimest effort of the Lyric Muse' and that it combined a 'forcible conception, a fervor of enthusiasm, and a terrible greatness'.[10] The same critic later agreed with Johnson's strictures on Gray's language, finding it 'encumbered and harsh' and thought that 'The Bard' had been wrought into a 'false, at least not true, sublime'. Yet, in the same work, Potter castigates Johnson for a narrow-mindedness in his aproach to poetry: 'Johnson seldom writes to the fancy ... but in a continual jog-trot of didactic, allowing no holiday. He constantly addresses himself to the understanding; makes no excursions into the regions of spirits, beyond "this visible diurnal sphere", ... nor even wishes to stray beyond the walks of mere modern life, back to the regions of Gothic fancy'.[11] Johnson was not insensitive to or unaffected by the 'sublime' in poetry, but he would not allow his critical judgement to be moved by it at the expense of sense.

The kind of language Gray uses in his Pindaric odes is to some extent determined by the form itself. One of the charac-teristics of the Pindaric ode was its deliberately lofty tone. In this it differed from the form more popular earlier in the century, the Horatian ode, which was simple, precise, and couched in familiar language. Pope's 'Ode on Solitude', which Pope claimed to have written 'at about twelve years old', usefully makes the contrast between the two forms. Pope's poem deals with the popular theme of simple country pleasures to be found in 'a few paternal acres'. His last stanza expresses a conventional wish:

> Thus let me live, unseen, unknown;
> Thus unlamented let me dye;
> Steal from the world, and not a stone
> > Tell where I lye.
> > > (ll. 17–20)[12]

The simplicity of both the language and the wish contrasts with Gray's more complex and more self-conscious treatment of remote rustic death in his *Elegy*. Gray's wish is not only for a stone to tell where he lies, but for the stone to express in its epitaph the nature of his vocation as a poet. Likewise, an obscure death is hardly the wish of the Bard:

> 'To triumph, and to die, are mine.'
> He spoke, and headlong from the mountain's height
> Deep in the roaring tide he plung'd to endless night.
>
> (ll. 142–44)

The remoteness of the ode's theme from common human experience contributes to a sense of distance which makes the elevated diction all the more appropriate. Gray also uses such language for parodic effect in his 'Ode on the Death of a Favourite Cat', in which part of the effect is gained by implicit contrast with more elevated treatments of death.

The preference for the Horatian ode is characteristic of the Augustan taste for simplicity and order, whereas to those unsympathetic to its 'mystery' the Pindaric ode could look like lazy writing or high-flown nonsense. Johnson says something much like this when discussing Cowley's odes: 'This lax and lawless versification so much concealed the deficiencies of the barren, and flattered the laziness of the idle, that it immediately overspread our books of poetry; all the boys and girls caught the pleasing fashion, and they that could do nothing else could write like Pindar'.[13] But Gray was no more enamoured of this style of versification than was Johnson. Mason noted that 'there was nothing which [Gray] more disliked than that chain of irregular stanzas which Cowley introduced, and falsely called Pindaric; and which from the extreme facility of execution produced a number of miserable imitators'.[14] But while they agreed on the necessity for strict form, they held widely divergent views on the diction associated with the Pindaric ode.

Johnson's views look superficially similar to those expressed by Wordsworth in the Preface to the *Lyrical Ballads*, especially where Wordsworth is criticizing the language of Gray's poetry. Wordsworth can sometimes seem to be offering a view of poetry that reverts to an earlier Augustan view with his emphasis on 'ordinary things ... presented to the mind in an unusual way' and his reference to the common reader, but Wordsworth's objection to Gray's poetry is based on a different concept of the function of language in poetry from that held by

Johnson. However he may have departed from the principle in practice, it was Wordsworth's aim to write poetry using 'a selection of the language really used by men', and he explicitly rejected those 'phrases and figures of speech which ... have long been regarded as the common inheritance of poets'.[15] Far from finding fault with poetic diction, Johnson endorses it and, in fact, criticizes Gray's translations of Norse and Welsh poetry on the ground that in them 'the language is unlike the language of other poets'.[16]

Johnson's criticisms of Gray's poetry centre on his supposed lack of linguistic craft. In his 'Ode on the Spring' his language is 'too luxuriant', in the 'Ode on the Death of a Favourite Cat' he calls the cat a nymph 'with some violence both to language and sense', in the *Ode on a Distant Prospect of Eton College* his use of the epithet 'buxom health' is considered 'not elegant; he seems not to understand the word', and in general condemnation Johnson offers the view that 'Gray thought his language more poetical as it was more remote from common use'.[17] All these criticisms spring from a view of language and its semantic function which makes Gray look linguistically eccentric. The obscurity which others found appealing was to Johnson at best a discourtesy to the reader and at worst an arrogant perversity which, if indulged, would eventually undermine language itself as a means of communication.

Johnson's views on wilful obscurity are clearly stated in *Idler* 70: 'If an author be supposed to involve his thoughts in voluntary obscurity, and to obstruct, by unnecessary difficulties, a mind eager in pursuit of truth; if he writes not to make others learned, but to boast the learning which he possesses himself, and wishes to be admired rather than understood, he counteracts the first end of writing, and justly suffers the utmost severity of censure, or the more afflictive severity of neglect'.[18] Perspicuity is not the only thing Johnson values; the language should also be appropriate to the form and theme of poetry. He criticizes Milton's language in *Samson Agonistes* because it 'seems to want elevation'. As a general principle he argues: 'All allusions to low and trivial objects, with which contempt is usually associated, are doubtless unsuitable to a species of composition which ought to be always awful, though not always magnificent'.[19] This is the kind of reasoning that led

to the pleonastic description of fish as 'the finny tribe', but
there is more to it than artificial elevation through euphemism.

An example of this is the criticism Johnson makes of a
passage in *Macbeth*:

> Come thick night
> And pall thee in the dunnest smoke of hell,
> That my keen knife see not the wound it makes
> Nor heav'n cry through the blanket of the dark
> To cry, hold, hold!

He argues that 'No word is naturally or intrinsically meaner
than another ... Words become low by the occasions to which
they are applied, or the general character of those who use
them; and the disgust which they produce, arises from the
revival of those images with which they are commonly
united'.[20] It is because a knife is an implement used by
'butchers and cooks in the meanest employments' and so
evokes images inappropriate to the awful nature of regicide,
that Johnson cannot 'conceive that any crime of importance is
to be committed with [it]', and he can 'scarce check [his]
risibility' at the thought of the 'avengers of guilt "peeping
through a blanket"'. If such everyday objects must be
mentioned in verse, they should be disguised in words with
appropriately dignified connotations. Johnson clearly believed
that there are words which are appropriate to poetry because
they have the requisite associations of dignity and propriety,
and they have these qualities precisely because they are not
'the language really used by men'. The elevation of Gray's
diction was evidently not a problem to Johnson, but he accuses
Gray of having 'a kind of strutting dignity, and [being] tall by
walking on tiptoe'[21] because Gray uses language which is too
dignified and tips the balance from proper elevation into
pomposity. This is particularly so in the Pindaric odes, where,
according to Johnson, 'the images are magnified by affectation,
the language is laboured into harshness'. Both Gray and
Johnson thought that poetry should be marked off from prose,
not only by its metrical form, but by its language, and this
language should be appropriately elevated in the 'higher'
poetical forms such as epic and tragedy.

Johnson seems to have the same expectation of a certain

kind of ode which he calls the 'greater' ode. In the *Dictionary* he remarks under 'ode': 'The less is characterised by sweetness and ease, the greater by sublimity, rapture and quickness of transition'. The lesser ode usually dealt with subjects such as love, wine and music, and the harmony of the subject was reflected in the diction which was natural, easy and unaffected. Following Burke's distinction it was often associated with the 'beautiful', while the greater ode was associated with the 'sublime'. The subjects of the greater ode were often remote in time or space, isolated, exotic, religious, and awe-inspiring in their immensity. Gray's 'Bard' reads almost like a treatise on the sublime, it includes so many of the requisite elements. The diction was expected to have the appropriate connotations of vastness, power, wildness and irregularity, and many of the judgements expressed on the obscurity of Gray's Odes seem to reflect this expectation. Anna Laetitia Barbauld writes of what she calls 'pure Poetry', by which she means lyric poetry, in terms which seem to set it above other forms and establish its diction as the standard of all poetical language:

> It deals in splendid imagery, bold fiction, and allegorical personages. It is necessarily obscure to a certain degree; because, having to do chiefly with ideas generated within the mind, it cannot be at all comprehended by any whose intellect has not been exercised in similar contemplations; while the conceptions of the Poet (often highly metaphysical) are rendered still more remote from common apprehension by the figurative phrase in which they are clothed.[22]

To Barbauld, not only has lyric poetry become the type of all poetry, but obscurity and figurative language have become signs of sensitivity and characterize the highest form of poetic diction.

Johnson, the detector of the fraud of Macpherson's *Ossian* poems, was unsympathetic to such views, and to understand why requires some investigation of his views on language in general. Many of his linguistic assumptions were derived from Locke: words stand for ideas, not things, and meaning is established by the association in the mind of a word with a particular idea. When meaning rests on an arbitrary agreement to associate particular ideas with particular words, not only do dictionaries seem like an obvious requirement, explaining the development and efflorescence of such works in the course of the eighteenth century, but tendencies which seem to break down that common agreement can seem like a breach of contract or dangerous conspiracy. Johnson's *Dictionary* resides on the authority of custom, which is a social codification of the agreement to associate certain ideas with certain words, but the prescriptive aim is to reduce slippage by anchoring the words in their ideas as permanently as possible. Johnson wished that 'signs might be permanent like the things they denote', but he recognized that 'words are hourly shifting their relations, and can no more be ascertained in a dictionary, than a grove, in the agitation of a storm, can be accurately delineated from its picture in the water'.[23]

Locke foresaw the dangers inherent in his theory:

> 'Tis not enough that Men have *Ideas*, determined *Ideas*, for which they make these signs stand; but they *must* also take care to *apply their Words*, as near as may be, *to such* Ideas *as common use has annexed them to*. For Words, especially of Languages already framed, being no Man's private possession, but the common measure of Commerce and Communication, 'tis not for any one, at pleasure, to change the Stamp they are current in; nor alter the *Ideas* they are affixed to...[24]

Misuse of words or alteration of meaning is seen by Locke as equivalent to fraud and is as strongly condemned. Towards the end of the century the same desire for a stable language is expressed by Beattie: 'To speak as others speak is one of those tacit obligations, annexed to the condition of living in society, which we are bound in conscience to fulfil, though we have never ratified them by any express promise; because, if they were disregarded, society would be impossible, and human happiness at an end'.[25] There is an obvious parallel between this and Hobbes' social contract which is instructive. Just as, for Hobbes, moral obligation has no existence outside society and consists entirely in the hypothetical promise or contract we make regarding others' life, property and general welfare, so, according to Beattie, language has no existence outside society and meaning is entirely a social construct, relying on our agreement to associate in a regular manner words with ideas. Lord Monboddo's suggestion that language slowly progressed from its primitive beginnings among man's predecessors, including the notorious orangoutang, was treated with great scorn by Johnson, who clearly held the same views as Beattie about language being a development of society. Though he believed that the English language had had a golden age ('the wells of English undefiled'[26]) which was now past and that his own was an age of iron, his nostalgia was for a past period of *civilized society* when meaning had seemed more stable and the language less deformed.

One of the abuses of language noted by Locke for its tendency to breach the contract of meaning is 'an *affected Obscurity*, by either applying old Words, to new and unusual Significations; or introducing new and ambiguous Terms, without defining either; or else putting them so together, as may confound their ordinary meaning'.[27] It is easy to see why a critic with Lockean assumptions about language would find the archaisms and foreign idioms in poets such as Spenser and Milton a matter of censure. It is also easy to see the gulf between this view and Gray's belief that 'The language of the age is never the language of poetry; except among the French ... Our poetry, on the contrary, has a language peculiar to itself; to which almost every one, that has written, has added something by enriching it with foreign idioms and derivatives: Nay sometimes words of their own composition or invention'.[28] Language is not, in Gray's view, a social construct imposing obligations on its users; it is individual and expressive. Some of Gray's linguistic assumptions are derived from and related to the idea of the sublime, pervasive in the latter half of the century, so to understand these assumptions it is necessary to explore this context.

Johnson was not impervious to the attractions of the sublime either in nature or in poetry. His descriptions of the bare wildness of Scotland owe a great deal to the concept of the sublime, and he writes of the pleasurable terror he felt in moments of danger such as the visit to the Buller of Buchan. In Wales, at Sir Rowland Hill's seat, he reports 'a kind of turbulent pleasure, between fright and admiration' which is induced by 'the extent of its prospects, the awfulness of its shades, the horrors of its precipices, the verdure of its hollows, and the loftiness of its rocks', and he recognized in these features elements of the sublime: 'The ideas which it forces upon the mind, are the sublime, the dreadful, and the vast'.[29] He feels the same sort of awe when confronted by the sublime in Milton: 'The characteristick quality of his poem [*Paradise Lost*] is sublimity. He sometimes descends to the elegant, but his element is the great.'[30] He thought Milton incapable of the 'lower' forms of poetry which required graceful ease and elegance.'Milton', he told Hannah More, 'was a genius that could cut a Colossus from a rock; but could not carve heads upon cherry-stones',[31] but he did not make this a point of criticism.

A feature of the sublime which begins to become apparent towards the end of the century is its synthetic tendency. Vastness and immensity could not be encompassed by detailed description, and the awful grandeur of nature would be dissipated if minutiae were enumerated. Johnson makes this point when discussing the metaphysical poets, whom he criticizes for being too analytical: 'Sublimity is produced by aggregation, and littleness by dispersion. Great thoughts are always general, and consist in positions not limited by exceptions, and in descriptions not descending to minuteness.'[32] This synthetic tendency becomes much more complex in Romantic poetry, where concepts of fusion, integration and unity take it far beyond the general grandeur of the sublime. But when Coleridge says that images 'become proofs of original genius only . . . when they have the effect of reducing multitude to unity, or succession to an instant . . .',[33] he is describing a feature of poetry which begins to develop around the time of Gray. Francis Bacon thought that poetry was both analytic and synthetic: 'Poesy . . . doth truly refer to the imagination; which, being not tied to the laws of matter, may at pleasure join that which nature hath severed, and sever that which nature hath joined',[34] but the analytic tendency in poetry begins to drop away in the course of the eighteenth century.

The analytic faculty was associated with judgement and the synthetic faculty with wit or invention. Pope thought both wit

and judgement necessary to poetry, with judgement acting as a
check on the wilder excesses of imagination:

> 'Tis more to *guide* than *spur* the Muse's Steed;
> Restrain his Fury, than provoke his Speed;
> The winged Courser, like a gen'rous Horse,
> Shows most true Mettle when you *check* his Course.[35]

According to Locke, wit consists in 'the assemblage of *Ideas*,
and putting those together with quickness and variety, wherein
can be found any resemblance or congruity', whereas judgement is a discriminating power which separates ideas and
discovers their foundation in sense impressions.[36] It is evident
that Locke valued judgement higher than wit, and, in fact, he
often seems suspicious of wit, as though it had a dangerous
tendency to obscure truth. It is one of the reasons he mistrusts
the kind of figurative language found in poetry:

> Since Wit and Fancy finds [*sic*] easier entertainment in the
> World, than dry Truth and real Knowledge, *figurative
> Speeches*, and allusion in Language, will hardly be admit-
> ted, as *an* imperfection or *abuse* of it ... But yet, if we would
> speak of Things as they are, we must allow, that all the
> Art of Rhetorick, ... all the artificial and figurative
> application of Words Eloquence hath invented, are for
> nothing else but to insinuate wrong *Ideas*, move the
> Passions, and thereby mislead the Judgment; and so
> indeed are perfect cheat.[37]

There is little difference in Locke's account between the
operations of poetic language and the abuses of language
which he condemns for their fraudulence. In some respects
Johnson seems to share this uneasiness at wit's tendency to
discover 'occult resemblances in things apparently unlike', and
he notoriously criticized the metaphysical poets in whose
poems 'the most heterogeneous ideas are yoked by violence
together',[38] but his attitude towards wit in poetry is more
complex than Locke's.

Jean Hagstrum has noted Johnson's preference for the simile
over the metaphor, and this has to do with the synthetic
tendency of metaphors. Metaphors can easily become mixed
and the tenor and vehicle confused, but even a straightforward

metaphor tends to blur distinctions between separate realities. In a simile the images are kept separate, so the potential for confusion is reduced. In his own poetry Johnson did not avoid metaphoric language, but the images are distinct and both tenor and vehicle are true representations of nature. When Johnson criticizes Denham's famous lines,

> O could I flow like thee, and make thy stream
> My great example, as it is my theme!
> Though deep, yet clear, thought gentle, yet not dull;
> Strong without rage, without o'erflowing full,

it is because the words are 'to be understood simply on one side of the comparison, and metaphorically on the other'. In other words, it makes no sense to say of a poet that he is 'deep' or 'without o'erflowing full', though it may be true of a river.

The same thought is clearly behind Johnson's verdict on the opening stanza of Gray's 'The Progress of Poesy', of which he would 'gladly find the meaning':

> Now the rich stream of music winds along
> Deep, majestic, smooth, and strong,
> Thro' verdant vales, and Ceres' golden reign:
> Now rowling down the steep amain,
> Headlong, impetuous, see it pour:
> The rocks, and nodding groves rebellow to the roar.
>
> (ll. 7–12)

The metaphor 'stream of music' is within the acceptable limits of joining together disparate images which are separately true, but when Gray extends the metaphor so that the musical stream is winding through 'verdant vales' and 'rowling down the steep amain', Johnson objects to the confusion of images. The comparison is literally true of a stream, but when applied to music appears to make no sense: 'If this be said of Music, it is nonsense; if it be said of Water, it is nothing to the purpose'.[39] Gray's explanation that 'the subject and simile, as usual with Pindar, are united'[40] would have made no sense to Johnson. This is a linguistic trait of Gray's which is evident in his prose as well as his poetry. He falls easily into personification (itself a metaphoric habit) in his informal letters: 'Low spirits are my true and faithful companions; they get up with me, go to bed with me, make journeys and returns as I do; nay, and pay visits, and will even affect to be jocose, and force a feeble laugh with me; but most commonly we sit alone together, and are the prettiest insipid company in the world'.[41] He also thinks readily in extended metaphors, as when he writes in his playful proposals for printing an account of his travels: 'Description of the little Creature, called an Abbé, its parts, & their uses; with the reasons, why they will not live in England, & the methods, that have been used to propagate them there'.[42]

Swift's works show the lunacy of translating metaphors into literal fact and the satiric possibilities of the uncertain relation between the world of words and the world of objects. For Swift it is a matter of stripping language of its illusions, but for Gray there is a sense that it is language which is inadequate because it is incapable of expressing what he feels. The shift in emphasis is shown in a movement away from an interest in the relation between language and nature and toward a fascination with the relation between language and emotional or cognitive states. The theory of association of ideas, introduced by Locke, emphasizes the relations between sense impressions formed in the mind. Johnson, in common with writers earlier in the century, wished those images to remain distinct, even while they were being drawn together by the mind, and to be ranged in ordered succession. As Johnson puts it: 'To proceed from one truth to another, and connect distant propositions by regular consequences, is the great prerogative of man'.[43] By the time Gray is writing in mid-century, this way of thinking about language is beginning to change. The emphasis moves away from the syntactic and synchronic toward the diachronic interest in universals. In poetry, the metaphor begins to be regarded as the sign of a sensitive soul and a mind impassioned by an amplitude of sensation, and is viewed by some as the essential characteristic of poetry. To Johnson the analytical tendencies of the metaphysical poets led to fragmentation and loss of grandeur in minute description, but the confusion of images in Gray's more synthetic linguistic habits, particularly in his figurative language, was equally reprehensible.

Sublimity may deal with the grandeur of generality, but, significantly, Johnson says that this generality is 'produced by aggregation', not unity; it does not produce immediate effects. The 'first authors of lyric poetry' are censured by Johnson because 'they applied themselves to instruct, rather by short sentences and striking thoughts, than by regular argumentation'. Their contemporary followers 'neglect the niceties of transition, ... start into remote digressions, and wander without restraint from one scene of imagery to another'. The supposed prerogative of the sublime or 'greater' ode to 'quickness of transition' seems to be denied here. Not only must the images be distinct, in Johnson's account, but they must be concatenated in coherent order, otherwise they have the same effect on the mind as the fragmented images of the metaphysical poets: 'Independent and unconnected sentiments flashing upon the mind in quick succession, may, for a time, delight by their novelty, but they differ from systematic reasoning, as single notes from harmony, as glances of lightening from the radiance of the sun'.[44]

The tendency of the sublime, as it was being developed in the latter half of the century, was to be synthetic, to blur distinctions between things, represented in the 'greater' ode by an abundance of figurative language in which the boundaries between images and their corresponding reality are confused. It was a tendency to which Johnson was unsympathetic; his notions of sublimity did not include loss of clarity, as is indicated by a comment to Boswell in which he asserts that 'The obscurity in which [Gray] has involved himself will not make us think him sublime'.[45] The difference between the two views is articulated to some extent by Robert Lowth: 'The language of Reason is cool, temperate, rather humble than elevated, well arranged and perspicuous, with an evident care and anxiety lest anything should escape which might appear perplexed or obscure', whereas the 'language of the Passions' expresses 'whatever is impetuous, vivid, or energetic', and he concludes that 'Reason speaks literally, the Passions poetically'.[46] Apart from the fact that Johnson would have expected the language of poetry to be elevated rather than humble everything that Lowth says of the 'literal' language of reason is what Johnson would have expected of poetry. Gray, on the other hand, could assert that 'Sense is nothing in poetry, but according to the dress she wears, & the scene she appears in'.[47]

It is no wonder, then, that Johnson found it difficult to accept that Gray's obscurity and confusion could be poetic.

NOTES

1. Norton Nicholls's 'Remiscences of Gray', Appendix Z, *Correspondence*, III, 1290.

2. Letter to Walpole, July 1756. *Correspondence*, II, 469.

3. *Gentleman's Magazine*, January 1782, quoted in James E. Swearingen, 'Johnson's "Life of Gray"', *Texas Studies in Literature and Language*, XIV (1972), 285; *Monthly Review*, LXVI (1782), 124–26.

4. R.W. Ketton-Cremer, *Thomas Gray: A Biography* (Cambridge, 1955), p. 130.

5. Letter to Wharton, August 1757. *Correspondence*, II, 518.

6. *The Yale Edition of Horace Walpole's Correspondence*, ed. W. S. Lewis, 48 vols (New Haven, 1937–83), XXI, 120; XXXIII, 287. When Walpole gathered together a group of 'the intelligent' to hear Gray read his Odes, one of them leaned towards another and said, 'What is this? It seems to be English, but by Gd I don't understand a single word of it'(*The Diaries of Sylvester Douglas, Lord Glenbervie*, ed. Francis Bickley [London and New York, 1928], I, 135, quoted in W. Powell Jones, 'The Contemporary Reception of Gray's *Odes*', *Modern Philology*, XXVIII [1930–31], 66). On another occasion Mr Fox, later the first Lord Holland, was overheard to remark that if the bard sung his song only once, he did not wonder if Edward I did not understand him (Powell Jones, op. cit., p. 67).

7. *Thraliana The Diary of Mrs Hester Lynch Thrale (Later Mrs Piozzi), 1776–1809*, ed. Katherine C. Balderston, 2 vols (Oxford, 1951), I, 188, 172.

8. *The Notebooks of Samuel Taylor Coleridge*, ed. Kathleen Coburn, 2 vols (London, 1973), I, 383, 1016.

9. Letters to Mr Brown, 17 February 1763; to Wharton, December 1754; to Walpole, 11 July 1757; to Beattie, 1 February 1768. *Correspondence*, II, 797; I, 416; II, 508; III, 1002.

10. *Inquiry into Some Passages in Dr Johnson's Lives of the Poets* (1783), pp. 30–33.

11. *The Art of Criticism* (1789), facsimile reprint (London, 1974), pp. 184, 193.

12. *The Poems of Alexander Pope*, ed. John Butt (London, 1963).

13. 'Life of Cowley', *The Works of Samuel Johnson, LL.D.*, 6 vols (London, 1825), III, 183–84.

14. Letter to Wharton, 9 March 1755. *Correspondence*, I, 421, n.4.

15. Preface to *Lyrical Ballads*, ed. R. L. Brett and A. R. Jones (London, 1963), p. 238, n.11 (1802 version), 245.

16. 'Life of Gray', *Works* (1825), IV, 402.

17. Ibid., IV, 398–99.

18. *The Idler and The Adventurer*, The Yale Edition of the Works of Samuel Johnson, ed. W. J. Bate, John M. Bullitt and L. F. Powell (New Haven, 1963), II, 217.

19. Rambler 140, *The Rambler*, The Yale Edition of the Works of Samuel Johnson, ed. W. J. Bate and Albrecht B. Strauss (New Haven, 1969), IV, 379.

20. Rambler 168, op. cit., V, 126.

21. 'Life of Gray', *Works* (1825), IV, 402.

22. Preface to *The Poetical Works of Mr William Collins* (London, 1797), p. v.

23. Preface to *A Dictionary of the English Language* (1755), facsimile reprint (London, 1990), sig.B2r.

24. *An Essay Concerning Human Understanding*, ed. Peter H. Nidditch (Oxford, 1975), Bk. III, ch. xi, section 11.

25. 'The Theory of Language', in *Dissertations Moral and Critical* (London, 1783), p. 269.

26. Preface to *Dictionary*, sig.C1r.

27. *An Essay Concerning Human Understanding*, III, x, 6.

28. Letter to West, 8 April 1742. *Correspondence*, I, 192.

29. *Boswell's Life of Johnson*, ed. G. B. Hill, 6 vols (Oxford, 1887), V, 434.

30. 'Life of Milton', *Works* (1825), III, 270.

31. *Boswell's Life of Johnson*, IV, 305.

32. 'Life of Cowley', *Works* (1825), III, 162.

33. *Biographia Literaria*, ed. J. Shawcross, 2 vols (Oxford, 1907), I, 16.

34. *The Advancement of Learning*, ed. Arthur Johnston (Oxford, 1974), II, iv, 1.

35. *An Essay on Criticism*, ll. 84–87.

36. *An Essay Concerning Human Understanding*, II, xi, 2.

37. Ibid., III, x, 34.

38. 'Life of Cowley', *Works* (1825), III, 161.

39. 'Life of Gray', *Works* (1825), IV, 399.

40. *The Poems of Gray, Collins and Goldsmith*, ed. Roger Lonsdale (London, 1969), p. 161.

41. Letter to West, 22 August 1737. *Correspondence*, I, 66.

42. Letter to Wharton, 12 March 1740. *Correspondence*, I, 138.

43. Rambler 158, *The Rambler*, V, 78.

44. Ibid., V, 77, 78.

45. *Boswell's London Journal, 1762–63*, ed. F. A. Pottle (London, 1950), p. 283.

46. Robert Lowth, *Lectures on the Sacred Poetry of the Hebrews* (London, 1787), Lecture XIV, pp. 308–09.

47. Letter to Mason, 9 November 1758. *Correspondence*, II, 593.

'A Man of Genius': Gray and Wordsworth

ANGUS EASSON

Gray and Wordsworth are inexorably linked by the latter's use in the *Lyrical Ballads* Preface of the 'Sonnet on the Death of Richard West' to exemplify those 'who by their reasonings have attempted to widen the space of separation between Prose and Metrical composition', at whose head (presumably as both the worst offender and the most eminent) was Gray, a man 'more than any other ... curiously elaborate in the structure of his own poetic diction'.[1] Wordsworth's discussion is not quite the wholesale dismissal of eighteenth-century poetry and of the 'inane and gaudy' phrases of Gray's poetic language that it is sometimes taken to be. Indeed, Wordsworth is at pains to stress, by use of italics, that part of the poem is in a language which 'in no respect' differs 'from that of prose'. Despite the implied censure (Gray could have written entirely and always as the poet of *Lyrical Ballads*, had he chosen), what the typographical division also reveals, despite Wordsworth's silence, is that the sonnet's distinction of language marks its double structure: the language of 'poetry' for the world indifferent to Gray's sorrow; the language of 'prose' for Gray's isolation of grief. As the best of adverse criticism can, Wordsworth's illuminates the very object of reproach.[2]

Gray's classic status in modern English poetry, when Wordsworth was young, made him as obvious an example in a polemic like the *Lyrical Ballads* Preface as he had been a model for the teenage Wordsworth, groping his poetic way:

A Winter's Evening—
FRAGMENT OF AN ODE TO WINTER

—But hark! the Curfew tolls! and lo! the night
Mounts the black Coursers of the stormy North
Now down the pathway brown
I bend my pensive steps
cetera desunt[3]

Wordsworth presumably decided, in ending so abruptly, that this was too much like writing the *Elegy* again, and there is even another touch of Gray in the (perhaps) self-mockery of '*cetera desunt*' (compare the 'lost' five hundred stanzas of 'A Long Story'). Yet, if Wordsworth abandoned poetry in the mode of Gray and if, in early bloom, he felt the strong father so much a threat that he attacked Gray's poetic language, one might expect an accommodation with the elder poet in later career, sign that, the threat past, he could forgive and forget. If so, the evidence is not in the various rescensions of the *Lyrical Ballads* Preface. The Preface was Wordsworth on Gray in 1800 and it was, publicly at least, as stubbornly Wordsworth on Gray in 1850, since Wordsworth made no change in this passage for the final text of *Poetical Works*.[4] Yet this seeming consistency of rejection by no means settles Wordsworth's responses to Gray. As late as May 1838, when George Ticknor, the Boston publisher, visited Rydal Mount and, at Mrs Wordsworth's urging, asked Wordsworth why he did not finish *The Recluse*, the poet responded, 'Why did not Gray finish the long poem he began on a similar subject? Because he found he had undertaken something beyond his powers to accomplish. And that is my case.'[5]

The poem in question, 'De Principiis Cogitandi', set out to investigate the mind's processes, and it is the Mind ('My haunt, and the main region of my song')[6] that clearly links Wordsworth's unfinished endeavour and Gray's; while Lucretius, the only poet to produce, in *De Rerum Natura*, an extended metaphysical or philosophical poem, was a common model for both poets. Gray refers jokingly to his offspring as 'Master Tommy Lucretius ... but a puleing Chitt yet', while Wordsworth's engagement with Lucretius in general and in *The Excursion* in particular has been the subject of some attention.[7] There is the appropriateness of parallel in enterprise here: two philosophical projects abandoned. But Wordsworth presumably also felt he was not diminished in the comparison of himself with Gray, by implication a poet capable of tackling and accomplishing such a task if anyone was. That it was beyond the powers of either need be no reproach. Another detail in this complex, though, may refer us back to the 1800 Preface, for the incompletion of *The Recluse* is tangled up with loss, most obviously (even if never admitted directly by Wordsworth) the loss of poetic power. There is the loss too of Coleridge, the prompter and driving force behind *The Recluse*, the loss of friendship in the breach that had been repaired but never effaced, and a sense of loss too in Coleridge's abandonment of poetry and (as Wordsworth might feel it, given Coleridge's public production) the atrophying of his intellectual powers. If the ever unwritten *Recluse* was an unsung elegy for Coleridge, so for Gray 'De Principiis Cogitandi' had become a memorial of friendship, its unfinished state a broken column on the grave of Richard West. The whole poem was addressed to Richard West, and the fragmentary second book, 'the last and the greatest of all his Latin writings',[8] is a lament on West's death: 'I can do no more, so long as my only desire is to lament here beside thy tomb and to address these vain words to thy silent ashes.'[9]

Making a negative point as he was in the Preface about Gray's Richard West sonnet, Wordsworth yet allows five lines some value, for their language in 'no respect' differs 'from that of prose'. By implication at least some value must lie in *what* these lines say and not only in *how* they say it. What is naturally expressed is, for the Wordsworth of the 1800 Preface, powerfully expressed, and he surely recognizes in that plain language the grief Gray feels for West's loss, even if he finds the sonnet elsewhere artificial. The experience and meaning of loss in Gray and Wordsworth draw them into community, even when apparently riven apart by the wedges of poetic theory and practice.

If we widen out from these instances of rejection in 1800 and parallelism in 1838, we find many passing references to or quotations from Gray in Wordsworth. The index of Wordsworth's collected *Prose* gives over half a column of references, which even with the editors' commentary allowed for, gives a significant *number* of citations. These surely are some evidence

of Wordsworth's high estimate of Gray. One such seems
unequivocal, when Wordsworth writes (and again the note of
loss is sounded) of 'that pensive interest with which the human
mind is ever disposed to listen to the farewell words of a man of
genius' (*Prose*, II, 207). It proves on closer examination, since
this is from *A Guide through the District of the Lakes*, that
Wordsworth is citing not the poetry but Gray's own journal of
his Lakes tour, unlikely though it is that Gray's topographical
interest would of itself earn him the title of 'genius'. The
interest, the human interest yet an interest surely stimulated
by Gray's poetic ability ('a man of genius'), is again provoked
by resonances of loss, for Gray 'died soon after his forlorn and
melancholy pilgrimage' (*Prose*, II, 207). The many citations of
Gray by Wordsworth that play around this Lakes journal,
though slight (often only the use of single words), yet form a
cluster of admiration. In particular, and not unnaturally,
Wordsworth was taken by the praise of the Vale of Keswick
and of the Vale of Grasmere. The phrase, 'the Vale of Elysium',
which Gray uses to describe the Vale of Keswick, picked out by
Dorothy Wordsworth in a letter of 1794, when she was reading
Mason's *Life and Letters*, is used by Wordsworth himself in a
prose fragment (? *c.* 1799); while with his strongly held ideas on
architecture and rural ornament (hatred of houses painted
white; recommendation of round stone chimney pots), Wordsworth responded delightedly to Gray's condemnation of flaring
gentlemen's houses and garden-walls, so happily absent in the
'peace, rusticity, and happy poverty' of Grasmere.[10] Here were
elective if not poetic affinities.

And yet that Wordsworth knew Gray's poetry and knew it
well is not, of course, in doubt, and that he referred to him
constantly and naturally, and in particular to the *Elegy*, is
clear. In the 1798 Conversations with Klopstock, predating the
Preface but at a time when he was involved with the poetic
principles that underlie its writing, Wordsworth observed that
the German poet knew little of Gray 'except the churchyard'
(*Prose*, I, 94), as if perhaps he ought to have known more.
Though at least the German poet did know the touchstone, a
poem so familiar that when Wordsworth quotes it in *The
Convention of Cintra* (*Prose*, I, 300) its identification is unnecessary. There it stands as an appropriate hint, in 'noble rage'

(*Elegy*, l. 51), to the rousing of the Spanish people, who might otherwise have remained in their collective obscurity. Again, the tag, 'the short and simple annals of the poor', came so readily to Wordsworth that in 1835 he did not bother even to mark it as a quotation, while a deleted passage in the *Guide through the Lakes* appendix, giving an account of resistance to encroachment, confirms how far the *Elegy* was taken by Wordsworth to be part of common cultural reference as he alludes to how 'these Hampdens withstood the powerful Tyrants of their fields' (*Prose*, II, 204 fn+ and 265). For Wordsworth, the radical or at least democratic element that lies in Gray's poem, released by our equality in death, might be summoned up when the society of the Lakes was threatened, when the passing of statesmen meant not politicians but small owner-occupiers, like his own Michael. Again and again, it seems, there is the resonance of loss when Wordsworth cites Gray, partly because of the centrality of that condition in Gray, partly because of Wordsworth's own engrossing concern with loss, whether personal (abandoning *The Recluse*) or poetic (in 'Michael' the plough has gone through the house that was the Evening Star). And yet, whatever Wordsworth's reservations about Gray's language might be, the references are there. Gray comes to hand unpremeditated upon such occasions and not only because of Gray's and the *Elegy*'s classic status. Both poets share a concern for the elegiac and the sepulchral: this commonality allows Wordsworth to use Gray to clinch arguments by reference to a framework of authority, which is acceptable to him in content and often, though not always, in language.

The *Elegy* necessarily feeds into Wordsworth's own church-yard vein, utilized as a narrative device in *The Excursion* (Bks VI and VII) or taken up in his 'Essays on Epitaphs'.[11] Naturally enough, the *Elegy* provided an epigraph to the 'Essays',[12] one which stresses the chronicling even of the obscure, whose 'annals', though they the 'place of fame and elegy supply', yet implore 'the passing tribute of a sigh'. The epitaph peculiarly draws together the record of human presence and human feeling, of memory and emotion. In *The Excursion*, as in so much else, Wordsworth recognizes the impulse to associate the memory of the dead with place, whether it be the landscape of

the living or the grave of the dead, for both landscape and
memorial stones are historians of the fact of human presence:

> —The Poets, in their elegies and songs
> Lamenting the departed, call the groves,
> They call upon the hills and streams to mourn,
> And senseless rocks; nor idly; for they speak,
> In these their invocations, with a voice
> Obedient to the strong creative power
> Of human passion.
>   (Bk I, ll. 475–81)

Even to unmarked stones may belong a history, as in the
'Poems on the Naming of Places' or more insistently in
'Michael'. The epitaph is a meeting of subject, writer, and
reader; an emotional and historical nexus, to tie the dead to the
living, the past to present and future. Epitaphs, Wordsworth
insists, are both public and permanent: 'an epitaph is not a
proud writing shut up for the studious'; while the emotion they
express should be 'strong, indeed, but nothing ungovernable or
wholly involuntary' (*Prose*, II, 59–60). It was these qualities, as
well as purity 'from vicious diction', that led Wordsworth in
the third Essay on Epitaphs to praise Gray's 'Epitaph on Mrs
Clarke' [*sic*], and in particular its last four lines:

> A pang to secret sorrow dear;
> A sigh, an unavailing tear,
> Till time shall every grief remove,
> With life, with memory, and with love.[13]

As though Gray, while an obvious point of reference, were not
allowed to escape, Wordsworth then censures severely and at
some length Gray's prose epitaph on his mother for a particu-
larity and oddness that ends by being 'lurking and sickly
selfishness' (*Prose*, II, 87–88). The *Elegy* itself ends with the
poet's epitaph, public and permanent, suitably contained by
being set within the narrative of the 'hoary-headed Swain', who
in turn invites the kindred spirit to read it. Like *Lycidas*, the
Elegy is a self-referential poem, about poetic power and about
the figure of the poet. Whatever Wordsworth's ambiguities
about Gray, then, it is no surprise that the young poet used the

Elegy approvingly in *The Prelude* and there numbered its author amongst 'the poets'. The episode concerned, in Bk X, is at a point of particular complexity, a mingling of the poem's larger themes of poetic education and failure in poetic stewardship, of past hopes and present fears, of public and private history. The *Elegy* acts within it to reflect and focus these concerns.

The naming of Gray and the *Elegy* comes in Bk X of *The Prelude*,[14] the second of two Books devoted to 'Residence in France' and Wordsworth's experiences of the Revolution. The Book ends (after a review of France's progress to the prospective coronation of Napoleon) in celebration not of politics but of poetry, with an address to Coleridge in Sicily and a roll-call tribute invoking the 'One great Society alone on earth', of 'The noble Living and the noble Dead', among them Archimedes and Empedocles and Theocritus, Greeks of Sicily that stand as strong and loving fathers to Wordsworth. Within Bk X, the *Elegy* reference is enclosed by the account of Robespierre's death (or rather, Wordsworth's account of how he learnt of Robespierre's death). The news of Robespierre's fall provides the exultant way out (at least in the short term) from Wordsworth's doubts and perplexities, into which he has been cast by the Revolution's progress and by his personal situation. The episode (Bk X, ll. 467–567) tells how, staying near Barrow-in-Furness, Wordsworth was returning from Cartmel, when he casually asked a traveller amongst a crowd crossing Ulverston sands at low tide, 'if any news were stirring' (l. 534), to be told '*Robespierre was dead*' (l. 536). Exulted by feelings of vengeance and eternal justice, Wordsworth poured forth a 'Hymn of Triumph' (l. 544) and looked forward to the unimpeded progress of 'The mighty renovation' (l. 557) that the Revolution had promised.

This key episode yet devotes twenty-five of its one hundred lines to the embedded episode (ll. 489–515) of William Taylor's grave, resting place of one of Wordsworth's Hawkshead schoolmasters, who had died in 1786 aged thirty-two (Robespierre, we might note, was thirty-six at his death, Wordsworth in his mid-thirties when writing the 1805 *Prelude*: their respective ages might invite comparison). The tribute to Taylor and the details and effects of his grave are not gratuitous or merely autobiographical, but crucial rather in the development and

meaning of the whole passage, as they are crucial too in an
episode that so irradiates both the Revolutionary Books of *The
Prelude* and the whole poem's themes and purposes. The life of
Robespierre, a famous (at least, a notorious) man, is set against
that of Taylor, an obscure one, as the life of a famous poet
(Gray) is set against an as-yet obscure one (Wordsworth).
Taylor's presence acts upon Wordsworth's depressed state of
mind and momentarily exults it, so making him the more
receptive to the news of Robespierre's death ('so feeling comes
in aid of feeling'). Depressed by the political, public and
personal situations, Wordsworth's mind is yet enlivened at this
point by memory, affection, the example of a poet (Gray), and
by renewed hope in his own poetic vocation, confirmed for him
(since the poet has a public duty as 'a man speaking to men') by
the renewal of hope in public life that the downfall of
Robespierre gives. And at the heart of all this is situated the
poet Thomas Gray.

Wordsworth had played no part in the big history of the
Revolution, despite his political conversion by Beaupuy (*The
Prelude*, Bk IX) or his later statement that he had known the
revolutionary journalist, Gorsas.[15] At the time of Robespierre's
death,[16] Wordsworth was staying with cousins at Rampside in
Furness, troubled by his enforced desertion of Annette Vallon
and by the outbreak of war between the two countries to which
he was bound by ties of love, friendship, family, and patriot-
ism. Rampside was a 'far-secluded privacy' (Bk X, l. 474),
more obscure than the village of Stoke Poges. For himself, he
had proved to be no Hampden or Cromwell, while still less, in
1794, in the context of *The Prelude*, with its seeking to understand his poetic preparation and his failure in production, was
he a Milton, unless mute, inglorious, a 'false steward' (*The
Prelude*, Bk I, l. 270) who suppressed that 'one talent which is
death to hide'. Yet even at a time when he might be depressed
or cast down, Wordsworth declares he gazed on the immediate
beauty of nature,

> with a fancy more alive
> On this account, that I had chanced to find
> That morning, ranging thro' the churchyard graves
> Of Cartmell's rural Town, the place in which

An honour'd Teacher of my youth was laid.
                                    (Bk X, ll. 489–93)

William Taylor lay beneath a stone where, along with a simple biographical statement,

> a slip of verse was subjoin'd,
> (By his desire, as afterwards I learn'd)
> A fragment from the Elegy of Gray.
>   (Bk X, ll. 498–500)

The lines, de Selincourt's note tells us, were the poem's final four lines, slightly adapted and (if de Selincourt reproduces the transcription accurately) garbling the meaning by omitting the brackets of the penultimate line. Here for Wordsworth are memory and love, entwined with his own poetic vocation, for Taylor, as his epitaph shows, 'loved the Poets' and if yet alive 'Would have loved me, as one not destitute of promise' (Bk X, l. 512). That line plays interestingly between 1794, the date of the episode's events, and the time of writing when Wordsworth has indeed justified his own and others' faith (the dead Taylor's and the living Coleridge's, amongst others) that he should be, 'else sinning greatly, / A dedicated Spirit' (*The Prelude*, Bk IV, ll. 343–44)—while within the episode the line plays between the varying threats of Robespierre. First, Robespierre was the threat to everything Wordsworth held dear—the Revolution; Annette; his own life and poetic being (potentially—if he had stayed in France, he might have perished, 'A Poet only to myself, to Men / Useless' [Bk X, ll. 200–01]). Second, as atheist, he threatened the 'Spirit and Wisdom of the Universe' that Wordsworth invokes within *The Prelude*. In a humble world of seclusion, Taylor had lived his worthy life; in the great world there is Robespierre, more than a Cromwell guilty of his country's blood. Wordsworth himself might have perished, whether by the guillotine or (as Taylor had) in the course of nature, to be as obscure as the unknown 'poet' whose epitaph Gray wrote and Taylor used.

As already stressed, the presence of Taylor's grave in the passage is no merely autobiographical record, diary-like demanding to be chronicled. The whole episode is one of *The*

Prelude's 'spots of time' and is carefully structured. Though the reader is forwarned of it, the news of Robespierre's death is for Wordsworth a sudden and unexpected revelation. The state of Wordsworth's mind has been quickened to creative vitality by familiar scenes of his youth and memories stimulated by Taylor's grave. He is peculiarly prepared to receive and to shape significance. The 'spot of time' comes unexpectedly and yet, as Wordsworth again and again demonstrates in these 'spots', its revelation is the more powerful for the mind not anticipating this particular experience (though quickened by circumambient experience or expectation), so that shock as well as creative alertness plays its part. Downcast (though with 'a fancy more alive'), there comes a reversal of feelings to a new height of exultation in the unexpected. Past and present intertwine through a complex of reference. Three individuals, Robespierre, Taylor and Wordsworth, are linked not only through temporal proximity and experience, but also through poetry, as Gray and Milton are invoked—the first named, the second imitated. Milton is linked to Robespierre through poetic allusion, Gray to Taylor by his epitaph, and both poets, as figures of creative genius, to Wordsworth, the poet potential of 1794, the poet actual of 1805.

The architectonic structure of the passage is reinforced, besides the reference to Gray and beside Wordsworth's own poetic fulfilment (asserted in the very achievement of *The Prelude*), by sympathizing poetic echoes. Robespierre and his crew are Miltonically 'this foul tribe of Moloch' (l. 470), who demand innocent blood as sacrifice, while their just fall is anticipated—'o'erthrown / And their chief Regent levell'd with the dust' (ll. 470–71), Robespierre crawling Satan-like on his belly.[17] Set against these demonic figures are the restorative powers of nature, elevated by Miltonic allusion to the heavenly force that threw down the guilty angels—sky, cloud, and mountain tops clad in 'one inseparable glory',

> Creatures of one ethereal substance, met
> In Consistory, like a diadem
> Or crown of burning Seraphs, as they sit
> In the Empyrean.
> (Bk X, ll. 481–84)

—a virtuous council to set against Satan's vile consult in hell. The diabolical nature of Robespierre is further suggested in counter images of security as the crowd crosses Ulverston sands, near a chapel (Romish, it is true, a place where masses were said, but still a bulwark against the godless Robespierre).[18] The travellers form a loose 'procession', in safe keeping of a guide, the sea itself 'at a safe distance, far retired' (1. 530), unlike the deluge that, under Robespierre's atheist crew, overwhelms France (1. 440).

It is following these Miltonic representations of false powers and true, of devils and of nature (evocations that deliberately summon up Milton the poet as well as the allusive power of *Paradise Lost*), that Wordsworth names Gray. Memory entwines not only with Taylor, who provides a link with his childhood, but with the very scene itself, the sands of Ulverston where, again returning from Cartmel, as a schoolboy he rode on horseback (Bk II, l. 108), a physical delight that is recalled at the end of the present passage (ll. 560–67). Wordsworth, in a context of perverted power and its poetic representation by a supreme poet, one of the tutelary presences of *The Prelude* (as Milton was a presence also for Gray), has been fulfilling the command of Taylor's epitaph, the wish of Gray, and so been preserving Taylor alive. 'Some pious drops the closing eye requires', and Wordsworth responds to the compulsion of nature: 'so that some few tears / Fell from me in my own despite' (Bk X, ll. 506–07)—not because hard-heartedly he would seek to deny Taylor this tribute, but because they are the result of spontaneous impulse rather than design, of an inner power greater than his conscious mind. With another death, the newly announced end of Robespierre, Wordsworth is overtaken by fresh impulses, joy and glee (a key Wordsworthian term, startling in this context, where we scarcely expect such animal exuberance), the future vision of France's progress being closed up by the ecstatic energy of horseriding. That energy and power of the horses and their speed, is a physical analogy to the sense of mental and spiritual liberty given by the relief at Robespierre's end. Instead of the 'atheist crew', we have 'a joyous Crew', who 'Along the margin of the moonlight Sea, / ... beat with thundering hoofs the level Sand' (Bk X, ll. 566–67). Exultation and liberation are given back to him from the past.

And so indeed the past closes up this episode, but it is a vital past, just as Taylor, living in Wordsworth's memory, had enlivened his fancy and made it capable. Political liberation seems also to offer the hope of poetic liberation: the Revolution may be truly fulfilled and Wordsworth truly become a poet. The *Elegy* lies at the heart of all this, in its parallels of the famous and the obscure, and in its projection of a persona (close to and yet not exactly Gray himself), a poet in temperament if not in achievement, who dying unknown did not even write his own epitaph (and yet who paradoxically within the poem's projected future, since Gray formally completes the poem, does write it). Such a silent poet Wordsworth might have been, as he projects himself in *The Prelude*, yet as in writing the *Elegy* Gray became a great poet, so Wordsworth did in writing *The Prelude*. Each finds a way out in expressive poetry, however more complex and subtle *The Prelude* is. In this key passage, without specific imitation, Wordsworth yet acknowledges and uses Gray to explore and exemplify his themes of vocation and poetry.

The Prelude is a poem about loss of powers, loss of direction, but it is also about restoration and discovery, proclaiming finally the greatness of the human mind, itself in turn the declared theme of the never-written *Recluse*. Loss is something to which Wordsworth turns again and again, and it is a condition of which Gray is painfully aware. For both poets, loss is tied up with memory, that very ability of the mind to retain what has been suffered and to organize that suffering—whether to understand it or to make it, even if declared incomprehensible, the subject of poetry. Yet there remain fundamental differences between the two, for Gray's model of the mind is ultimately static, contemplative, confining, where Wordsworth's is dynamic, dramatic, exploratory. Allowing for all that occasion and creative circumstances produce, the differences can be recognized in their respective sonnets on Richard West and on Catharine Wordsworth ('Surprised by Joy'). Even in structure, the dynamic differences are striking. Gray has a simple and effective systole/diastole between objective indifference (first and third stanzas) and personal grief (second quatrain and closing two lines), without syntactic disturbance of the formal architecture. Wordsworth, in a Miltonic form, breaks violently across from octave to sestet. The rhyme resists a division of the octave into quatrains, while the sestet's seeming opposition to the octave (the pang and the one yet worse) proves to be a reinforcement of pain, not a recovery from it. The contrast of external and internal is evident in Gray, enforced, as Wordsworth has shown us in the *Lyrical Ballads* Preface, by distinctive dictions. Yet within Wordsworth's sonnet is a world of creative paradox. The division is against himself, so that the impulse of joy, sudden, so seemingly desirable, certainly natural (compare the tears forced from him at Taylor's grave), proves to be part of a 'beguiling' that anaesthetizes, that is not desired, since in memory however painful lies love. Love, inseparable from sorrow at the sense of loss, is yet part of a vital life of mind and self. The imagery enforces this sense of a paradox that, far from being mere wordplay, lies at the core of our being. In forgetting his daughter, however momentarily, Wordsworth has been blind. His memory lapse, tied to sensory deprivation in its metaphor ('blind'), is hateful, for while 'sight' and pain are inextricable, they are yet necessary constituents in the active mind's sustaining of Catharine alive. Sight is used in double sense, the first, that implies pain, being contrasted with the sensory faculty, as Wordsworth recalls the moment, when death removed her, at which he lost sight of the child Catharine. His sharpest pang was at the instant of her dissolution, knowing

> That neither present time, nor years unknown
> Could to my sight that heavenly face restore.

Process, which for earlier poetry had been the enemy, is welcomed by Wordsworth, even the mental process of pain, for immutability is not a human condition: Catharine is indeed safe from vicissitude—'in the silent tomb'. Death imposes temporal blindness; memory, giving sight, sustains life.

Again, the differences are as obvious in two 'Prospect' poems, *Eton College* and 'Tintern Abbey'. Both review the past within a physical scene. Gray, in a place full of association, evokes the human condition ('they are men', 'all are men'), yet implies that 'ignorance' may be better than to see into the life of things or to hear 'the still sad music of humanity'. There is no conviction that intensity of feeling, even if it is suffering, can make us strong (as Wordsworth claims, and for the 'spots of time' in particular). Nor does Gray's structure allow development: the children are enclosed in their 'distant prospect', physically and temporally separated from the poet's adult self, where Wordsworth in 'Tintern Abbey' not only reviews his own progress, but has a doubling and renewal through his 'Dear, dear Sister' (l. 121).[19]

How far Wordsworth could take the 'Prospect' poem (including, in this case, elements of that earlier genre, 'Instructions to a Painter'), can be seen in the 'Elegiac Stanzas Suggested by a Picture of Peele Castle' (1806), one of the poems of loss prompted by the drowning of his brother John in the wreck of the *Earl of Abergavenny*. Casually at least, it can be linked to admiration of Gray, since Peele Castle (the subject of his friend Sir George Beaumont's painting) is near Barrow-in-Furness and Rampside, where Wordsworth was staying in summer 1794 at the time of Robespierre's death (*The Prelude*, Bk X). Wordsworth is able to manipulate the scene in recalling it: by imagining how (given a painter's power) he would have fixed it *then*; by considering how grief has changed his responses; by applauding Beaumont's depiction of the castle in a mood corresponding to his own at present. By contrast, Gray's Eton College remains an unchanging place, an Eden where no bullying or early death intrudes. The opening section of the 'Elegiac Stanzas' recalls Wordsworth's 1794 experience of the castle and how he might, in his tranquil mood,[20] have painted it as a poetic image of 'lasting ease, / Elysian quiet, without toil or strife', adding to the physical reality

the gleam,
The light that never was, on sea or land,
The consecration, and the Poet's dream . . .

(ll. 14–16)

The sea, which is both fact and a concealed metaphor in a poem prompted by John Wordsworth's drowning, offers a surface tranquillity as the painted surface would, that conceals the truth. The disturbance of John's death ('A deep distress') not only lends new meaning to 'This sea in anger, and that dismal shore', but makes Beaumont's stormpiece into a metaphor of Wordsworth's own condition, a metaphor that seeks not to be imaginatively poetic but, as so often in Wordsworth's rhetoric of sincerity, poetically real. The gleam is lost that the conventional poetic mind provides—

> I have submitted to a new control:
> A power is gone, which nothing can restore;
> A deep distress hath humanized my Soul.
>
> (ll. 34–36)

The disturbing force of that final line (was Wordsworth not humane before? what has he been as a man and as a poet? what does it mean?) is characteristic of Wordsworth's hard sayings and of how his poetry, again and again, forces poetry to cease to be merely poetic:—and hence his scorn of diction that removes us from a sense of reality. For Wordsworth's own commentary, we can turn to a passage in the second of the 'Essays on Epitaphs' (written 1810), which the editors (*Prose*, II, 105) link to the 'Elegiac Stanzas':

> Amid the quiet of a Church-yard thus decorated ... by the hand of Memory ... I have been affected by sensations akin to those which have risen in my mind while I have been standing by the side of a smooth Sea, on a Summer's day. It is such a happiness to have, in an unkind World, one Enclosure, where the voice of detraction is not heard...

Even here, though, the enclosure proves artificial, for the mind has flashed in on him the ills by which the dead 'must have been agitated':

> The image of an unruffled Sea has still remained; but my fancy has penetrated into the depths of that Sea—with accompanying thoughts of Shipwreck, of the destruction of the Mariner's hope, the bones of drowned Men heaped together...
>
> (*Prose*, II, 63–64)

For Wordsworth, there is a universal truth, but it lies more disturbingly than in humble acceptance of a common lot.

Poetry is not consolation: it shows vicissitude to be a condition, yet a proof of life. Disturbance is part of being human and the way to the palace of Wisdom lies through vital suffering, a new power, in place of that 'which nothing can restore' (l. 35). The heart that lives alone, as Gray's poetic heart too often seems to do, 'Is to be pitied; for 'tis surely blind' (l. 56). Wordsworth, through a poetry that at times denies it is poetry—if poetry be a form that separates us from the experience recalled by a man speaking to men—asserts that experience of suffering joins us in community, so that 'Not without hope we suffer and we mourn' (l. 60).

Necessarily, this has been a brief survey, taking a few examples. Whole areas have been only momentarily touched on—poetic language; loss; the effect of experience—and others not at all. Is it significant that Wordsworth acknowledges that his 'Ode to Duty' is 'on the model of Gray's Ode to Adversity' or that he added firmly that the latter 'is copied from Horace's Ode to Fortune',[21] so anticipating suggestions that Gray was his immediate or ultimate model? And is there a common line of thought between Adversity and Duty, Gray's goddess and Wordsworth's:

> Flowers laugh before thee on their beds
> And fragrance in thy footing treads;
> Thou dost preserve the stars from wrong;
> And the most ancient heavens, through Thee, are fresh
>   and strong.
>
>   (ll. 53–56)

To find a nightingale and a cuckoo in the 'Ode to Spring' might seem little more than a coincidental link with 'The Solitary Reaper', while the 'common sun' in the 'Ode on the Pleasure Arising from Vicissitude', though more worth pursuing, does not have the key resonance of Wordsworth's use of 'common' in 'all the sweetness of a common dawn' (*The Prelude*, Bk IV, l. 337) or 'fade into the light of common day' ('Ode: Intimations of Immortality', l. 77). Yet, for all Wordsworth's scorn of Gray's poetic diction, they have a common interest in the primitive, which led Gray to Norse and Welsh (with the resulting experiments in translation and poetic language) and which led Wordsworth to the life of ordinary men and women and to language 'such as men do use'. The violent rejection of Gray in the *Lyrical Ballads* Preface may have been a necessary part of shrugging off the strong influence of a great poet of the preceding age (one whose status meant Klopstock *should* have been more familiar with him), while that so many of the Gray references are to the Lakes Tour journal suggests that Wordsworth both marginalized the elder poet and drew upon work which least challenged what he sought to do. But after the tentative start of most poets, Wordsworth found a poetic vein and purpose, a dramatic process, a progression often made through contraries, which meant that for all his admiration and responsiveness to Gray ('a man of genius'), he was not intimidated by him and was confident enough, in outstripping him, to quote him and to praise him. What we have between the two is not so much influence, such as can be seen in the powerful though very differently absorbed presence of Milton in both later poets, but a relationship, rather, in which Thomas Gray had both his uses and his meaning for William Wordsworth.

NOTES

1. *The Prose Works of William Wordsworth*, ed. W. J. B. Owen and Jane Worthington Smyser, 3 vols (Oxford, 1974), I, 132; hereafter referred to as *Prose*.

2. For another such illumination, see Samuel Johnson's focus on 'knife' as a butcher's implement in *Macbeth*, *The Rambler*, No. 168.

3. William Wordsworth, *The Poems*, ed. John O. Hayden, 2 vols (Harmondsworth, 1977), I, 68; hereafter referred to as *Poetry*.

4. *Prose*, I, prints the two versions of the Preface in parallel; see I, 132–35 for the Gray passage.

5. George Ticknor, *Life, Letters, and Journals*, 2 vols (Boston, Mass., 1876), II, 67; quoted in Jonathan Wordsworth, *William Wordsworth: The Borders of Vision* (Oxford, 1982), p. 376, to which I owe this reference.

6. *The Excursion*, Prospectus, l. 41 (*Poetry*, II, 38).

7. See, e.g., Paul Kelley, 'Wordsworth and Lucretius' *De Rerum Natura*', *Notes and Queries*, N.S. 30 (1983), 219–22; Willard Spiegelman, 'Some Lucretian Elements in Wordsworth', *Comparative Literature*, 37 (1985), 27–49; Angus Easson, '"The Crown of Wisdom": Lucretius and *The Excursion*', paper at the Wordsworth Conference, 1986. Gray's remark is *Correspondence*, I, 225.

8. R. W. Ketton-Cremer, *Thomas Gray: A Biography* (Cambridge, 1955),

p. 58. Wordsworth was of course a great reader of Latin; late in life he quoted Lucretius, amongst others, at length and with pleasure (see the testimony of the Rev. R. P. Graves, in Christopher Wordsworth, *Memoirs of William Wordsworth*, 2 vols (London, 1851), II, 482–83.

9. '. . . quod possum, juxta lugere sepulchrum / dum juvat, et mutae vana haec jactare favillae' (Gray, *Complete Poems*, pp. 170,169). See Ketton-Cremer, p. 58 note, for another translation, by John Sparrow. Mason's *Life and Letters*, which follows Gray himself in calling this brief fragment of a second book, 'the fourth Book', may have led Wordsworth to think Gray had got further than was the case: see Gray, *Complete Poems*, p. 168 Title note, and p. 266.

10. Quoted *Prose*, II, 208; the two previous references are *Letters of William and Dorothy Wordsworth: The Early Years, 1787–1805*, ed. E. de Selincourt, revised Chester L. Shaver (Oxford, 1967), I, 114–15, and *Prose*, I, 8 (and p. 13 notes). Elsewhere 'flaring' is used by Wordsworth, apparently in deliberate allusion to Gray: *Prose*, II, 217, 323; for other references to Gray's tour, see *Prose*, II, 156, 157, 261 (note to l. 52), 274, and III, 353, where 'flaring' is brought against the threatened onslaught of the Kendal and Windermere Railway; see also *Prose*, II, 401 (note to l. 1260). For Gray's account, see *Correspondence*, III, 1079.

11. See further on Wordsworth and Epitaphs, Geoffrey Hartman, 'Inscriptions and Romantic Nature Poetry' in *From Sensibility to Romanticism: Essays Presented to Frederick A. Pottle*, ed. F. W. Hilles and H. Bloom (New York, 1965), pp. 389–413, reprinted in Hartman's *The Unremarkable Wordsworth* (London, 1987), pp. 31–46; D. D. Devlin, *Wordsworth and the Poetry of Epitaphs* (London & Basingstoke, 1980); and Angus Easson, *The Lapidary Wordsworth: Epitaphs and Inscriptions* (Winchester, 1981).

12. Though to the second Essay, rather than the first: *Prose*, II, 63; *Elegy*, ll. 77–84.

13. *Prose*, II, 87; Gray, *Complete Poems*, p. 52 (where the name is 'Clerke').

14. All quotations are from the 1805 version, ed. Ernest de Selincourt, revised Helen Darbishire (London, 1960). I am not unaware, of course, in the discussion that follows, of the problems in distinguishing between Wordsworth's version of his life in *The Prelude* and the events upon which that account is based: see Stephen Gill, *William Wordsworth: A Life* (Oxford, 1989), for the most recent and best discussion.

15. Gorsas is mentioned in *The Prelude*, Bk IX, l. 178; see Stephen Gill's discussion of the episode (*Wordsworth: A Life*, pp. 77–78) and Nicholas Roe, 'Wordsworth's Secrecy: Gorsas and "The Philanthropist"', *The Politics of Nature: Wordsworth and Some Contemporaries* (Basingstoke & London, 1992), pp. 101–16.

16. 28 July 1794; the news and facts of his death were only known in England as late as 16–19 August: see *The Prelude*, p. 304 note.

17. How far (horrid thought) might the poem's image suggest, even be intended to suggest, the manner of Robespierre's death, strapped to the plank of the guillotine?

18. Robespierre was not an atheist, but Wordsworth so represents him: see J. M. Thompson, *Robespierre* (Oxford, 1988 [1935]), pp. 429–30.

19. There are problems in all this; and we must face the 'hard sayings' in Wordsworth: for instance, 'The Old Cumberland Beggar' with its 'As in the eye of Nature he has lived, / So in the eye of Nature let him die!' (ll. 196–97).

20. Interestingly different from the state of mind of 1794 represented in *The Prelude*; another reminder that Wordsworth's primary concern is with poetry, not autobiography.

21. Isabella Fenwick note, *Poetry*, I, 1004; Horace, 'O Diva, gratum quae regis Antium', *Odes*, Bk I, xxxv.

Unheard Voices, Indistinct Visions: Gray and Byron

BERNARD BEATTY

Byron takes Johnson's line on Gray in his letters and comments: 'Gray's elegy pleased instantly, and eternally.—His Odes did not, nor yet do they please like his elegy.'[1] His relationship with Gray's poetry is, however, much more thoughtful than this comment suggests. The invocation of Gray's name usually served either one of two contrary purposes. Wordsworth used him to attack poetic diction and 'polished' poetry in general. But he could be invoked by Southey, Cowper, Langhorne, the Wartons and a host of others as a poet of sublimity vastly superior to the 'polished' Pope. Byron, however, declared that we should believe in 'Milton, Dryden, Pope',[2] which means that we should not, in Byron's view, oppose 'polish' to 'sublimity'. For Byron, Gray is not so much either part of an antithesis as a ground of connection. Byron's poetic practice is built up from subtle, overt, or outrageous connections.

Byron's first collection of poetry puts us on the right track at once. 'Fugitive Pieces' was withdrawn and burnt because of the uproar and anxieties of recognition some of the more erotic poems caused in Southwell where Byron was staying. Some manuscripts survived and Byron, in any case, retained and reprinted some of these poems in subsequent chastened collections. One of these, 'The Tear', had an addition when reprinted in *Hours of Idleness*. It was now prefixed by Gray's four-line 'Tears (Latin Alcaic) fragment on them'.[3] The subject-matter obviously links the two poems but the effect of reading Gray's exquisite lines as a controlling introduction to Byron's rollicking pathos is puzzling. How far, we wonder, is this incongruity intended and to what purpose? Here is the

fragment as printed, together with the first, second, eleventh
and twelfth quatrains of Byron's poem:

> O lachrymarum fons, tenero sacros
> Ducentium ortus ex animo; quater
>   Felix! in imo qui scatentem
>   Pectore te, pia Nympha, sensit.

GRAY

(1)

> When Friendship or Love
> Our sympathies move;
> When Truth, in a glance, should appear,
>   The lips may beguile,
>   With a dimple or smile,
> But the test of affection's a Tear.

(2)

> Too oft is a smile
> But the hypocrite's wile,
> To mask detestation, or fear;
>   Give me the soft sigh,
>   Whilst the soul-telling eye
> Is dimm'd, for a time, with a Tear.

(7)

> Sweet scene of my youth,
> Seat of Friendship and Truth,
> Where love chas'd each fast-fleeting year;
>   Loth to leave thee, I mourn'd,
>   For a last look I turn'd,
> But thy spire was scarce seen through a Tear.

(11)

> When my soul wings her flight,
> To the regions of night,
> And my corse shall recline on its bier;
>   As ye pass by the tomb,
>   Where my ashes consume,
> Oh! moisten their dust with a Tear.

(12)

May no marble bestow
The splendour of woe,
Which the children of vanity rear;
No fiction of fame
Shall blazon my name,
All I ask, all I wish, is a Tear.

The 'spire' in the seventh stanza refers to Harrow and thus recalls Gray's Eton. Elsewhere in *Hours of Idleness* a poem called 'On a Distant View of the Village and School, of Harrow, on the Hill' invites us to compare the two. This is just what Brougham did in his review of the collection which, in turn, provoked *English Bards and Scotch Reviewers*:

> Lord Byron should also have a care of attempting what the greatest poets have done before him ... Gray's Ode on Eton College, should really have kept out the ten hobbling stanzas 'on a distant view of the village and school of Harrow' ... In like manner, the exquisite lines of Mr. Rogers, '*On a Tear*,' might have warned the noble author off those premises ...[4]

Brougham is on easy ground here. Byron invites comparisons with Gray and Rogers but looks gauche beside them. After Gray's *Ode* and *Alcaics*, 'The Tear' may well seem trite in sentiment, careless in diction, propelled by an inappropriate metre, and remorselessly inventive at a low level. The fact that the last stanzas project the speaker into an unostentatious tomb observed by others is uncomfortably close to the final manoeuvre of the *Elegy*. 'The Tear' seems to invite these casual, confident criticisms and yet it also cocks a snook at them. It is a consumable that wishes to be used and then be beyond its date as a whimsical reminder of the tone only available on that date. It belongs in the drawing-room as an exercise of amateur talent but is, there, a *tour de force*. More specifically it belongs to the sedate but prurient circle that Byron knew in Southwell, much as 'A Long Story' belongs to Gray's Stoke Poges. Regency Southwell, like Regency society in general, ironized and tainted its inheritance of Augustan forms of decorum by mingling staged revivals of Restoration flashiness with them. Southwell, like Mansfield Park, enjoyed amateur dramatics.[5]

Byron's immediate predecessor in this spoiler's art was Thomas Moore whose rather fey versions of Anacreon (1800) and mildly risqué collection of songs attributed to 'Thomas Little' (1801) were widely read. Henry Kirk White's reaction to these poems is instructive. He was at St John's College whilst Byron was next door at Trinity. His own poetry, which Byron admired, is full of half-hearted borrowings from Gray. In the letter quoted (1806), he casts himself as the Jeremy Collier of Regency taste but his understanding is surprisingly sharp:

> But literature has of late years been prostituted to all the purposes of the bagnio ... I call to witness Mr. Moore, and the tribe of imitators which his success has called forth, that my statement is true ... You may remember the reign of Darwinian poetry, and the fopperies of Della Crusca. To these succeeded the school of *simplicity* in which Wordsworth, Southey, and Coleridge, are so deservedly eminent ... Moore's poems and his translations will, I think, have more influence on the female society of this kingdom, than the stage has had in its *worst period*, the reign of Charles II ... The broad indecency of Wycherley, and his contemporaries, was not half so dangerous as this *insinuating and half-covered mock*-delicacy, which makes use of the blush of modesty in order to heighten the charms of vice.[6]

White's letter gives us a curious but representative perspective on literary history. It is certainly one that the eighteen-year-old Byron understood. His *Hours of Idleness* poem 'to the Earl of [Clare]' sticks up for 'Poor Little! sweet, melodious bard!' against the reviewers who brand him 'As void of wit and moral'.[7] Byron defends Restoration theatre too. We find him using the same metaphor as White but for reverse purposes when he complains that contemporary theatre does not now 'dare to call the blush from Beauty's cheek'.[8] In a curious poem entitled 'Soliloquy of a Bard in the Country, in an Imitation of Littleton's Soliloquy of a Beauty', he casts himself as the bard

whose talents go unrecognised in rural Southwell. He, too, is
the subject of an attack like that made by Kirk White:

> What though, she said, for one light heedless line,
> That Wilmot's verse was far more pure than mine!
> In wars like these, I neither fight nor fly,
>
> (ll. 31–33)

At the end of the poem (ll. 77–82), relying on the indirectness
of its mode to cover his presumption, he boasts that he is like
Pope, Gray, and Dryden in that they too were subject to
vicious criticism by their inferiors. What is striking here is that
Byron, from the beginning, should align himself both with the
Restoration and the Regency, and with Pope, Gray, and
Dryden. He defends both the indelicacy of Moore and the
chastity of Rogers's diction. Byron instinctively acknowledges
and nurtures an inclusive tradition. By and large, he would
remain true to this and, as a consequence, oppose 'the school of
simplicity' and Romantic rejection of eighteenth-century practice or classical norms. Kirk White's violent attack on Moore,
on the other hand, is the harbinger of Southey's attack on the
'Satanic School' and of Victorian distaste for *Don Juan*. Phrases
from one can be transferred quite easily to either of the others.
We should note too how White's acute criticism of the '*half-
covered mock*-delicacy' of Regency lyrics is used as a flaunted
defence by Byron. It is, he demurs, only 'one light heedless line'
that gives him a reputation worse than Rochester's.

This is sufficient evidence to make us suspect an almost
political charge in Byron's transcription of Gray's chastest
Latin as an epigraph for his own light heedless lines. A kinship
of sentiment and attitude is being established through an
evident disjunction. In miniature we already have here a
foretaste of *Don Juan* as a considered, practical riposte to
Wordsworth's critique of Gray's diction in the Preface to *Lyrical
Ballads*. That preface was the manifesto of 'the school of
simplicity'. It made suspect that intermediate self-consciousness about diction which is the condition of Byron's verse as
much as Gray's. In the first version of 'The Tear', Byron wrote
'my body shall sleep' in stanza 11 and then replaced it with the
more decorous and euphonious, 'my corse shall recline'.[9]
Gray's impeccable Latin is added, presumably, as an endorse-

ment of such routine polishing. But it works, too, as a marker against which to set the bouncy unrestraint of Byron's lyric. Margaret Doody has argued that the Augustan Ode characteristically sets different idioms against one another.[10] To carry on doing this in Byron's day, when the trick is being lost or diverted to the coy realm of 'comic verse', involves precision in panache. This is exactly what Byron cultivates with increasing confidence and increasing isolation. Gray's 'pia Nympha', ostensibly 'scatentem', freezes the genial current she epitomizes in the petrification of a graven epigram. Byron's displayed polish helps his heedless lines to glide with ease and casual feeling. There is an ironic, spirited relationship between the lapidary and the evanescent mutable. This relationship, roughly speaking, is 'tradition' as Byron understood it. He called it 'precedent'.[11] Tradition consists in transforming the influences which you have been unanxiously formed by and lovingly accept. The case of Samuel Rogers may help us here by its contrasting straightforwardness. He admired Gray, and Byron admired him, at any rate as a poet. It is easy to understand why Rogers admired Gray and why Brougham coupled the two poets together. Brougham could *see* the connection between Gray and Rogers, but saw only crass imitation of them in Byron's early poems. Brougham, according to Hazlitt, could only produce a popular effect by sailing 'with the stream of prejudice' and venting 'common dogmas'.[12] Rogers, despite his lifelong admiration for Gray, had his own prejudices too. He complained that 'with all Gray's care in composition' the word 'shade' occurred three times in the course of the first eleven lines of the *Eton College Ode*.[13] Rogers himself, as scrupulous in diction as in his interior furnishings, would not make this mistake. What may surprise is that Byron should have so much admired this correctness. He wrote to Thomas Moore (5 September 1813) in renewed admiration of Rogers's *The Pleasures of Memory*: 'His elegance is wonderful—there is no such thing as a vulgar line in his book'. It is Rogers's coldness and deliberated delay in composition which Byron here prefers to printing 'piping hot from Southey's school'.[14] Yet, as Rogers wryly observed, 'Byron had prodigious facility of composition ... after going home, he would throw off sixty or eighty verses, which he would send to

press next morning'.[15] Byron wrote like Dryden, not like Pope
or Gray. Only his translation of Horace's *De Arte Poetica* was
the product of protracted labour and published, as it hap-
pened, Horace's requisite nine years after composition. This
may well be the main reason behind Byron's high regard for
this dull work. It was necessary for him to recognize and
establish negatively a sustained single diction ('no such thing
as a vulgar line') in order to generate the counter-stressed
incongruities of the *ottava rima* poems. Byron's defence of
Rogers's elegant diction, as opposed to Wordsworth's 'simplicity' and, later, Keats's 'vulgarity', is not in the name of an
elegant tradition of verse as such but in the name of a wider
tradition which needs to be able to recognize the decorous and
the colloquial. There has to be something more surprising in
real continuity than Brougham, for instance, could imagine.
We can see something of this in 'Prometheus', which is the only
poem of Byron's formally comparable with one of Gray's Odes.

The relation between Gray and Byron in this poem is not
immediately obvious. Brougham would miss it, but he would
see immediately the connection between Wordsworth's 'Ode to
Duty' and Gray's 'Ode to Adversity', and perhaps he would
mock Gray's presence in Coleridge's 'Ode to the Departing
Year'. Wordsworth intends us to recall Gray's Ode, and
Coleridge, to our embarrassment, is pretending to be Gray's
Bard equipped with a journalist's vision of current affairs.
Wordsworth deliberately uses the same stanza form as Gray.
Byron uses octosyllables but has no alexandrines and writes in
three irregular paragraphs. Nevertheless Gray's transformed
cadence can be heard more distinctly within 'Prometheus' than
'Ode to Duty'. This can be detected in the first line of each
poem:

> Daughter of Jove, relentless Power
> > (Ode to Adversity)

> Stern Daughter of the Voice of God!
> > (Ode to Duty)

> Titan! to whose immortal eyes
> > (Prometheus)

Wordsworth uses the same metre but alters the cadence. His poem is more thoughtful, more even, less vocative, less energized by rhythm. Virtually all the poem is held within the circle of Wordsworth's self, whereas this is so only of the last stanza of Gray's Ode.[16] The mode of address, real and not decorative in Gray and Byron, is avoided by Wordsworth though apparently utilized. All he does to bring this about is put a strong word before 'Daughter' and yet not undermine the stronger stress on the first syllable of 'Daughter'. The effect is to make the reflecting self present as one in control of its own voice and attentive to its own act of hearing. The will is announced and maintained in this and the poem, as it proceeds, becomes an act of witness to its own steady pace. Hence, when Wordsworth repeats the appearance of Gray's imprecatory conclusion, much as he recalls his opening invocation, the effect once again is quite unlike Gray. The addressee is neutralized, virtually eliminated:

> Oh! let my weakness have an end!
> Give unto me, made lowly wise,
> The spirit of self-sacrifice:
>
> (ll. 60–63)

What 'weakness'? There is not, and never has been, any acknowledgement of weakness in the cadence of the poem.[17] But this is where we would encounter it if it were present. Again, the strong 'Oh!' weakens the preserved stronger sense on 'let', and the interposing 'have', as with 'made' in the next line and 'of the' and 'of' in the opening stanza, stops the lines from pointing to a needed or feared 'other'. On the contrary, the voice of address is here referred back to its confident origin. We have only to eliminate the measured interposing syllables in order to tell the difference: 'let my weakness end, make me wise, give me self-sacrifice'.

Byron's opening, like Gray's, inverts the accent. The voice is thrown forward to the addressee. 'Titan' recalls 'Daughter' and, perhaps, 'Ruin seize thee, ruthless King'. Gray loves trochees and places them at regular intervals in his major odes. Often he superimposes falling cadence on the declared rising rhythm.[18] The initial 'Daughter', like Byron's 'Titan', ensures that we will pick up this beat wherever it occurs. It will remind us of the directness of engagement within which the poem stands. Reflection and the reflecting self do not constitute Byron's or Gray's poem, they are secondary to a self-standing mode of address. Take these lines addressed to Prometheus for instance:

> What was thy pity's recompense?
> A silent suffering, and intense;
> The rock, the vulture, and the chain,
> All that the proud can feel of pain,
> The agony they do not show,
> The suffocating sense of woe,
>   Which speaks but in its loneliness,
> And then is jealous lest the sky
> Should have a listener, nor will sigh
>   Until its voice is echoless.
>
>   (ll. 5–14)

That certainly sounds like Byron. It is hard to imagine Gray as Prometheus. But Byron's metre, like Gray's, is instrumental. It directs our attention to referential voicing rather than contemplated meanings. Byron couldn't have written 'All that the proud can feel of pain' if Gray had not written 'The Proud are taught to taste of pain'. Voice directs attention in both. Byron's moral, needless to say, points away from Gray's. Byron (here at any rate) celebrates pride: Gray castigates it. Instead he relishes 'the rock, the vulture, and the chain' of adversity. The mythology, too, is different. We might almost say, if we cross-refer to 'De Principiis Cogitandi', that Gray is celebrating the midwife's forceps in 'Adversity'. Byron's scenario of pain is male. The 'Thunderer' imposes punishment on Prometheus who strengthens 'Man with his own mind' (l. 38). Gray, on the contrary, is an unmale 'Suppliant' who wants a softened not a wounded heart (ll. 33, 44). He is brought up by a stern rugged nurse and her younger sister, and is accompanied by four women. In 'De Principiis', the baby child is taken violently from its accustomed warm circumfusion in the womb into the iron embraces of maieutic 'Dolor' (ll. 72–80). Nevertheless, both the mythology and the violence here are real and attended to as they are in Byron's poem. And the moral in Gray's poetry does sometimes centre in defiance. His Bard refuses to accept Edward I's jurisdiction and, like Prometheus, preserves yet announces the prophetic secret of a tyrant's downfall by subsequent history. Byron's 'Prometheus' weds the rhetoric of Gray's Bard with the grim but pathos-haunted stoicism of 'Adversity' and shows us the connection between them. What we read is quite new but it brings out elements in its authorizing ancestors that we would not otherwise suspect. Consider, for instance, the relation between Prometheus's silence and the Bard's voice.

'The Bard' begins with inverted commas identified as 'sounds' in line 9, as speech at the end of the poem (l. 143), but categorized obliquely as song in line 22: 'Struck the deep sorrows of his lyre'. 'Sorrows' cannot be 'struck' and do not directly belong to the lyre. Gray wanted, presumably, the energy of 'struck' and the semi-visualization it produces. Trochaic cadence here picks up 'Stream'd' two lines earlier and forecasts 'Hark' which begins the next line. We hear this musical emphasis rather than hearing a voice of any particular kind. We hear sound pictures, imagine a tableau, attend an oratorio where the soloists do not look at one another. The obliqueness of 'Struck the deep sorrows' emerges as necessary to these effects. This is rather different from Byron's 'Prometheus' which is heavily voiced. Readers who try reading it aloud find that they have to produce marked registers of voice which are clearly not their own. The emotive power of the poem, which is considerable, depends upon this forceful, alien voice becoming the reader's. It will be seen that this has a telling, inbuilt irony. If we say Byron's poem aloud, we find ourselves speaking an unspeakable 'loneliness' which does not want even the sky to contain 'a listener' and will not allow itself the small exhalation of a sigh 'Until its voice is echoless'. So the poem is the strong voicing of a silence constituted by refusal of voice. These Byronic ironies return us at once to Gray's home territory, and here Byron's 'feel of pain' and Gray's 'taste of pain', though differentiated morally, reveal the same intense interest in transactions of suffering carried out in unresponding space. In so far as this silence is voiced, it is so 'in vain'. Yet there is a certain complicity in this. Energies of voice in dialogue are deliberately directed toward ears that cannot hear. That is why both Gray and Byron are, first and foremost, poets.

Of course, the differences between Gray and Byron are huge. Byron could make poetry out of the reciprocities of conversation and does so in *Don Juan*. Gray separates the voice of his letters (directed unmistakably to the person named in the letter) from the habitual voicings of his poems much as Byron does in *Childe Harold*. The Duke of Grafton would not find himself addressed in 'Hence, avaunt, ('tis holy ground)' and would not find it eerie to be welcomed to Cambridge later in the Installation Ode by the dead mother of Henry VII, because her voice, like all others in the poem, is separated from its ground. Much the same is true of 'The Bard', which is quite uninterested in Edward I's reaction to the voice which indifferently scatters 'wild dismay' over his 'crested pride'. The 'roaring tide' would drown the Bard's voice much as 'the noise of the river' in the Chartreuse gorge makes it impossible for Gray to 'distinguish' what the spectre of the still living West seems to say to him. 'West' is seen 'at a distance' and his voice 'seemed to have a cadence like verse'.[19] Gray is unconcerned with reciprocities, at least in his English poems. Like his Bard, he has eyes and ears for indistinct spectres and impermanent 'visions of glory'. When spectres and visions abandon the Bard ('leave me unbless'd', l. 102; 'expire', l. 134) he promptly flings himself into the annihilation ('endless night') and permanent sounding ('roaring tide') which are the elemental foundations of vatic voice. His sound and fury strictly signify nothing but he calls it a victory: 'To triumph, and to die, are mine'. The end of Byron's 'Prometheus' reworks Gray's conclusion to 'The Bard', rather than simply alluding to it as Wordsworth recalls the end of 'Adversity':

> Triumphant where it dares defy,
> And making Death a Victory.

> (ll. 58–59)

It is essential here that voice witnesses to a dialogue which it denies. Gray's *Elegy* paints pictures in 'darkness', hears voices in 'solemn stillness', sees gems in 'dark unfathom'd caves', finds perfume in deserts, and living fire in ashes. The elegiac mode of Gray and of Byron's Promethean poems (i.e. most of Byron's major poems except *Don Juan, Beppo,* and *The Vision of Judgement*) transfers the fruitfulness of these religious paradoxes from spiritual life to aesthetic spectacle. 'Progress' and 'Pilgrimage' move towards vanishing points. The noisiest stanzas in *Childe Harold,* for example, claim to be voiceless. They contrast the articulations of Thunder and Lightning in the great storm over Lake Leman with the silence and inarticulacy of the 'speaker':

> ...I would speak;
> But as it is, I live and die unheard,
> With a most voiceless thought, sheathing it as a sword.
>
> (III, 97)

It is a bit late in the day to convince Matthew Arnold that Byron, like Gray, did not 'speak out' and it seems a less evident premise. But Byron certainly meant 'I live and die unheard'. It is the lightning that speaks; Byron himself has nothing to say. Or, to put it more precisely, if a little preciously, Byron both has nothing to say and has Nothing to say. In this he is exactly like Gray. Their understanding of ennui is the same and Gray's sense of nothing (rather than Rochester's) is the prototype of Byron's.

Gray's well-known 'Nihilissimo' letter identifies nothingness with busyness, especially travel: 'If you choose to be annihilated too, you cannot do better than undertake this journey ... I shall be secure in my nothingness, while you, that will be so absurd as to exist, will envy me'. We find the same association in an earlier letter to West (8 May 1736): 'doing nothing is a most amusing business'; and again in a letter to Wharton (22 April 1760): 'to find oneself business (I am persuaded) is the great art of life'. This, he asserts, is only a problem for men rather than for women who 'have always something to do ... a variety of small inventions & occupations fill up the void, and their eyes are never open in vain'.[20] Business or busyness is, in Latin, 'negotium'. That is to say it is 'not-idleness' or 'not-leisure'. 'Otium' has a long and paradoxical history in Western moral thought. It is sometimes identified with contemplation as, perhaps, in Gray's 'And leave us leisure to be good'. At other times, it is the enemy of contemplative moral life, as in St Benedict's Rule, 'Otiositas inimica est animae'.[21]

Gray, who loved the orderliness of La Grande Chartreuse, made a detour to revisit it, and averred that he would have been a silent hermit there if he had lived at another time, would have agreed with St Benedict. He had a horror of idleness but a contempt for worldly business.[22] The word 'otiositas' was sometimes transferred to mean writings or poems as the fruits of leisure. Gray was a busy hermit at Cambridge. He neither lectured nor taught, but he was never idle. He is active in reading, writing, and classifying. He avoids conversation. Even on his travels he engages in 'a great deal of silence, and something that rather resembles, than is, thinking'.[23] His versification and diction form one part of this silent busyness and arise fitfully from the void which is his chosen frightful companion. Gray's voice makes no mark in public conversation but can be heard in silence and by silence. Without this palpable void, business is pointless and contemptible. It is the affair of 'the Busy and the Gay', 'some on earnest business bent', 'the busy housewife'. These represent humanity by a gradus epithet more usual for bees. We are the 'busy race'. Gray as poet and Byron as Harold stand apart from this humanity and pursue the privileged, noiseless tenor of their way.

Harold begins, on the other hand, as one of the flies in Gray's 'Ode on the Spring':

> Childe Harold bask'd him in the noontide sun,
> Disporting there like any other fly;
> Nor deem'd before his little day was done
> One blast might chill him into misery.
> But long ere scarce a third of his pass'd by,
> Worse than adversity the Childe befell;
> He felt the fulness of satiety:
> Then loath'd he in his native land to dwell,
> Which seem'd to him more lone than Eremite's sad cell.
>
> (I, 4)

This is the foundation of his compulsive travelling, as it was of Byron's and Gray's. Both are hermits who cannot stay still; silent men whose adherence to nothingness fosters the busy weaving of words. Harold later upgrades hermits, one of whom he sees much as Edward I sees the Bard:

> More blest the life of godly Eremite,
> Such as on lonely Athos may be seen,
> Watching at Eve upon the giant height,
>
> (II, 27)

Byron, from his childhood onwards, was drawn intensely to this stilled receptivity and could not have been a poet without it. But he resisted it. He wanted to be, and was, a man of action too. The first two cantos of *Childe Harold* reveal the pilgrim and the politician but, as first printed, they abound with scholarly notes and appendices on Romaic Greek and antiquarian detail. A surprisingly large amount of Byron's life was spent, like Gray, alone, silent, busy, in his room.[24] It is this spectral business which Byron takes with him into the public pageant of history:

> 'Tis to create, and in creating live
> A being more intense, that we endow
> With form our fancy, gaining as we give
> The life we image, even as I do now.
> What am I? Nothing: but not so art thou,
> Soul of my thought! with whom I traverse earth,
> Invisible but gazing, as I glow
> Mix'd with thy spirit, blended with thy birth
> And feeling still with thee in my crush'd feeling's dearth.
>
> (III, 6)

'Doing nothing' here is a very sublime business indeed. The Bard would clearly recognize himself in that famous declaration, or rather he would recognize not his 'self'—he has no self to recognize—but that 'more than human voice' which Gray ascribed to him in his Commonplace Book.[25] Byron's voice sounds most loudly in this stanza and the Lake Leman stanzas because his 'I', dissolved into 'Nothing', speaks out only as 'Soul of my thought'. The busy energies of voice mount up, fall, and are scattered into silence. From the reader's point of view, this is accomplished by recognizable diction and overt metrics which habituate us to a 'more than human' voice rather than to that of a man speaking to men. The Bard gains life by giving it. The religious formula for eternal life becomes an aesthetic stance giving temporary respite from extinction. As long as he

speaks and sings—to the dead, to the elements, to the future—
in ornate sound-pictures endowed with form, we feel intensely
the 'dearth' of feelings which he announces. We are taken
directly to the eye of the storm, the heart of this arid,
overflowing source by the stifled, consciously received vocabulary and vigorous metrics. The implications of Byron's early
use of Gray's Latin epigram now emerge more decisively
within Byron's peculiarly un-Wordsworthian enterprise in
Childe Harold.

The point may be granted for Byron but more hesitantly
affirmed of Gray. Let us try another tack. Both Gray's and
Byron's poems found, almost immediately, illustrators. Both
were set to music. In our century, Wordsworth's Immortality
Ode has been set to music by Gerald Finzi, but the connection
of Wordsworth's oeuvre with music and painting is not
intrinsic. No one would seek to paint or sing the 'visionary
dreariness' for which Wordsworth himself claims he would
need 'colours and words unknown to man'.[26] It is much easier
to set Gray's or Byron's verse. Their poetry is untethered
because of its mediating diction, and is so openly redolent of
the form with which it is endowed that it is naturally available
for further forming. Precedent authorizes the particularities of
composition, enables emergence, but retains what it newly
authorizes for further use. We can see something of this in
Gray's delighted reaction to Bentley's visual re-imaging of his
poems. We find it again in Gray's fertile suggestions for a
proposed musical setting of 'The Bard'. This came to nothing,
but the act of re-imagining the poem as music is impressive. It
was to have been performed by a Mr Smith, pupil of Handel,
but it sounds more like Berlioz:

> It should be so contrived as to be a proper introduction
> to the ode; it might consist of two movements, the first
> descriptive of the horror and confusion of battle, the last a
> march grave and majestic, but expressing the exultation
> and insolent security of conquest. This movement should
> be composed entirely of wind instruments, except the
> kettle-drum heard at intervals. The *da capo* of it must be
> suddenly broke in upon, and put to silence by the clang of
> the harp in a tumultuous rapid movement, joined with the

voice, all at once, and not ushered in by any symphony.
The harmony may be strengthened by any other stringed
instrument; but the harp should everywhere prevail, and
form the continuing running accompaniment, submitting
itself to nothing but the voice.[27]

This reminds me of nothing so much as George Steiner's
comment on the end of Byron's 'Heaven and Earth':

> Inevitably, one hears behind the words organ peals and
> the blast of trumpets ... The tableau is Victorian, like one
> of those vast, dim canvases by Haydon. But it is also a
> foreshadowing of Wagnerian opera.[28]

These acts of multiple imaginings—sounds for pictures, words
for both—hang in space and are contemplated by their busy,
void-filled constructors. In Byron's 'Prophecy of Dante',
'Dante' says that painters, sculptors, and anyone who creates
forms may all be called 'bards', for the line of poetry 'peoples
but the air' (IV, 20–36). The sublime panoply of Gray's vision
of the Bard submits 'to nothing but the voice'. But the voice
here fills aesthetic space as a contemplated mode of address
announcing history but quite cut off from it. In effect, it
'peoples but the air'. How else is *Childe Harold* locally conducted than this?

At this point, the connection between Gray and Byron is
very close and should be seen in its distinctness. Byron can side
with neither Warton nor Johnson about Gray. He is drawn to
Gray's sentiment[29] and he is equally drawn to the self-
consciousness of Gray's diction as a means of expressing
feeling, manifesting energy, and voicing the void in a calculated mix of metaphysics and fiction.

Gray's delicate reticence and Byron's immersion in conversation, and erotic and political life make it hard for us to take
sufficiently seriously their nurtured aridity as a busy, haunted
space of voice. Gray, in silent ruins, imagining himself as the
Abbot of Netley talking to himself[30] or Byron re-imagining the
ghost of Newstead Abbey as the Black Friar of Norman Abbey
seem period pieces. Both poets, we recall, loved Ossian. It is
harder to patronize their attitude to light. At the end of 'The

Progress of Poesy', Gray claims to be 'Beneath the Good', below Pindar, and certainly not in Milton's forbidden elevation from which he saw 'the saphire-blaze' until, like the Bard, his eyes too closed in 'endless night'. Nevertheless, Gray still makes an astonishing claim to light:

> Yet oft before his infant eyes would run
> Such forms, as glitter in the Muse's ray
> With orient hues, unborrow'd of the Sun:
>
> (ll. 118–20)

The only way in which this is distinguishable from Milton's presumption is that Gray is passively seeing (forms run before his eyes) and that the seeing seems to involve distance rather than Milton's rapacious proximity ('He pass'd the flaming bounds'). The stance of the infant poet is more or less that of his Bard who sees 'Visions of glory' run before his eyes as, from Snowdon's height 'Descending slow their glitt'ring skirts unroll'. Distance here guarantees the otherness of what is seen, much as the 'gales' that blow from Eton to poet retain their separate origin. It is not like Wordsworth's vision on the heights of Snowdon where the sea of mist, subdued, touches his feet and, like Gray's Milton, he stands daringly within what he beholds. Nor is Gray's infant and poetic vision like that of the Immortality Ode. It is both more vatic and more Lockeian. Real seeing (or ostensibly real seeing) in Wordsworth's poetry is midwife to the creative independence of consciousness. Hence there is no incentive to paint or sing what is seen. Gray, on the contrary, does not have to first establish that he is seeing anything. That is why Johnson, correct in noticing that Gray had not visualized his warps and woofs, is wrong to criticize. Someone else can paint them exactly. Gray receives forms, endows with form, and is prepared for his forms to be re-formed. He describes attitudes rather than perceptions. We would expect to find a certain blurring of the fields of perception and imagination, sunlight and 'Muse's ray', rather than the yielding of one as sign of the other (an 'image of a mighty mind', *The Prelude*, XIII, 69). This is exactly what Gray does in a remarkable passage in 'De Principiis Cogitandi'. 'Dolor', he says, brings us from warm womb to cold world, but we are given instantly the wonderful consolation of light (l. 81)

which the newborn eyes drink in ('bibunt'). This is perception
but is remarkably like the passage on 'infant eyes' in 'The
Progress of Poesy' and the unveiling of nature's face to the
infant Shakespeare who 'Stretch'd forth his little arms, and
smiled' (l. 88). It is the permanent newness of this light which
matters. Gray, alert to history and time, can never be a poet of
memory or nostalgia. He feels, as G. Wilson Knight said of
Byron and of him, 'the tingling nearness of any heroic past'.[31]
Distance is near. It is the present pictured scene rather than
past recollection which operates in the Eton College Ode. Gray
makes this clear to us in his fine set-piece description of a
sunrise.

> I set out one morning before five o'clock, the moon shining
> through a dark and misty autumnal air, and got to the sea-
> coast time enough to be at the Sun's Levee. I saw the
> clouds and dark vapours open gradually to right and left,
> rolling over one another in great smoky wreathes, and the
> tide (as it flowed gently in upon the sands) first whitening,
> then slightly tinged with gold and blue; and all at once a
> little line of insufferable brightness that (before I can write
> these five words) was grown to half an orb, and now to a
> whole one, too glorious to be distinctly seen. It is very odd
> it makes no figure on paper; yet I shall remember it as
> long as the sun, or at least as long as I endure. I wonder
> whether any body ever saw it before? I hardly believe it.[32]

The running together of perception, imagination, recollection,
the present act of writing, and the art of writing, is clearly
evident here. The diction is not that of Gray's poetry ('Levee',
'insufferable', 'smoky', 'got to the sea-coast') but the loyalty to
what is presently seen as forms and the registering of glories
which cannot be 'distinctly seen' unite Gray and his Bard.
There are too many 'I's in these sentences for it to be a prose
poem, though it is clearly offered to us as a self-standing piece
of fine writing. Perhaps too, despite Gray's disclaimer, there is
too much distinctness of vision in it. Gray, as a poet, hears and
sees intently but at a distance which lessens and loses what he
strains after. There are far more passages in Byron's poetry
which resemble Gray's prose than there are in Gray's poetry.[33]
Byron sees tears, for instance, much more closely and variously

than Gray does.[34] Nevertheless much of *Childe Harold* is seen in
Gray's blurred distinctness. Lake Leman is half-seen like this:

> It is the hush of night, and all between
> Thy margin and the mountains, dusk, yet clear,
> Mellowed and mingling, yet distinctly seen,
> Save darken'd Jura, whose capt heights appear
> Precipitously steep; and drawing near,
> There breathes a living fragrance from the shore,
> Of flowers yet fresh with childhood;
>
> (III, 86)

'Yet' in line 3 must mean 'still', as it does in the last line quoted,
if the syntax is to add up, but it parallels the 'yet' of line 2 and
we read it therefore as we read Denham's notorious 'Though
deep, yet clear; though gentle, yet not dull'. The ambiguity is
crucial. Are we contemplating an aesthetic chiaroscuro in
which distinct indistinctness is delighted in as such, or are we
and the landscape in changing time and light so that things
now ('yet') seen distinctly will soon not be so? Here the answer
is 'both'. Roughly speaking, this is the distinction between
Gray and Collins, whose evening draws 'The gradual dusky
veil' over 'all'. The sense of the landscape changing whilst
looked at is in Gray's letters but scarcely present in Gray's
poetry. It is not the landscape which alters but the poet who
fades away. The most that can be found in Gray's verse is a
willed synchronization of the two as in a line from a rejected
stanza in the *Elegy* ('With whistful Eyes pursue the setting
Sun')[35] or the Sapphic ode to West. In the latter, Gray, after
declaring himself to be a worshipper and servant of the sun,
says that he would be blessed if he could pass unnoticed into
death as the sun sets:

> O ego felix, vice si (nec unquam
> Surgerem rursus) simili cadentem
> Parca me lenis sineret quieto
>   Fallere letho!
>
> (ll. 45–48)

The stanza seems to picture the sunset fading of the initial 'ego'
into 'letho'. But this similitude is displaced. Gray adds a final
stanza in which the restored sun blazes the following morning

unenvied by the disappeared poet. The pattern is exactly that of the Bard who prophesizes the 'restoration' tomorrow of the 'golden flood' of light. Childe Harold is dissolved more quietly. A cloud descends between 'us' and the glow of vision and sunlight thus forming 'A melancholy halo ... on the verge of darkness' (IV, 165). This almost imperceptible light sends us fruitlessly 'prying into the abyss' (IV, 166) but, finally, 'my visions flit / Less palpably before me' (IV, 185) and the poem, in an appropriately lack-lustre stanza, lessens to a mannered full-stop. Harold's 'Pilgrimage', like Gray's 'Progress', peters out. Manfred announces the same manoeuvre with more bravura. His worshipping address to the sun concludes: 'He is gone: / I follow' (III, ii, 29–30). His actual death, though, when it comes, is a quiet, 'not difficult' disappearance not unlike Gray's imagined (and indeed actual) death.

Intertextuality licenses all connections. And literary scholarship, from the beginning, has tracked Gray's raids on the already articulated to their documented sites. Gray had little reason to love his father and Byron could not remember his. Despite or perhaps because of this, both poets generate their words out of their accepted patrimonies. They are neither random nor antiquarian in this. It is clear that Gray's personality forced him to separate his verse from his prose, his day-to-day life from his art, his imagination from his classification. His verse therefore announces its own alienation from its separated sources. His invocation is only held together, as Paul Fry so skilfully argued, by a circle with the motto *Nihilissimo*.[36] Like Edward I's army, his diction is suspended in what Byron called 'Battle's magnificently-stern array'[37] and yet 'mocks the air' which it peoples 'with idle state'. Byron, on the other hand, can seek an integration of his diversities or manipulate their incongruities. The reader of Gray's *Elegy*, his letters, Norse poems, Odes on Grafton and Walpole's Cat, and verses on Lord Holland's Seat, simply has to accept their disjunction. Byron, at a later time and with a wholly different energy, can solder them into *Don Juan*. Byron's Promethean poems, however, take from Gray their mode of spectral stylized address to the shifting panoplies of history and place, the preference for voices which go unheard, and rapt attentiveness to the indistinctly seen. The image which Byron picks out as the most 'striking' in Gray's *Elegy* is 'shapeless sculpture'.[38] It is this track, not opened up by Johnson's criticism, that I have tried to stay with in this essay, but it is only one track. Both Gray and Byron, whose eyes open to the strange light of the muse, keep their feet on earth, accept social forms, and presume that the intensity they relish remains subordinated to ethical life. Byron is not being disloyal to Johnson's precepts in working Gray's 'glittering accumulations' into his own words that burn. What is from one point of view aesthetic spectacle and, from another, the assertion of Promethean pride is, in *Don Juan*, the moral turning-point beyond which we can 'breathe and walk again':

> Must I restrain me, through the fear of strife,
> From holding up the Nothingness of life?
>
> (VII, 6)

NOTES

1. *Lord Byron: The Complete Miscellaneous Prose*, ed. A. Nicholson (Oxford, 1991), p. 109.

2. *Don Juan*, 1, 205. All quotations from Byron's poetry are taken from *Lord Byron: The Complete Poetical Works*, ed. Jerome J. McGann, 6 vols (Oxford, 1980–91).

3. The fragment is translated in *Gray, Collins and Goldsmith: The Complete Poems*, ed. Roger Lonsdale (London, 1969), p. 308: 'O fount of tears, that have their sacred sources in the tender spirit; four times blessed is he who has felt you, holy Nymph, gushing forth from the depths of his heart!'

4. *The Edinburgh Review*, January 1808. Quoted in T. Redpath, *The Young Romantics and Critical Opinion 1807–1824* (London, 1973), p. 209.

5. 'He [Byron] soon became involved in private theatricals with the Pigots and some of their friends, including Julia Leacroft, the organizer of the performances.' (Leslie A. Marchand, *Byron: A Portrait* [London, 1971], p. 41).

6. To R. P. Thompson, 8 April 1806. Kirk White, *Poems, Letters and Prose Fragments*, ed. J. Drinkwater (London, 1907), pp. 221–22.

7. *Poetical Works*, I, 96.

8. Ibid., I, 41. The line comes from a prologue written for an amateur production of Cumberland's *The Wheel of Fortune* in which Byron starred at Southwell. The prologue endorses the 'purer scenes' of 'this polish'd age', but does so with exactly that 'mock-delicacy' of which Kirk White complains. Elsewhere Byron, in the role of satirist, denounces 'Little's songs for flushing virgins' cheeks' (*English Bards*, I, 285).

9. *Poetical Works*, I, 40.

10. Margaret Anne Doody, *The Daring Muse* (Cambridge, 1985), p. 257.

11. See Byron's note to *English Bards*, l. 211 (*Poetical Works*, I, 403). See Bernard Beatty, 'Lord Byron: Poetry and Precedent', in *Literature of the Romantic Period 1750–1850*, ed. R. T. Davies and B. G. Beatty (Liverpool, 1976), pp. 114–34.

12. W. Hazlitt, *The Spirit of the Age*, ed. E. D. Mackerness (London, 1969), p. 226.

13. *Table-Talk of Samuel Rogers*, ed G. H. Powell (London, 1903), p. 18. Rogers claimed that he knew all Gray's poems ('I can repeat them all', p. 17), and he used to carry a pocket edition of Gray's poems on his walks.

14. *Hints from Horace*, l. 654, and letter to Moore, 5 September 1813.

15. *Table-Talk*, p. 178.

16. See for instance Geoffrey H. Hartman's comment on the 'Ode to Duty': 'yet the chief emotion expressed by him, and expressed movingly, is for a *self-devoted* dedication, and this eliminates the possibility that Duty's compulsion could stem from authority or the dictate of external law'. (*Wordsworth's Poetry 1787–1814* [New Haven, 1964], p. 278.)

17. This is true, for instance, of 'I long for a repose that ever is the same', where the cadence confirms 'ever is the same' rather than longing.

18. The interweaving of trochees and iambs derives from eighteenth-century interest in Milton's 'L'Allegro' and 'Il Penseroso'. I cannot find any other example of Gray's mathematical precision in their placing. 'The Progress of Poesy' places trochees every eighth line in the strophe and antistrophe, and at lines 1–3, 7–11 in the epode (with one irregularity in the final epode). 'The Bard' sustains a different but exactly repeated pattern. Trochees unite Gray's interest in primitive metres with his taste in diction for well-placed disyllables. We can see how Byron's use of Gray's diction brings trochaic suggestions in such examples as these:

> When Health affrighted spreads her rosy wing,
> And flies with every changing gale of spring;
> Not to the aching frame alone confin'd,
> Unyielding pangs assail the drooping mind:
> What grisly forms, the spectre train of woe!
> Bid shuddering Nature shrink beneath the blow,
> ('Childish Recollections', ll. 3–8)

> To lips where Love had lavished all his breath,
> To lips—whose broken sighs such fragrance fling,
> As he had fann'd them freshly with his wing!
> (*The Corsair*, III, 552–54)

Hopkins's comment that Gray's sonnet on West is 'remarkable for its falling or trochaic rhythm' is well-known (*Gerard Manley Hopkins* [The Oxford Authors; Oxford, 1986], p. 248).

19. Gray to West, 16 November 1739. *Correspondence*, I, 128.

20. The 'Nihilissimo' letter is Gray's continuation of a joint letter with Walpole to West, 31 July 1740, *Correspondence*, I, 172–73. The other letters are *Correspondence*, I, 39; II, 666.

21. *The Rule of Saint Benedict*, ed. J. McCann (London, 1952), p. 110.

'Idleness is the enemy of the soul'. Dom Jean Leclerq comments, '*Otium* lies midway between the two perils *otiositas* and *negotium*, which is the very denial of *otium*—*Otium* is the major occupation of the monk, it is a very busy leisure, *negotiosissimum otium* as St Bernard and so many others have repeated'. (*L'Amour des lettres et le désir de Dieu* [Paris, 1957], trans. C. Misrahi, *The Love of Learning and the Desire for God*, 3rd ed. [New York, 1982], p. 67.) Leclerq pursues the subject with his usual erudition in *Etudes sur le vocabulaire monastique du moyen âge* (Rome, 1961).

22. See Gray's letters to his mother, 13 October 1739, and to West, 16 November 1739 (*Correspondence*, I, 122–23; I, 128), and also his Alcaic ode, 'O Tu, severi religio loci'. In a letter to Wharton (5 June 1748, *Correspondence*, I, 304), he quotes approvingly from Gresset's 'La Chartreuse': 'Entre les jeux de la folie, / Et l'ennui de l'oisiveté'. Gresset casts himself ironically as a Carthusian hermit in his Paris attic.

23. Gray to West, 21 April 1741. *Correspondence*, I, 181.

24. 'I do not know that I am happiest when alone; but this I am sure of, that I never am long in the society even of *her* I love, (God knows too well, and the devil probably too,) without a yearning for the company of my lamp and my utterly confused and tumbled-over library ... I have not stirred out of these rooms for these four days past ... The more violent the fatigue, the better my spirits for the rest of the day; and then my evenings have that calm nothingness of languor, which I most delight in' (Byron's Journal, 10 April 1814. *Byron's Letters and Journals*, ed. L. Marchand [London, 1973–82], III, 257).

25. Ed. Lonsdale, p. 178.

26. Wordsworth, *The Prelude* (1805), XI, 309.

27. *The Poems of Thomas Gray*, ed. J. Mitford (London, 1814), p. 80. Mason is responsible for this information. It is not clear how much of the ideas and words here belong directly to Gray. He had at least some hand in this conception: see Ed. Lonsdale, p. 183. There was a vogue for elaborate musical settings in the mid-eighteenth century: 'L'Allegro' and 'Il Penseroso' were set to music by Handel.

28. G. Steiner, *The Death of Tragedy* (London, 1951), p. 210.

29. It is not accidental that Byron associates Gray with 'The Tear'. In particular, Gray's vein of sentiment associating friendship with lost school-days and with death clearly appealed to him. Byron has a Latin poem on his dead Cambridge friend Edleston (*Poetical Works*, I, 354), which is based on Catullus but strongly recalls Gray's passionate Latin on West's death in Book II of 'De Principiis Cogitandi'. In general Byron is careful in his English 'Thyrza' poems on this death to alter 'he' discreetly to 'she'. Gray helps us to see that this can be read both ways. In *The Corsair* we first encounter Medora singing a version of Gray's epitaph:

> 'My fondest—faintest—latest accents hear—
>   Grief for the dead not Virtue can reprove;
> Then give me all I ever ask'd—a tear,
>   The first—last—sole reward of so much love!'

(I, 359–62)

Medora dies without reason whilst *The Corsair* is away, much as Edleston died whilst Byron was on his Levantine travels. Biographical conjecture is a dangerous business, but the allusion to Gray here gives us some grounds to make this connection.

30. Letter to Nicholls, 19 November 1764. *Correspondence*, II, 852–53.

31. G. Wilson Knight, *Poets of Action* (London, 1967), p. 187.

32. This was printed by Mason as a postscript to the letter to Nicholls (see n. 30), but it is not with the original letter. It is printed in *Correspondence*, II, 854 n.10.

33. E.g. *Childe Harold*, III, 27–29; *The Curse of Minerva*, 1–18; *Don Juan*, II, 183.

34. Even in 'The Tear' we learn that tears blur sight, blur the eyes of the one we behold weeping, drop and moisten dust, can be kissed on eyelids, and sparkle. This is typical of Byron. Tears are not thus individuated or attended to in Gray's poetry. We can mark the difference by noting that Byron can scarcely see the spire of Harrow through a tear and recall how impossible it would be for Gray to disclose his situation like this in the Eton College Ode.

35. Ed. Lonsdale, p. 136.

36. Paul Fry, 'Thomas Gray's Feather'd Cincture: The Odes', in *Poets of Sensibility and the Sublime*, ed. H. Bloom (New York, 1986), p. 91.

37. *Childe Harold*, III, 28.

38. *Collected Prose*, p. 135.

Gray Among the Victorians

MALCOLM HICKS

The pronouncements of a critic of 'great eminence' provide the
central focus for a modern reader's assessment of Victorian
attitudes to Thomas Gray. The acknowledgement is W. J.
Courthope's in a forthright attack on the usefulness of his
contemporary, Matthew Arnold's, famous 'touchstones' as
guides to discrimination in poetry—his snippets, culled from
the great masters of Western literature, and applied as a means
of measuring the level of 'high poetic quality' in the writings of
lesser lights.[1] It is in the essay in which they are proposed,
originally published as the introduction to T. Humphry
Ward's popular anthology, *The English Poets* (1880), and known
subsequently as 'The Study of Poetry',[2] that the reader is first
likely to encounter one of Arnold's several evaluations of Gray
in the context of his age. The paragraph on Gray bridges the
gap between Dryden, Pope and Burns—all of whom fail the
touchstone test. The 'classic' Gray is not subjected to the trial.
What we get is a distillation of Arnold's views on the poet and
the period in which he struggled to find a voice. Born in an age
overshadowed by poetry of prose status (with Dryden and
Pope the chief executants) Gray, in retreat, catches the Greek
manner and, derivative though this makes him, he thus
becomes the 'scantiest and frailest of classics in our poetry'.[3] In
exploiting the ambiguity of 'poetical classic', Arnold accords
Gray his fragile place in the first rank because he turned for
sustenance to Arnold's own admired Greek predecessors.
Significantly, snatches of the *Iliad* bear the palm as touchstones.

Doubtless Courthope's exceptions to Arnold had been
prompted by the latter's slighting of Pope, whom Courthope
had edited. His objections to the arbitrariness of touchstones,
and the narrow ethical standards they represent, are fuelled by
his concern over the dissemination of pernicious 'advice to

presumably large numbers of readers'.[4] As part of the wide
educative enterprise in which Arnold was frequently engaged,
his remarks on Gray had been rehearsed four years previously
in his preface for an edition of Johnson's *Lives of the Poets*. Like
the introduction to Ward's anthology, this was intended for, if
not a popular, then certainly a wide and impressionable
audience—'all young students of literature'.[5] But six months
earlier, in reviewing Stopford Brooke's *English Literature* (in a
'Literature Primers' series), Arnold had questioned Brooke's
judgement of the poems of Gray and Collins as '"exquisite
examples of perfectly English work wrought in the spirit of
classic art"', detecting in Gray, even in the *Elegy*, the occasional lapse into the 'false poetical style of the eighteenth
century'.[6] Arnold's neglecting to stoop to precise explanation—rather than precise exemplification—is often at odds
with his desire to instruct. Yet what Gray clearly enough fails
here is the test of 'genuineness': a quality which, for example,
Arnold found (at times) in Wordsworth (and which Wordsworth himself found lacking in Gray's sonnet on the death of
his close friend, Richard West). The quality is as much
'classic'[7] as English Romantic, and is permanently registered
in those touchstones which the sometime Professor of Poetry at
Oxford encourages the general reader to seek out if he or she
has 'any tact' so to do. Gray's alleged lapses into 'false poetical
style' are accentuated by Arnold's alterations introduced in the
process of modernizing his text. In the offending lines from the
Elegy's 'Epitaph', in contrast to the editions at his disposal,
Arnold employs a dash to exaggerate the effects of 'a tear',
followed by a semi-colon rather than a comma, and ekes out
the effect with the full forms of 'Misery', 'gained', and
'Heaven':

> He gave to Misery all he had—a tear;
> He gained from Heaven ('twas all he wish'd) a friend.

'Style' for Arnold means sentiment, true or 'false', in a
confusion of form and subject matter. In an earlier essay of
1863, reflecting on the eighteenth century, style is discussed
more closely in terms of its component parts. 'The main vehicle
for their high poetry [was] a metre inadequate ... for this
poetry,—the ten-syllable couplet'. Gray, whom Arnold singles

out for wearing best, and for giving the 'most entire satisfaction ... hardly uses that couplet at all ... he is a poetical nature repressed and without free issue'. In the earliest version of the essay, in his eagerness to be sympathetic to Gray's predicament, Arnold had wrongly said he 'does not use that couplet at all'.[8] Several critics have reminded the reader that he does: in the 'Hymn to Ignorance' and 'The Alliance of Education and Government' (besides some epitaphs and translations), but it is significant that these are fragments.

What we have here is the first phase in a circular discussion of the man and the milieu. The reticence of Gray the poet is extended to Gray the man, as the starting point of Arnold's essay on Gray which prefaced Ward's selections from his work, in order to explain, in social and historical terms, the reticence of Gray the poet. This essay begins by quoting from a letter from one of the poet's friends, James Brown, to another, Thomas Wharton, meditating on the loss of Gray some fortnight before. After leaning towards the mood of the *Elegy*, Brown says: 'He never spoke out, but I believe from some little expressions I now remember to have dropped from him, that for some time past he thought himself nearer his end than those about him apprehended'.[9] This 'simple statement', as Duncan C. Tovey called it,[10] suggests that Gray's reserve and sensitivity restrained him from distressing others with possible presentiments of an end which they would be powerless to prevent. But Arnold pounces on '*He never spoke out*' (Arnold's emphasis, not Brown's). 'In these few words is contained the whole history of Gray, both as a man and a poet ... let us dwell upon them, and press into their meaning'. Not 'press them into meaning', which would have been a more accurate indication of his intentions. Brown's 'he never spoke out' appears to refer to particular restraint over possible forebodings, rather than to accepted estimations of Gray's character in general. But Arnold is keen to advance the latter reading. More importantly, neither interpretation of Gray's reticence is the same as that 'scantiness of [poetic] production' which Arnold proceeds to make Brown's observation mean. The eager desire to interrelate the personal and the poetical seems to disclose a late Romantic earnestness on Arnold's part. But his exploitation of 'he never spoke out' is not caught up in any complaint at the absence of the confessional in Gray's poetry. That mode is too often exhibited as 'false poetical style' (to use Arnold's phrase about eighteenth-century practice) and is firmly rebuked in the Romantic Byron's 'pageant of his bleeding heart' in Arnold's *Stanzas from the Grande Chartreuse* (1853). Shelley's 'lovely wail' has helped none of the 'inheritors of his distress', and Arnold's acute sense of his own shortcomings in this way was the principal reason for his own renunciation of poetry. Perhaps Arnold implicitly detects oblique confessional expression struggling within the 'false poetical style' of the lines from the *Elegy* quoted earlier.

There is, however, a decidedly Victorian matter which intervenes. Arnold mentions Adam Smith's wish for Gray 'but to have written a little more'. Victorians could not find it in themselves to be so indulgent. It is not that quantity necessarily equals quality. Something of the positive side to Gray's paucity is glimpsed in both Arnold's and Stopford Brooke's choice of 'exquisite' to describe it. But work, and what it creates, at base testify to the abiding presence of the divine. A seminal text, in support of what is inevitably a generalization, is Carlyle's *Sartor Resartus* (1833). Teufelsdröckh's affirmation at the close of the chapter, 'The Everlasting Years', is worth quoting:

> I too could now say to myself: Be no longer a Chaos, but a World, or even Worldkin. Produce! Produce! Were it but the pitifullest infinitesimal fraction of a Product, produce it, in God's name! 'Tis the utmost thou hast in thee: out with it, then. Up, up! Whatsoever thy hand findeth to do, do it with thy whole might. Work while it is called Today; for the Night cometh, wherein no man can work.

For Arnold, Gray, whatever his occasional blunders, like the great masters embraces what might seem to be antithetical ideals. He is a 'classic' and a 'born poet'; his own poetry fit, indeed, to function as touchstones. (Remember that he is excused the test.) What is wanting, however, as Carlylean energies falter and the institutionalized fabric of Christianity founders, is more of it 'to console us, to sustain us': to augment that body of poetry which will increasingly replace 'what now

passes with us for religion and philosophy'—as Arnold maintains at the start of 'The Study of Poetry'. To be deprived of so
much more of Gray's sublime, even enviable, combination of
the lyrical and the sententious because of the superficial 'age of
prose' in which he suffered might suggest why Arnold is so
critical—to say nothing of his emphasis also on Gray's own
melancholy. The censure is arguably as much a moral as an
aesthetic one; and although Arnold's has been challenged,
principally by Tovey, for developing his premises out of
Brown's letter, his is merely the strongest voice in the universal
notice of Gray's small output.

Mitford quotes, apparently with approval, a letter of Gray's
friend, William Mason, to Lord Harcourt in the 1790s, where a
motto appears that is rarely lost sight of thereafter. 'Mason . . .
says " 'To be employed, is to be happy,' said Gray; and if he
had never said anything else, either in prose, or even in verse,
he would have deserved the esteem of all posterity" '.[11] It is
mentioned by Arnold, and by Gosse as 'one of his finest
sayings'.[12] Gray's busying himself in extensive scholarly
inquiry was the main form this employment took. But for the
American James Russell Lowell, in an acute essay on Gray first
published in 1886, this labour is demoted to 'dilettantism',
which enervated the 'intense energy' of the 'genius' he possessed and should have been possessed by. 'This rare combination of qualities in Gray . . . accounts for both the kind of
excellence to which he attained, and for the way he disappointed expectation, his own, I suspect, first of all'. What is
worth notice is that Lowell's Shelleyan conception of the way
inspiration operates leads him unhistorically to ascribe the
cause of Gray's 'scantiness'—for it is this to which he alludes—
not to the age but to the personality.[13]

Letter writing was an art cultivated in the 'age of prose', and
Gray did 'speak out' in this medium, to employ Arnold's
misinterpretation of the phrase. However, in discussing Gray's
letters he still manages to sustain a sense of Gray out of tune
with prevailing sentiment. You will find, Arnold implies, no
display in the manner, say, of Gray's friend Walpole. Gray's
letters '[make] it possible for us . . . to know him, and to
appreciate his high qualities of mind and soul'. Victorians lived
with frequent bereavement, and Arnold is not alone in warmly

observing Gray's models of tact, of 'excellent seriousness' in matters of condolence. His acute literary critical faculties are singled out in a letter to West disputing the latter's praise for Racine because of his alleged ease with the age in which he lived, 'for using in his dramas "the language of the times..."'. 'The language of the age is never the language of poetry...' is the celebrated reply. This proves to be a clever enlistment of Gray in what increasingly looks to be as much Arnold's cause as Gray's own. It prepares the ground for a later crescendo of blatant misapplications of Brown's innocent 'he never spoke out', which lead into Arnold's explanation. 'Gray, a born poet, fell upon an age of prose', resounds Arnold, echoing his preface to Johnson's *Lives* and the introductory essay to Ward's anthology. Arnold's description of Dryden and Pope as the 'classics of our prose' in that essay has become notorious. By citing the 'born poet['s]' own recognition of the division in any age between poetry and prose, and by contrasting (implicitly at least) Gray's scantiness with the easy abundance of a Dryden or a Pope, Arnold would manoeuvre Gray into confirming his evaluations. (Notwithstanding the need for a substantial body of work expressive of the 'deepest powers of mind and soul', Wordsworth wrote too much for Arnold. But his response is to make a judicious selection of the pieces of 'high merit' from Wordsworth's 'seven volumes', and certainly not any full-scale denial of poetic value.) Arnold conceives of Gray as a near mute inglorious Milton, oppressed by whatever confusions of social and literary circumstance an historically indeterminate 'age of prose' implies. At the same time Arnold darkly discloses what had proved to be his own difficulties in finding an adequate voice in his own dispirited age of prose. The Victorian Arnold voices his own sense of belatedness by reaching back to a Romantic precursor. Qualities we associate with Keats (the other poet Arnold introduced for Ward), and those he sees in Wordsworth, wasted in the desert air of Gray's 'age of prose' and were powerless to be born in his own: 'Poetry ... was intellectual, argumentative, ingenious; not seeing things in their truth and beauty, not interpretative. Gray [like Arnold himself] with the qualities of mind and soul of a genuine poet, was isolated in his century'.

In defence of what might at best appear to be Arnold's clever irresponsibility, John Mitford, whose editorial work on Gray spans some forty years, inclines towards Arnold's notion of the poet brought low by an age of prose. In the preface to his last edition of Gray's writings, the correspondence of Gray, Mason, and Brown (1853), he mentions how Gray was obliged to explain to Norton Nicholls why he failed to finish 'The Alliance of Education and Government'. The poet appealed to his own lyric aptitude and his habit of polishing as the reasons for the absence of any lengthy composition.[14] If we concede that the long poem lapses into prose—and many Romantic commentators have emphatically supported the idea[15]—and if we notice how attempts at long poems invariably call forth from the conservative, didactic Gray the 'ten-syllable couplet' (rather than blank verse), we begin to see why Arnold was tempted to deplore Gray's predicament. (Of Wordsworth he said that 'his poems of greatest bulk are by no means [his] best work'.) The trouble is that the evidence mustered for Arnold's unqualified conclusions is arguably too slender to admit of anything more than Arnold's own prejudices. Before supplying these reasons, Gray had responded to Nicholls's question by merely stating that he 'could not' complete the fragment. Is there anything more here than simple resignation to lyric gifts? Is the ensuing explanation a complex and defensive extenuation of guilt, or merely polite second thoughts following a rather abrupt reaction? 'How simply said, and how true also', remarks Arnold, but Gray's answer is incorporated into Arnold's campaign on behalf of a poet in conflict with his age and its forms. When Arnold's contemporaries see Gray as a precursor of the 'Romantic School' they limit their reference to the forms and content of the poetry.[16] Arnold alludes to a Romantic personality who, at odds with the spirit of the age, still achieved the frailest 'classic' status in a slender volume of universal worth. Had he examined the poetry he might have been able to resolve these apparent contradictions. Mitford is on surer ground in pursuing the implications of Gray the poet's self-assessments, as a result of which Gray emerges as a writer noticeably uncharacterized by his own or any other period. Mitford is content to observe how the lyric Muse, visiting Gray fitfully, is unsuited to desiderated epics. He declines to endorse the view that the scholar overwhelmed the poet, but he does appreciate the temptation for a man of Gray's temperament to forego the effort of writing poetry with the libraries of Cambridge at his disposal.[17]

Close on a century before the arrival of reader-response criticism, Oscar Wilde had observed, in his preface to *The Picture of Dorian Gray* (1891), that 'the highest, as the lowest, form of criticism is a mode of autobiography'. Perhaps Arnold's engagement with Gray and the eighteenth century is an amalgam of the two, and reveals as much about Arnold as it does about Thomas Gray. (The problem here is one of infinite regression: my reflections on Arnold are themselves a 'mode of autobiography', as are the reader's on my writings. But we can put a stop to this, even if an arbitrary one, by declaring the obvious: it is Gray and Arnold who are the focus of general interest.) Although Arnold does not gather sufficient evidence for his assertions, and seems to be unaware of their complexity, relativists would maintain that the evidence is always insufficient. But this 'cognitive atheism', as E. D. Hirsch has called it,[18] is as intolerable as absolute conviction. With the interrelated problems of the conditions of critical practice and datagathering in mind, I suggest that Arnold was writing, consciously and perhaps unconsciously, of his own anxieties as much as of those he attributes to his subject. He often compared himself with Gray, and his contemporaries confirmed the similarity. Mowbray Morris, editor of *Macmillan's Magazine*, appraises Arnold's situation in exactly the terms in which Arnold had appraised Gray's own:

> He has said that Gray's poetical production was checked and limited by the circumstances of his life and of the age into which he was born. Some such influence may, one fancies, have had power over Matthew Arnold; and this may help to account for the perversity and flippancy of some of his prose-writing.[19]

The tone is hesitant, in keeping with the difficulties involved in reaching conclusions which I have emphasized above, and no comment is offered on Arnold's estimation of Gray and his period. The focus is rightly on Arnold, and it is interesting to see it suggested that Arnold's 'perversity and flippancy', for which many commentators have found cognate terms, are possibly the symptoms in his prose for his frustrations as a poet. One might 'fancy' Gray's melancholy, his cold reserve, an equivalent reaction. His response to what was a friend's inquiry as to why he never finished 'The Alliance of Education and Government' would then take on darker colouring.

In an essay on the interaction between Gray and Victorian writers, it is worth pressing these unhistorical parallels to note how the sense of isolation and melancholy in Gray's poetry surfaces in Arnold's own.[20] In passing, we might recall Arnold's removal of 'Empedocles on Etna' from his 1853 *Poems* for its failure (as he says in the Preface) to 'inspirit and rejoice' the reader. A letter of J. C. Shairp's to Clough (1849) notices Arnold's tendency to appropriate his subject-matter— Empedocles's 'name and outward circumstances are used for the drapery of his own thoughts'.[21] And Arnold, again to Clough (1853), criticizes his own 'Scholar Gypsy' for 'at best awaken[ing] a pleasing melancholy'. What the 'complaining millions of men' need, he says, is 'something to *animate* and *ennoble* them—not merely to add zest to their melancholy or grace to their dreams.—I believe a feeling of this kind is the basis of my nature—and of my poetics'. Writing in the same year to his favourite sister, who had worried over her piecemeal approval of her brother's poetry, Arnold replied: 'The true reason why parts suit you while others do not is that my poems are fragments—i.e. that I am fragments, while you are a whole; the whole effect of my poems is quite vague and indeterminate—this is their weakness'.[22] The earnest Victorian takes himself to task for failing coherently to 'speak out' in a way we could never expect Gray to do in a less ostensibly troubled age and circumstances. Arnold would wrest himself from a general disposition he might share with Gray. If we imagine the latter as, paradoxically, the strong weak precursor, it might be useful to pursue their relationship in terms of the oedipal complexities of modern revisionist criticism which is, however, noticeably unhistorical in practice.

The connection between the two poets is made at a more accessible universal level by Edmund Gosse, in his book-length study of Gray which appeared in 1882. The life of the poet is brought to a close in Gosse's penultimate chapter. The final inscription is taken from Arnold's 'To Marguerite—Continued':

> Gray 'never spoke out,' Brown said; he lived, more even
> than the rest of us, in an involuntary isolation, a pathetic
> type of the solitude of the soul.
>> Yes! in the sea of life enisled,
>> With echoing straits between us thrown,
>> Dotting the shoreless watery wild,
>> We mortal millions live *alone*.
>> The islands feel the enclasping flow,
>> And then their endless bounds they know.[23]

Arnold's dispiritedness here was prompted by his parting from
a real, if obscure, Marguerite.[24] Love, if not a panacea for
Victorians' spiritual troubles, was certainly valued as a consolation prize, not least by Matthew Arnold. It is Gosse who
relates that Bonstetten, the young friend of Gray's final years,
attributed the

> discord between Gray's humorous intellect and ardent
> imagination on the one side and what he calls a 'misère de
> coeur' on the other ... to a suppressed sensibility, to the
> fact that Gray never—
>> anywhere in the sun or rain
>> Had loved or been beloved again,
> and that he felt his heart to be frozen at last under what
> Bonstetten calls the Arctic Pole of Cambridge.[25]

Arnold's critical tactics with Gray were to come under
sustained attack from the Cambridge scholar and editor of
Gray's letters, Duncan Crookes Tovey. He allows that contemporary interest in Gray is 'indeed a little disproportionate
to the scant and fragmentary nature of his positive achievements', but this is because he is a '*modern*', especially in his
letters. We might anticipate further inquiry along Arnold's
lines, but his variations on 'he never spoke out', are firmly
reprimanded. They 'read like fanciful homilies on an inappropriate text'.[26] Perhaps Tovey neglects to mention Arnold's
name as a mark of scorn, but the fact that he can do so indicates
the general currency of the eminent late critic's remarks. For
all Tovey's matching of Arnold's Olympian manner—'we

cannot indeed believe ... that ... good Mr Brown had anything in his mind but the fact that Gray did not acknowledge to his friends how near he felt his end to be...'—his reflections are equally impressionable, speculative. What Tovey's standpoint licenses is a denial that Gray was in any way hampered by the age in which he lived. And to ascribe '*Weltschmerz*' is premature. He quotes the humorous James Russell Lowell twice to the same effect: ' "Responsibility for the Universe had not yet been invented" '. Arnold's Gray is clearly detected as a Romantic. The partiality of Arnold's position masquerades as social and historical appraisal. Tovey insists that Gray the man was at home with his world and his personality, and would have been the same in any epoch. 'Gray's *momentum* comes from within; he writes to please himself; publicity is with him always quite a secondary matter.' And yet the antagonists are not always poles apart. Tovey's passage about modernity runs: 'He fascinates us still, because he is one of us; because he shows himself ... a *modern*; because we feel that in his company we are at the sources of a familiar stream'.[27] Arnold had maintained that Gray's poetry wears best from the eighteenth century.[28] The abiding relevance of Gray for both commentators seems to endorse some kind of neo-classic criteria of universality and timelessness, which are standards of excellence we most readily associate with what is better called at this point the age of Johnson rather than the age of prose. What Tovey refuses to allow is for the 'classic' Gray to be compromised by Arnold's pretence at historical method and glib characterization of epochs.

John Bradshaw, the last of Gray's Victorian editors, echoes Tovey in offering a simple, reasonable answer for Gray's 'small quantity'. 'But Gray wrote only for himself or his friends, and it was merely when pressed by them or by the booksellers that he published anything.'[29] The number and variety of extenuations which Gray's 'small quantity' receives is as singular as the phenomenon itself, yet if Gray resembles anyone in this matter it is the late Victorian A. E. Housman. Similarly circumstanced as a scholar of adequate but not considerable means, Housman resisted publication and, like Gray,[30] refused money with gentlemanly reserve and disavowal for what proved to be a scanty output. 'In barrenness, at any rate, I hold a high place among English poets, excelling even Gray', Housman wrote in 1910.[31] The parallels extend to the mood of their poetry. The plaintive notes of *A Shropshire Lad* are first caught in Gray's 'The Death of Hoël'.

The poetry of Collins in Ward's *English Poets* was introduced by Swinburne, who extols his virtues at the expense of Gray. Arnold might consider Gray to be a 'born poet', but Swinburne will have none of it. 'As an elegiac poet' Gray is eternally supreme, he admits, but thereafter seeks to carry the day on Collins's behalf with a bluster of rhetoric more than equal to anything of which poor Gray is accused. 'The fanfaronnade and falsetto which impair the always rhetorically elaborate and sometimes genuinely sonorous notes of Gray were all but impossible to the finer touch of his precursor.'[32] If Arnold moulds Gray in his own image, Swinburne interacts similarly with Collins. To some extent they are carrying on wars with themselves. Courthope had noted, with a show of bewilderment, that whereas Arnold advances 'touchstones' as criteria for excellence in poetry, Swinburne counters with 'imagination and harmony'.[33] Swinburne admits Gray's 'high seriousness' of substance on occasions (to use Arnold's phrase), but it is Collins the lyricist who is enviably supreme. 'Gray is simply unworthy to sit at [his] feet.' Collins 'could not be taught singing like a finch: but he struck straight upward for the sun like a lark'. Swinburne is an unrepentant latter-day Romantic of the *poeta nascitur, no fit* school. Arnold prefers a balancing act. In his letter to Gosse in praise of *Gray* he says: 'You are right in remarking that the secret of Gray's superiority lies in his having read, thought and felt so very much more than Collins'.[34] Both, however, choose to see their protégés as endeavouring to flourish in stony ground. 'Living both in an age and after an age of critical poetry...', says Swinburne, echoing, with a trifle more precision, the judgements of Arnold.

An anachronistic wish emerges on our part for some early stirrings of detailed scrutiny of texts among Victorian critics to support broad observation. Even in the 'Study of Poetry', intended for a wide reading public, Arnold says disconcertingly that 'touchstones' are 'infallible' guides if we have 'any tact' in their discovery and their application. What if we have

not—or feel we have not? Courthope's attack on the arbitrariness of Arnold's touchstones was not obliged, and made the
point of not being able, to provide any particular alternatives.
Gosse's *Gray*, in Macmillan's 'English Men of Letters' series,
gives the most critical illustration; but, significantly, even
Gosse rises to an impassioned denunciation of what he regards
as pedantic analysis. Gray's own lines from 'William Shakespeare to Mrs Anne, regular Servant to the Revd Mr Precentor
of York', attributing to Shakespeare a distrust of critics, are
conscripted in support:

> For criticism of the type which has now become so
> common, for the counting of syllables and weighing of
> commas, Gray, with all his punctilio and his minute
> scholarship, had nothing but contempt:-

> > Much have I borne from cankered critic's spite,
> >   From fumbling baronets, and poets small,
> > Pert barristers, and parsons nothing bright:-
> > But what awaits me now is worst of all.[35]

A haughty, complex alliance of gentleman commentator and
creative artist is maintained here, at the expense of analysis
which might provide the enlightenment to which Gosse himself
is supposedly committed. Would that the 'counting of syllables
and weighing of commas' were 'so common' as Gosse
declares—especially where scholarship and the criticism that
might have depended on it are concerned. 'William Shakespeare to Mrs Anne' was first published in Mitford's *Correspondence* (1853). Gosse was the first to publish it among Gray's
poetry, in volume one of his four-volume *Works* of 1884,
misleadingly stating that 'it had never before been included
in Gray's Works'.[36] His *Gray* furnishes an untitled, variant
excerpt two years earlier. Bradshaw's *Works*, published in 1894
at the dawn of the development of English studies at university, speaks of 'many inaccuracies' in *Gray*, and of the text of
the poems in Gosse's *Works* as being 'far from accurate'.
Interestingly, unlike his *Gray*, Gosse's edition 'does not aim at
being popular on the one hand, or educational on the other';
whereas Bradshaw's 'is designed to meet the requirements of
students as well as others'.[37] If there is the faint germ here of a

complicated social-historical critique of literary-critical practice, it must be cultivated elsewhere.

Victorian writers generally lack the inquisitive critical pursuit of Arnold. They are most content with biographical commentary larded with occasional literary judgement. Bradshaw's own scholarly introduction is much less than half the size of his 'Life and Writings' which succeeds it. In contrast to Wordsworth's criticism of the sonnet on the death of West for its falsity of expression, Bradshaw calls it 'the first [sonnet] of any value written since those of Milton'. This leads to wider biographical notice of the dissolution of Gray's friendships (the break-up of the celebrated 'Quadruple Alliance'). In general terms this is taken to explain the melancholy hues of the *Ode on a Distant Prospect of Eton College*. 'It is a distorted view and a one-sided picture, with no bright side; as was well observed by the Earl of Carlisle', says Bradshaw. An intriguing scene is conjured. He evokes a lecture on the writings of Gray by the noble Lord, delivered over forty years before to the Sheffield Mechanics' Institute. In this early instance of adult education, poor unpatriotic Gray is rebuked for not having exercised a happy prescience to dispel the gloom: '". . . of the last six Prime Ministers four have been Eton men, and not very long after the Poet had cast his desponding glance upon that boyish group, among those who disported on the 'margent green' was Arthur Wellesley, Duke of Wellington"'. An irresistible piece, where reverent assent is commanded by the fact that the lecture was given late in the year of the aged Duke's demise. The views expressed, with Bradshaw's approval, are at least as 'one-sided' as anything attributed to Gray. What Bradshaw both suggests and falls short of is any investigation in detail of the manner in which the Romantic Gray appropriates his subject matter.[38]

Approving, if oblique, reference is made to what we might think to be Arnold's questionable detachment, in Gosse's prefatory survey of Gray's writings and his editors in *Gray*. Gosse compliments Arnold's 'brief summary' (for Ward) as being 'by far the best account of Gray, not written by a personal friend'. Arnold was quick to respond by letter with praise for *Gray*. A passing remark on Swinburne's 'nonsense', with regard to Collins's 'Ode to Liberty', offers indirect support for Gosse's various challenges of Swinburne for his 'deeply and extravagantly unjust' estimation of Gray. Gosse's nicest thrust has all the more point for occurring in the context of relatively detailed analysis of 'The Progress of Poesy':

> This manner of rhyming, this rapid and recurrent beat of song, was the germ out of which have sprung all later metrical inventions, and without which Mr. Swinburne himself might now be polishing the heroic couplet to its last perfection of brightness and sharpness.[39]

Gosse's Gray is an innovatory lyricist and precursor of the Romantics in both form and subject matter. Where the letters are concerned, he is pleased to confirm Arnold's notice of the occasional 'full tone of the romantic solitary' (quoting the same description of Derwentwater). Gray's admired learning happily leads the poet to the 'romantic lyrics, paraphrased, in short measures, from Icelandic and Gaelic sources', and in this regard Gosse is the first extensively to mention Gray's pioneering work in the Romantic revival of interest in primitiveness.[40] 'The Latin poetry of an Etonian is generally reckoned at that school, the chief test of his literary talent.' Thus wrote the father of Arthur Henry Hallam in an 1834 preface to his late young son's *Remains in Verse and Prose*. Gosse is unique among Victorians in noticing Gray's school exercises in Latin. He searches out a 'play-exercise at Eton' among Gray's MSS at Cambridge, for example, and observes how 'this early effusion ... prefigures its author's maturer moral and elegiac manner'. What is also of interest is how, in a work designed for a wide spectrum of readers, Gosse's generous quotation from the original is prefaced by a brief synopsis of the whole in the vernacular. Where appropriate, Arnold himself provided translations of his touchstones.[41]

Despite the sensitivity of his methods and his appraisal, Gosse is of *mens sana in corpore sano* inclinations. He deplores eighteenth-century gentlemen's lack of exercise, and declines to investigate Gray's anxieties in Arnold's manner. More precisely occupied with stylistic matters, he specifically employs the term 'Gray and his school' when discussing a common tendency to personify abstract qualities witnessed in the so-called school's 'assumption that a mythology might be formed out of the emotions of the human mind'.[42] The collective term is casually borrowed from Leslie Stephen, by whom it is employed in a much more comprehensive social-historical sweep than Arnold wished to attempt, and in discussion of 'general tendencies' rather than literary characteristics. Much more firmly of a Tom Brown turn of mind than either the ex-Rugeiban Arnold, or Edmund Gosse, Stephen attributes Gray's 'singular want of fertility' largely to the fact that 'he belonged to the class fop or *petit-maître*, mincing, precise, affected, and as little in harmony with the rowdy fellow-commoners [at Cambridge] as Hotspur's courtier with the rough soldiers on the battle-field'. These manly summaries from the avowed promoter of an historical, rather than judicial, criticism, are far removed from Mitford's sympathetic suggestion that 'academic bowers' are not the 'most favourable residence of the Muse'.[43] The substance of genius for Stephen is agreeably down-to-earth. The 'secret' is in the style: in giving us what often was thought but never so well expressed. 'No English poet has ever given more decisive proof that he shared that secret of clothing even an obvious thought in majestic and resounding language, which we naturally call Miltonic.'[44] The (moral) aesthetic exhibited is curiously unhistorical, and ironically shades towards support of Gray's candidature for touchstone status. But Stephen's combination of substance and sombre song is an uneasy one, and could strip down at a critical extreme into unexalted expressions of an 'age of prose' on the one hand, decked out in 'false poetical style' on the other. The American Lowell is defensive in expressing similar notions:

> The thought in Gray is neither uncommon nor profound, and you may call it beautiful commonplace if you choose. I shall not contradict you. I have lived long enough to know that there is a vast deal of commonplace in this world of no particular use to anybody, and am thankful to the man who has the divine gift to idealize it for me.

Lowell had previously detected in Gray the unproductive alliance of genius—Romantically fancied as possessing a 'certain fanaticism of temperament'—and dilettante, 'admirable for observation, incapable of turning it to practical account'. But any attempt to see here a veiled effort to reconcile them is unpersuasive. It is also difficult to see whether Lowell's defence of Gray is a concession to, or rescue from, the philistine. What Gray lacks in bulk he makes up for in popular appeal. In discussion of Gray's letters Lowell is on more certain ground, where praise of the poetry is introduced under their protection. Echoing Arnold, he says that 'in his letters of condolence, perhaps the most arduous species of all composition, Gray shows the same exquisite tact which is his distinguishing characteristic as a poet'.[45] Victorians' frequent exercise in, and receipt of, letters of sympathy would make them as appreciative of expressions of melancholy good taste as competent to sense when the right tone had been achieved.

Victorian commentators are united in their assumption of authority in their polemical assessments of Gray and the age to which he is ascribed. A charitable explanation would be because literature matters; because it 'console[s] us ... sustain[s] us', either as Arnoldian 'criticism of life' or Swinburnian lyric effusion. Despite the subversive challenge to the Arnoldian position by Pater and his late nineteenth-century aesthetic disciples, the fundamental position of literature as 'moral barometer' persists. Stephen, regarded as the first man of letters following Arnold's death in 1888,[46] directly challenges the Arnoldian position from a sociological standpoint in the first of his Ford lectures of 1903:

> To say the truth, literature seem to me to be a kind of by-product. It occupies far too small a part in the whole activity of a nation, even of its intellectual activity, to serve as a complete indication of the many forces which are at work, or as an adequate moral barometer of the general moral state. The attempt to establish such a condition too closely, seems to me to lead to a good many very edifying but none the less fallacious conclusions.[47]

In advancing art for art's sake against Arnoldian art, literary art, as 'criticism of life', the late nineteenth century still claimed for literature an aesthetic centrality. For Stephen's sociological 'high seriousness', the next step is to maintain that literature scarcely signifies, a mere embellishment in the Marxian superstructure. The workings of Arnoldian assurance, which would enmesh Gray's writings in vague social-historical notions such as the 'age of prose', are rendered suspect, slapdash, on all counts.

A modern reviewer has said that 'growing knowledge has made us more cautious' than our Victorian predecessors.[48] Had they grounded their controversies in Gray's poetry, their broad statement might have gathered persuasion. Notwithstanding the poet's rehearsal of commonplaces, 'The Alliance of Education and Government' (particularly ll. 84–87) states clearly enough that man is moulded by his milieu; the 'Stanzas to Mr Bentley' bemoan the uninspired, or uninspiring, age, as does III, 3. of 'The Progress of Poesy'. These—and other—indications of Gray's acute sense of belatedness in a powerful poetic tradition are not examined by Victorian critics. With reverberations of 'Il Penseroso' (appropriate in a poem celebrating the installation of a new Chancellor at Milton's Cambridge), the *Ode for Music* evokes an agreeable association of 'Contemplation', 'cloisters', 'Freedom' and 'soft-ey'd Melancholy' (ll. 27–34), while sympathetic resignation to life's misfortunes is proposed in a brief retrospect on the lives of the princely great (ll. 35–56). The list is of necessity limited, crude, but it gives momentary sight of the lines of exploration that are lacking. Pronouncements on Gray's psychology, which support larger, or literary, judgement, might have benefited from similar inquiry. This argues a Romantic, confessional Gray, but without the need to force theories of the unconscious on ages which knew nothing of them. It has already been suggested how Bradshaw's biographical material on bereavement required a complementary analysis of the *Ode on a Distant Prospect of Eton College* to forward any discussion of Gray's creative turn of mind. Gosse hinted at the way in which poetry can be revelatory when he selected a stanza from Arnold's 'To Marguerite—Continued' as envoy to illumine Gray's 'solitude of the soul'. Ever anxious about the utility of their art, as performers or consumers, Victorians much admired the *Elegy* for its ability to sugar the pill: for its union of lyricism and serious reflection. 'Tennyson would rather, it is reported, have written the "Elegy" than all Wordsworth.'[49] Victorian critics could have gained some knowledge of Gray from the *Elegy*—and provided themselves with a greater understanding of the poem in the process. This is not the place to examine the complex narrative identities of the *Elegy*; but Victorian writers could have seen, in pursuit of their psychological interest in Gray, that speculations on those beneath the soil disclose something of the character of the spectator. (Dickens's Pip shows the way at the beginning of *Great Expectations*; Lockwood, unconsciously so, at the end of *Wuthering Heights*.) Again, brief reference is crude, but it gives some idea, perhaps, of the way an Arnold might have supplemented the alleged evidence that Gray's letters contain.

But, as outlined earlier, gentlemen critics do not stoop to particulars. At first it looks as if it is only Arnold's extempore brilliance which is served by taking as his point of departure the slender evidence of a letter from one of Gray's friends to another. But ' "He never spoke out" ' and 'age of prose' proved to be memorable shorthand developed out of the creative engagement of one clever man in his milieu and moment with another.[50] Reviewing Bradshaw's edition of Gray's *Poetical Works*, Lionel Johnson reflected that Arnold's notion of Gray stifled by his age is 'as nearly the truth, in all likelihood, as any answer can be'.[51] I said at the start that the reader is first likely to experience Gray among the Victorians via Arnold. It remains, in a fruitful sense, the most provocative encounter.

NOTES

1. W. J. Courthope, *The Liberal Movement in English Literature* (London, 1885), p. 11.

2. So called when republished in *Essays in Criticism: Second Series* (1888), and thereafter.

3. Quotations are taken from 'The Study of Poetry', *Matthew Arnold: English Literature and Irish Politics*, ed. R. H. Super (Ann Arbor, 1973), pp. 161–88. (Vol. IX of *The Complete Prose Works of Matthew Arnold*).

4. *The Liberal Movement in English Literature*, pp. 11–12. The papers which comprise the book had first appeared in the monthly 'National Review'.

5. First published as 'Johnson's Lives', *MacMillan's Magazine*, XXXVIII (June 1878), 153–60. See *Matthew Arnold: Essays Religious and Mixed*, ed. R. H. Super (Ann Arbor, 1972), pp. 318, 459–60. (Vol. VIII of *The Complete Prose Works of Matthew Arnold*.)

6. See 'A Guide to English Literature', *Matthew Arnold: Essays Religious and Mixed*, pp. 249–50. Arnold loftily advises several revisions, and the compliment to Gray and Collins was erased from subsequent editions.

7. 'Classic' is, however, an indefinite term in the vocabulary of approval. John Mitford, the long-term editor of Gray in the first half of the nineteenth century, speaks of the room Gray occupied in his mother's house at Stoke Poges as 'piously preserved, as a spot of classic interest...'. See *The Correspondence of Thomas Gray and William Mason* (London, 1853), p. viii.

8. The comments appear in 'Maurce de Guérin', first published in *Fraser's Magazine*. See *Matthew Arnold: Lectures and Essays in Criticism*, ed. R. H. Super (Ann Arbor, 1962), pp. 12–39, in particular pp. 14–15. See also p. 409.

9. Quotations from 'Gray' are taken from *Matthew Arnold: English Literature and Irish Politics*, pp. 189–204.

10. Duncan C. Tovey's term in his edition, *Gray and His Friends: Letters and Relics* (Cambridge, 1890), p. 21.

11. *The Correspondence of Thomas Gray and William Mason*, p. xix.

12. Edmund W. Gosse, *Gray* (London, 1882), p. 195.

13. Quoted from 'Gray' in Lowell's *Latest Literary Essays and Addresses* (London, 1891), pp. 13–14. Gray's 'dilettantism' is disparaged by the robust Leslie Stephen in the context of a discussion of 'taste for the "Gothic"'. See 'Gray and his School', in *Hours in a Library*, 3 vols (London, 1892), III, 125. See also the brief notice in Stephen's *English Literature and Society in the Eighteenth Century* (London, 1966), p. 125 (Ford Lectures, 1903; first published 1904). A pejorative sense of 'dilettante' was well established in the nineteenth century. The *O.E.D.*, for example, quotes Ruskin's 'mere dilettante' (1886).

14. *The Correspondence of Thomas Gray and William Mason*, pp. xxi–xxii.

15. Coleridge, in *Biographia Literaria*, ch. xiv, says: 'A poem of any length neither can be, or ought to be, all poetry'. J. S. Mill says that lyric poetry is 'more eminently and peculiarly poetry than any other' in 'Thought in Poetry and its Varieties', in *Dissertations and Discussions* (1832). Newman speaks of a 'word [having] a power to convey a world of ... imagination ... [with] no need of sustained fiction', in 'Poetry with Reference to Aristotle's Poetics', which first appeared in the *London Review* (January 1829). Poe maintained that '"a long poem" is simply a flat contradiction in terms' in his essay 'The Poetic Principle' (1850).

16. Courthope, for example, *The Liberal Movement in English Literature*, pp. 223–24. Edmund Gosse, generally, in *Gray*, in particular pp. 121, 217.

17. *The Correspondence of Thomas Gray and William Mason*, pp. xx–xxv.

18. In the essay 'Faulty Perspectives', in his collection *The Aims of Interpretation* (1976).

19. See Carl Dawson (ed.), *Matthew Arnold, The Poetry: The Critical Heritage* (London, 1973), pp. 23, 325–36. Mowbray Morris's evaluation appeared in October 1888, six months after Arnold's death.

20. John Heath-Stubbs quotes stanzas from the *Elegy*, and says: 'The great solitaries that haunt Wordsworth's poetry, as well as Arnold's Scholar Gypsy, are implicit here...'. See Thomas Gray, *Selected Poems*, ed. John Heath-Stubbs (Manchester, 1981), p. 11.

21. From Clough MSS. See *Matthew Arnold: Poetry and Prose*, ed. John Bryson (London, 1954), p. 794.

22. Ibid., pp. 743, 745.

23. Gosse, *Gray*, p. 210.

24. See, for example, *Matthew Arnold: Poetry and Prose*, p. 787.

25. Gosse, *Gray*, p. 198.

26. *Gray and His Friends: Letters and Relics*, p. 21.

27. Ibid., pp. 21, 25–29, 31.

28. In 'Maurice de Guérin'. See *Matthew Arnold: Lectures and Essays in Criticism*, p. 14.

29. John Bradshaw (ed.), *The Poetical Works of Thomas Gray: English and Latin* (London, 1894), p. lxii. 'Aldine' edition.

30. See, for example, Gosse, *Gray*, p. 179.

31. *The Letters of A. E. Housman*, ed. Henry Maas (London, 1971), p. 108. There is unwitting humour in Arnold's letter to Gosse in praise of his *Gray*: '"Simonidean" is the right word to express the note struck by Gray—you could not have taken a better' (*Matthew Arnold: English Literature and Irish Politics*, pp. 386–87). Simonides of Ceos (*c.*556–*c.*468 BC), one of the most celebrated lyric poets of Greece, is said to have made literature a profession and been the first to take money for his poems, particularly his eulogies, which he wrote to order.

32. Quotations are taken from Algernon Charles Swinburne, 'Collins', in *Miscellanies*, 2nd edn (London, 1895), pp. 56–62.

33. *The Liberal Movement in English Literature*, pp. 9–10.

34. *Matthew Arnold: English Literature and Irish Politics*, p. 387.

35. Gosse, *Gray*, p. 170.

36. *The Works of Thomas Gray: In Prose and Verse*, ed. Edmund Gosse, 4 vols (London, 1884), I, 132–33.

37. Bradshaw, *Poetical Works of Thomas Gray*, p. xvii, xviii, xxii; Gosse, *The Works of Thomas Gray*, I, xvi.

38. Bradshaw, *Poetical Works*, pp. xxxiii–xxxiv. The lecture was delivered on 14 December 1852.

39. *Matthew Arnold: English Literature and Irish Politics*, p. 387. Gosse, *Gray*, p. 121.

40. Gosse, *Gray*, for example pp. 57, 59, 63 and pp. 160–63, 188–89. The Arnold cross-reference is in 'Gray', *Matthew Arnold: English Literature and Irish Politics*, pp. 196–97.

41. Quoted from Arthur Henry Hallam, *Remains* (London, 1869), p. xii. See also Gosse, *Gray*, pp. 6–7, 21.

42. Gosse, *Gray*, pp. 6, 13–14, 21. 'If I do not write much it is because I cannot' passes at face value, p. 178. See also p. 132.

43. Quoted from Leslie Stephen, 'Gray and His School', *Hours in a Library*, 3 vols (London, 1892), new edn, III, 114. See also III, 109 and f/n 17. Stephen's 'Hours in a Library' essays first appeared in the *Cornhill Magazine*, which he edited 1871–1882. It is true that Stephen expresses some sympathy for Gray's well-known suffering of a false fire alarm, played out as a cruel joke at Cambridge; but Gosse, significantly, is far more sensitive about it. See *Hours in a Library*, III, 114; Gosse, *Gray*, pp. 124–26.

44. 'Gray and His School', p. 116.

45. 'Gray', *Latest Literary Essays and Addresses*, pp. 13, 27, 39.

46. Noel Annan, *Leslie Stephen: The Godless Victorian* (London, 1984), p. 112.

47. Quoted from Leslie Stephen, *English Literature and Society in the Eighteenth Century* (London, 1966), p. 13.

48. Quoted from Alastair Macdonald's useful survey 'Gray and his Critics', in *Fearful Joy: Papers from the Thomas Gray Bicentenary Conference at Carelton University* (Montreal, 1974), p. 190.

49. Ibid., p. 172.

50. Sometime following the Restoration, Virginia Woolf's poet *manqué*, Orlando, finds 'his floridity ... chastened; his abundance curbed; the age of prose was congealing those warm fountains'. Quoted from *Orlando: A Biography* (London, 1992), p. 69. First published 1928.

51. 'Gray and his Critics', p. 189.

Index of Proper Names
and Works